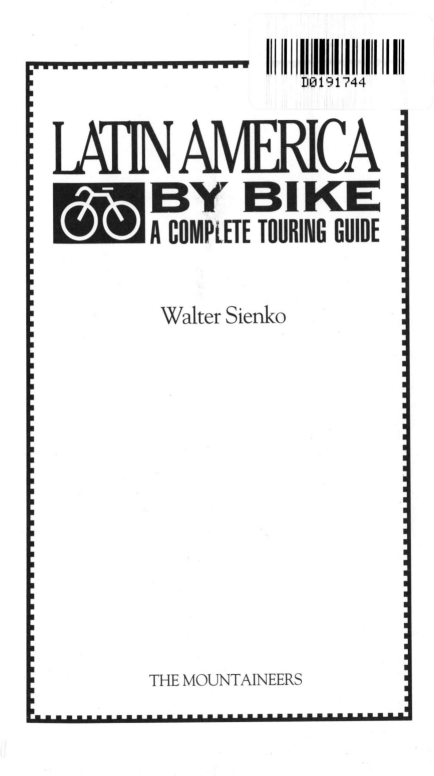

LATIN AMERICA
BY BIKE
A COMPLETE TOURING GUIDE

Walter Sienko

THE MOUNTAINEERS

To Kathleen

© 1993 by Walter Sienko

5 4 3
5 4 3 2 1

Published by The Mountaineers
1011 SW Klickitat Way, Seattle, Washington 98134

Published simultaneously in Canada by Douglas & McIntyre, Ltd., 1615 Venables Street, Vancouver, B.C. V5L 2H1

Published simultaneously in Great Britain by Cordee, 3a DeMontfort Street, Leicester, England, LE1 7HD

Manufactured in the United States of America

Edited by Meredith Waring
Maps by the author
All photographs by the author except as noted
Cover design by Watson Graphics
Book design and typesetting by The Mountaineers Books

Cover photographs: Mayan pyramids in Tikal, Guatemala; inset: drawing a crowd in Minas Gerais, Brazil

Library of Congress Cataloging-in-Publication Data
Sienko, Walter
    Latin America by bike : a complete touring guide / Walter Sienko.
        p.   cm.
    Includes index.
    ISBN 0-89886-365-1
    1. Bicycle touring--Latin America--Guidebooks. 2. Latin America--Guidebooks.
I. Title.
GV1046.L29S57   1993
796.6'4'098--dc20   93-14257
                                                    CIP

CONTENTS

PART I
Introduction

PART II
Argentina
Belize
Bolivia
Brazil
Chile
Colombia

Uruguay

Venezuela

PART I

Enjoying one of the natural swimming holes at Agua Azul, Mexico

INTRODUCTION

I wish I had had this book when I started bicycle touring in Latin America. Before I started I could find only guides telling me where the best nightspots and "funkiest" hotels were. My preparations had to be gleaned from the information in these general guides. My initial reason for writing this book was to give the reader an idea of what to expect when traveling in Latin America. I designed it as a manual. Rather than focus on what to do, where to go, and where to sleep (there is always a Hotel Centro), I chose to explain how to find accommodations, restaurants, and interesting regions. Most travelers' adventures happen en route, and cycling makes the most of these opportunities.

I cannot imagine wanting to travel any other way but by bicycle. The intimate contact with the land, people, and elements is the essence of traveling. Distances between destinations are reduced to more human proportions; 100 kilometers means something again. A cyclist's toil brings appreciation for both human nature and the universe.

As you ride quietly down an empty road in Bolivia, llamas stare, curious at your passing. Late at night, camping in Baja, you watch the heavens unleash a million stars, and the distant howl of a coyote twitches a primitive instinct that sends a chill up your spine.

You gain more respect for humanity, and the people sense it in your openness to them. On the road you make contact with real people. You bring the twentieth century with you, igniting their curiosity, and the interchange awakens both of you.

Bicycle touring promotes everything that is best about traveling; it is a slowly evolving tableau of sensual experiences.

This book was based on two major expeditions to Latin America. The first was an eight-month overland tour by bus and train. On the most recent, the Tierra del Hielo a Tierra del Fuego tour, my spouse and I traveled from Inuvik, Canada, to Ushuaia, Argentina. I don't expect you'll experience exactly what we did, but this book gives the bicycle tourist an idea of what to expect in Latin America.

Bicycle tourists are an independent lot, so I didn't want to pull you around by the nose, telling you where to eat and sleep. Other guides base their notion of quality and value on opinion and possibly happenstance (maybe that hotel proprietor was having a bad day). Instead, I want to teach you how to prepare, how to live, and where to go, based on your interests.

I have designed the tours in this book for those with a limited amount of time to explore an area. I think this book offers the best cycling experiences in Latin America.

Regrettably, one country I did not visit was El Salvador. Hopefully, in the near future this troubled country will be secure enough to visit.

Finally, I would like to thank Dr. Marc Lewin, traveler, doctor, and friend, who has recently worked with Mother Theresa in Calcutta, India. His expertise and help with the book's health sections is gratefully appreciated.

¡Vaya con Dios!

PREPARATION

The first key to a successful trip is making the right decisions before you leave. Almost every decision you make at home will have an impact when you're traveling in Latin America. Ignorance and poor preparation can cause frustration, expense, and health problems.

There's no need, however, to pack your pannier with paranoia. Knowledge about what to expect will prevent unnecessary worry. The more you prepare, the more you'll appreciate your trip. Your preparations will prime you for the thrills of exploring new lands, responding to different cultures, and wallowing in adventure.

HOW TO USE THIS BOOK. The first part of the book explains the general preparations and expectations for bicycle touring in Latin America. Its information is applicable from Mexico to Chile.

The second part of the book is divided alphabetically by country. After a brief introduction, the country is subdivided into cycle zones, which are usually geographic. Within the zones the book describes the terrain, cultural interest, and weather of the zone. The "General Information" section states how to get to the country by air and from neighboring countries, documentation needed, the range of accommodations (both hotels and camping), food (including restaurants, meal habits, markets, and food availability), drinks, health risks, photography, money (including economics, exchange procedures and costs, operating hours of shops and banks, postal services, and national holidays), and security concerns, including an overall security rating.

Each country chapter also includes specific bicycling information: availability and quality of parts and mechanics, road conditions and traffic, maps, and alternative transportation, which describes the policies about loading your bike.

Most countries have at least one tour; some have more than one. Some tours incorporate more than one country. Each tour has an information block that includes the total tour distance, where the tour starts and finishes, the best time to visit, the general terrain, scenery rating (maximum three stars), interest rating (maximum three stars), and a difficulty rating, based on terrain, road conditions, and availability of provisions.

In the tour logs, kilometers are not cumulative but are the distances between locations. Locations in boldface provide full provisions, while locations in regular type provide only food and water. Scenery and cultural interest between locations are also rated. If no provisions are available, that is stated in the "Comments" column. The "Comments" column also gives market days.

MONEY. One major mistake travelers make concerns the type of money they bring. Options you can choose from include the local money of the visiting country, any number of foreign currencies, and the American dollar.

First, by purchasing local money in your home country, you trade at a lower exchange rate than you would in the destination country. New York ignores any need for Venezuelan bolivars compared to La Paz's voracity for American dollars. Another problem is that some countries have astronomical inflation rates; money you buy before arriving quickly loses its value.

Foreign currencies such as Canadian dollars, Deutsche marks, English pounds, and Japanese yen are horrendous to exchange. In large cities you might find exchange houses or banks reluctantly accepting uncommon bills, but the rates you receive, compared to the U.S. dollar, are criminal. Lastly, this unofficial exchange, the parallel market, accepts only American dollars.

The U.S. dollar dominates in Latin American economies. Banks treat it as the international currency. Every local knows the current exchange rate. You can cash American dollars almost anywhere—exchange houses, banks, hotels, and the parallel market. The U.S. dollar is the most versatile, worry-free currency to carry.

Travel stores sell an array of items in which to carry your money and documents. The most useful is a money belt that attaches around your waist. The wallet section can rest snugly on your lower back when you are cycling. You can also buy neck pouches, which are inconvenient, and leg pouches, which are conspicuous if you wear shorts. Do not rely only on your money belt for keeping your valuables safe. Keep emergency funds stashed elsewhere: in a pannier or in the seat post. We slit an opening in the inside of our boots and stashed a few American bills in the hole.

Most of the funds you carry should be in traveler's checks. A traveler's canon preaches carrying only as much cash as you can afford to lose. Lost or stolen money is irretrievable, and plenty of stories abound about travelers who tried to save a few dollars on traveler's checks and ended up destitute. Bring a list of refund centers and keep a separate list of all your check numbers. Bring your receipts too; some institutions won't change your checks without them and you'll need them if you lose the checks.

You'll find credit cards a magnet for thieves, but you can't deny their usefulness in large cities. With a credit card you can withdraw cash in local currency. If you carry a credit card, know how to report its loss.

Some credit cards offer extra services that can be very valuable to the traveler. For example, some allow you to write a personal check on your home bank account.

Don't rely on wiring money from your home bank. The pitfalls of the method are enormous: the search for the right bank in a foreign country, the bureaucratic delays, the import and exchange restrictions.

The amount of money you need for a trip depends on two major factors. The first is your reliance on hotels and restaurants. If you sleep in a lot of hotels and eat in a lot of restaurants, your costs will be higher than if you camp and cook your own food. The second, less predictable factor is the country's economy. A country may adopt a new economic policy and within days the cost of living explodes.

HEALTH. Prepare for your trip by visiting a travel clinic. Staffed by doctors specializing in travel, they have the latest information on diseases, parasites, and drugs and dosages needed for traveling in Latin America. If you choose to go to a general practicioner, he or she will probably consult a travel clinic to get the same information. Don't take chances with your health—you will face unusual bugs and viruses and you need to prepare yourself beforehand.

Doctors in the clinic will evaluate your health needs based on your trip's duration, your destination, and your traveling style. Bicycle touring ranks as a high health risk. Cyclists usually travel for longer than a month, concentrating on undeveloped, rural areas. The physical demands of cycling, which include dealing with bad weather and pests, often in isolated areas, require you to be scrupulous in health preparations.

Health needs are constantly changing. The risk of different diseases increases and decreases; preventive methods change; scientists introduce new drugs and deem old ones ineffective. All these variables mean you should obtain the latest information possible. A thorough, independent source is the International Association for Medical Assistance to Travelers, known as IAMAT. The organization will send you a worldwide list of English-speaking doctors who offer their services to travelers on a basic fee structure (excluding drugs or hospitalization). IAMAT retains offices in Canada, New Zealand, Switzerland, and the United States. See Appendix A for addresses.

Inoculations break down into two categories: mandatory and recommended. The first mandatory shot is an updated DPT, a combined diphtheria, polio, and tetanus shot. The vaccine is good for five years. A solo tetanus booster is effective for ten years. You should receive a gamma globulin inoculation, effective for four to six months against hepatitis A. Typhoid, the last mandatory vaccination, requires two pokes one month apart if you have never received the shot before. If you need only a booster, you'll get just one injection. Each regime lasts for three years—longer than some Latin American governments.

Cholera has erupted throughout Latin America. Doctors no longer recommend the cholera vaccine because it has lost its effectiveness and often causes side effects. Health-travel specialists advise eating only well-cooked food and drinking only water that you know has been cleansed through filtration, boiling, or bottling.

Yellow fever, borne by mosquitoes, is endemic in the Amazon basin and on the tropical coasts of South America and Panama and on the desert coast of Peru. A one-jab inoculation lasts for ten tears. Authorities restrict entry into the Amazon region of Brazil unless you can prove that you've had a yellow fever vaccination.

The type of hazards you expect determines the types of voluntary vaccinations you should receive. Health officials and others with intense human contact, including sexual contact, should consider a hepatitis B vaccine.

Doctors may recommend a rabies vaccine if you anticipate contact with animals. When you see the large number of wild dogs that roam throughout Latin America, you might be thankful for having gotten a rabies vaccine. Shortly before leaving get a test for tuberculosis.

Malaria poses a serious problem in every country of Latin America except Chile and Uruguay. As doctors introduce new drugs against the mosquito-borne parasite, the parasite mutates and develops an immunity to them.

Malaria has two major strains. The easiest to deal with is the chloroquine-sensitive strain. In areas that the mosquitoes inhabit, you need to maintain a strict chloroquine regime. Start taking a chloroquine dose one week before entering the area. Continue the regime weekly during your stay and continue for four weeks after leaving the area. Chloroquine has unpleasant side effects, including minor stomach upsets, itchy skin, nausea, diarrhea, headaches, and blurry vision. IAMAT recommends that if you take chloroquine for a prolonged period, you should have your eyes examined yearly.

In areas where chloroquine-resistant malaria is present but less than 25 percent of known cases, continue with the same regime as above, but also carry a treatment dose of Fansidar. Take the full dose if you begin suffering symptoms of malaria: fever, nausea, headaches, and general malaise. Fansidar provides an effective treatment for chloroquine-resistant malaria but has serious side effects and should not be taken as a prophylactic.

Travelers visiting areas with a high incidence of chloroquine-resistant malaria should follow a mefloquine regime a week before entering the area, continue weekly, and continue for four weeks after leaving the area. Mild side effects include nausea, headache, and dizziness, while serious side effects—skin rashes, seizures, psychosis, and diarrhea—are rare. If you take a mefloquine regime for long-term prophylaxis and a malaria outbreak occurs, do not use the drug as treatment; see a doctor as soon as possible. Finally, if you use Lariam for a long period, you should have a liver-function test and an eye examination.

When traveling, everybody expects to pick up diarrhea; it's rare not to have a run-in with it. For mild diarrhea, take an Imodium regime. However, Imodium does not eradicate an infection, it only brings your bowels under control. If you contract severe diarrhea, take an antibiotic regime. Although you can obtain Imodium and antibiotics throughout Latin America, carry regimes with you, as you will invariably succumb in some far-off area. See Appendix G for a list of first-aid items to pack.

Appendix B charts disease conditions through Latin America.

Birth control remains a touchy issue. The region is heavily influenced by the Catholic church. This factor, along with the *machismo* of fathering as many children as possible with as many women as possible, inhibits availability of birth control. Condoms and birth-control pills are slowly becoming more widely available, with each country progressing at its own pace.

Sexually transmitted diseases are no different in Latin America than anywhere else in the world. The combination of ignorance and *machismo* ensures the proliferation of AIDS and other STDs. Be careful with any sexual encounter: Don't fool yourself into thinking it couldn't happen to you.

Get a dental checkup before leaving on your trip, especially if you plan an extended tour, because a lot of sugar is packed into the Latin diet. Dentists abound throughout the continent, but their knowledge, equipment, and hygiene standards are usually below what you're probably accustomed to.

The final health issue to consider before you leave is medical insurance. First, check into your current medical coverage; some policies apply no matter where you are. (Remember that medical costs in most Latin American countries are inexpensive, so your health insurance dollars may go further.) As a safety measure, you should always carry enough funds in case you have a medical emergency that forces you to return home immediately. If your current policy doesn't cover foreign medical bills, check your credit cards. Most cards offer health plans that are cheaper than those of insurance companies, but you must buy them separately and reimbursement occurs only when you return home.

So, what if you have no policies and no credit cards? For short trips, I'd highly recommend purchasing coverage. The few dollars it costs will pay off if you need to use it. But for long extended trips, the cost of health insurance is more than hospital stays in most countries.

DOCUMENTS. If you are North American, you need a passport to enter every country in Latin America except Mexico. Some countries require a minimum validity period on your passport before allowing entry. So, whatever trip length you plan, ensure the expiry date extends at least six months beyond the trip's expected length.

On longer trips obtain the maximum number of pages possible. Latin American officials love stamping papers, and when you travel with a bike, passports fill quickly. Count on one page per visa and one more page for entering and exiting the country. You will regret having to apply for a new passport while in another country because you simply ran out of space.

Plan enough time for processing the paperwork needed to obtain your documents. Don't wait until the last minute to apply for your passport, because you will also need to obtain required visas.

Visas are advance permission authorizing entry into the country. You can gather visa requirements from several sources. If you fly directly to the country, embassies and tourist offices will inform you of the proper requirements. If you travel overland, entry requirements can change before you arrive. At home, officials may tell you a visa isn't required; two months later, you arrive at the border from a neighboring country to find that the political winds have shifted and your nationality needs a visa. Always obtain the latest information just before your arrival. You don't want officials to refuse you entry and then have to backtrack 1,000 kilometers, all because you didn't carry the right documents.

You should carry two important health documents: the International Health Certificate and an IAMAT membership. A clinic issues the certificate, which outlines your inoculation history. Certain countries and areas require this proof before allowing access into a jurisdiction. The only place I was ever asked to produce it was Brazil's Amazonas region. (If I could not prove I had received a yellow fever vaccination, the officials would have inoculated me on the spot.)

You can obtain an IAMAT membership by making a donation to the association. IAMAT offers up-to-date literature on health concerns and is an excellent medical resource. The organization will send you a worldwide list of English-speaking doctors who offer their services to travelers on a basic fee structure that excludes drugs or hospitalization.

While traveling, carry copies of your passport, visas, traveler's check numbers, and bike information. That way, if they get lost or stolen, it is easier to replace them.

Carrying a registration document for your bicycle is an excellent idea. This document doesn't have to be anything official as long as it looks authoritative to the border personnel. Design an impressive card with your photo, a couple of stamps, and the bike's serial number and particulars.

Each country's border requirements change, depending on the crossing and even the individuals manning it. (See the "Getting to the Country" section in each chapter for that country's particular requirements.)

When you go through customs, be courteous and quiet. To avoid suspicion, answer all questions directly; don't offer extra information and state "pleasure" as the purpose of your trip. Finally, Latin American border procedures are full of red tape, forms, delays, and unfathomable bureaucratic procedures. Don't let any of it bother you.

GETTING THERE. Shop carefully for tickets when flying anywhere in Latin America. From North America, most flights connect through Miami. From Europe, you connect through New York or Miami. The cheapest flights are with the South American airline companies.

Theoretically, you can connect between any city in the world, but the more connections you make, the more problems develop. The excessive baggage handling that each connection entails increases the possibility of bicycle damage. Changeovers also increase the chance of having things lost or stolen. To minimize the problems and hassles of connecting flights, take the most direct flight.

Most airlines' policy is to limit baggage weight or number of pieces. What airlines allow in practice, however, is usually more generous. Flights to developing countries usually fill with returning vacationers intent on returning with a ton of goods. I've seen huge televisions pass through baggage checks without an official raising an eyebrow. To minimize problems before buying tickets, ask what the airline's bike policy states. Carriers vary tremendously in their allowances, and a cheaper ticket may cost you more if the airline charges for bicycles as excess baggage. If possible, obtain their policy in writing.

Usually, airlines leave packing the bike to you. One method, neat but expensive, uses a specially designed bike-bag. The disassembled parts fit neatly into the inside pouches of the bag. A notable drawback is that you need a place to keep your bag while you are touring.

The second method is to use boxes for packing. The major disadvantage with boxes is that baggage handlers have no idea what the box contains. Ignoring the hundred "fragile" stickers, the handlers may toss, drop, or crush the box. Boxes are the riskiest way to pack your bike.

Large plastic bags are useful packing material. Handlers, seeing what they are loading, tend to treat the bike with more care. Airlines like plastic bags too, as the plastic protects other passengers' bags from your bike's grease and dirt. Some airlines even supply plastic bike-bags.

My favorite way of transporting a bike is wheeling it to the baggage section, making it as thin as possibly by removing the pedals, loosening the headset so that the handlebars can be turned sideways, and deflating the tires. The airlines may ask that you deflate the tires so they don't explode if the airplane's pressure drops. Baggage handlers can wheel the bike instead of carrying it, so the possibility of its staying upright increases. You may increase your chances of paint scratches, but it's better than a crushed bike.

Most airlines carrying bikes absolve themselves of liability; some may ask you to sign a waiver. Airlines seem paranoid about bikes; they'll take skis, surfboards, and golf clubs without a fuss, but bicycles frighten them. Prepare yourself for any delays by arriving early to process your gear.

WHERE AND WHEN TO GO. Why do you want to travel? Do you want to see stunning scenery or exotic cultures? Do you want to cruise lazily, enjoying the sun and sand of charming beaches where the living is easy, or do you want the excitement of isolation and the challenge of adversity?

Simply, what and when determine where. You should research routes and areas until you find the spot that satisfies what you want. Climate conditions establish when you should travel. Examine temperatures and precipitation periods for the zone that interests you. Nothing throws a stick in your spokes faster than poor weather.

Appendix C rates the scenery, cultural interest, and bicycling difficulty of the areas covered in this book and lists the rainy season for each. Appendix H gives temperature and precipitation data for the representative areas of each country.

A good map, complete with topography lines, is indispensable for whatever country you plan to visit. You'll want to choose the most rewarding routes, and you'll need to plan for provisions and accommodations. If one good map is vital, two maps are ideal. When you compare maps, you can judge the reality of distances, towns, and road conditions more accurately. If both maps locate a town, you can be sure it exists; if only one map has the town marked, be cautious of what you'll expect to find there.

An excellent source of maps outside of Latin America is International Travel Map Productions. They produce excellent maps of some countries, and they're quickly expanding their line to include most of Latin America. You can reach them at P.O. Box 2290, Vancouver, B.C. V6B 3W5, Canada. The European distributor is Bradt Publications, 41 Nortoft Road, Chalfont St. Peter, Bucks SL9 OLA, England.

Cycling to Corcovado's summit in Rio de Janeiro, Brazil

ON THE ROAD

You'll find every type of bicycle touring in Latin America. Bolivia inspires the rider with undeveloped conditions: rough roads, isolation, and challenging topography. Argentina seduces you with dignity. The people strive to re-create a miniature Europe: sophisticated, genteel, a lifestyle aimed toward richness. When you know the characteristics of each Latin American region, you can then anticipate its challenge and enjoyment.

ACCOMMODATIONS. Simply, you have two sleeping options: finding a roof for over your head, or carrying your roof with you. Rarely can you use one option exclusively. Carrying camping gear allows you the freedom to call anywhere your home—if only for a night. Alternately, in large cities you will probably want a safe place to store your gear.

In Latin America you can find rooms ranging from Copacabana's five-star international hotels hosting rock stars to squalid Honduran *pensiones* doubling as whorehouses. The variety of accommodations depends on the density of prosperous tourists. Large cities and tourist areas offer rooms of every type. Away from these major centers, your choices diminish gradually to a point where some villages off the tourist itinerary lack any type of accommodation.

Every country calls its hotels by different names, and each has a different rating system. Obviously, the higher the rating, the more a room will cost and the more amenities and luxuries you should find. However, the less formal and less expensive ones are often unrated. The cheapest types of accommodations are family-run establishments trying to make extra money with their spare rooms.

Finding a good room is usually a combination of luck and perseverance. Guidebooks are a good method of finding rooms in large cities. Be aware that the high rate of hotel and staff turnover makes their recommendations hit-or-miss propositions. At the least, you can use the information to locate hotels and evaluate the cleanliness and comfort for yourself.

Another method of finding a room is by getting advice from the local tourist office, police, or people on the street. This is a good method in smaller cities, where directions are less confusing and the people more knowledgeable about their towns. The disadvantage to this method is that locals assume that as a foreigner you have money and therefore want luxury. They may recommend hotels out of your price range, but eventually your searching will lead to an adequate hotel.

In towns and villages it's helpful to know that hotels are usually found near the bus and train terminals and around the town's main plaza. Hotels near bus and train stations tend to be noisier and seedier, but it's guaranteed you'll find a place to stay. Rooms around a main plaza are usually the best value: the noise is minimal and the location is good for local color, restaurants, and markets.

When you've found a hotel, inspect the room before paying. Check the general appearance, particularly whether the sheets and bathroom are clean. Remember that cleanliness is not merely an aesthetic concern; it is a matter of health. Do the lights and fan work? What is the shower situation? Are there particular times when there's hot water? Does the shower actually work? Does the shower cost extra? One primary reason to rent a room is to clean up, and a good, hot shower is worth its price.

Latin Americans have two methods of heating water for showers. The most efficient method is the gas heater. Within the boxed unit, a small pipe delivers water through a heating flame and then sends it to the nearby showerhead. Make sure, by shaking the canister, there is enough gas. Second, when you turn on the water, the pilot flame should energetically ignite the rest of the gas line. Finally, keep the water pressure low enough so that the flames can heat the water volume passing through it.

The electric showerhead is tingling at best and shocking at worst. In theory, when you connect the electric current and turn on the water, it warms up as it passes though the showerhead's element. In reality, the shower's warmth depends on the age and efficiency of the gadget and the available electricity to operate it effectively. Most small towns have a meager supply of power, so the chance of a hot shower with these devices is low, but if you touch the wires, the meager shock won't kill you either.

Water temperature is not an important consideration when choosing a room in the lowlands. Imagine dusk is settling in after you've finished a tough day's riding, and you're ready to fall asleep for a well-deserved rest. It begins; you hear a single buzz that quickly turns into a steady drone that fills the room. You spend your night fitfully, trying to avoid an endless, bloodthirsty horde. The greatest factor in selecting a lowland room is its ability to keep insects off your body. Upon first entering a room, look for a fan somewhere, or at least a mosquito net over the bed. Only by using proper netting or a moving air current can you avoid the onslaught of insects and get some sleep.

Most rooms offer some type of fan, either a small, oscillating table model or a full-size ceiling model. Ensure it works before taking a room for the night; its self-assured presence doesn't guarantee anything.

Latin Americans love their noise and can't understand why *gringos* want tranquillity. Noise outside your room may include a blaring television, a crying baby or, nestled at the back of the hotel, the chicken roost, promising you won't miss the sunrise. Noise is unavoidable. Carry a set of earplugs to deaden the clamor, and before choosing a room get a feel for the noise potential. Usually, street-side rooms are the noisiest.

Hotel clerks play a variety of games. You want a single; they only have doubles. You want a room without a bath; they only have them with baths. Don't agree too easily, as clerks change their mind if they think they'll lose a customer. In cheaper hotels you can negotiate anything. In more expensive hotels, hidden taxes and services may appear in the final price.

Finally, assuming you'll sleep most nights in lower-quality hotels, two tips. Always keep toilet paper and soap with you; hotels rarely provide them. Secondly, pack your food when you're finished eating, because food scraps and unwashed dishes attract pests.

You've learned how to find a decent room and sleep comfortably, but where will you store your bike? Life is simple if you have the extra space in your room; just lock your bike in the corner and relax.

If you can't keep the bike in your room, the next best solution is asking the proprietor for a secure spot to store and lock your bicycle. Almost every hotel has a locked storage area with spare space for securing your bike. Before leaving it in a separate room, remove all the gear that anyone else can easily pilfer—remove the temptation.

Also, to help in securing your room, carry a small padlock with you. In the smaller hotels, there is usually a hasp to attach a padlock to, and you should use them to lock your room at every opportunity. Regardless of whether you are using your lock or the hotel's, always secure your room, don't leave the key with anybody, and don't leave any valuables in the room. Finally, when sleeping, keep your money belt or pouch tucked under your pillow.

Camping is another, often better, alternative. When I'm touring, I love camping. I love the independence of stopping when I want; I love the freedom of relying on my intuition; and I love interacting with people who are unaccustomed to seeing travelers. Camping facilitates everything that's right about bicycle touring.

Organized camping is common in Argentina, Chile, and Brazil. These countries offer private facilities, which may have pools, showers, and restaurants, and many municipal campgrounds, which may be only a designated field on the town's outskirts.

Mexico, Belize, Guatemala, Costa Rica, Uruguay, and Venezuela operate scattered campgrounds. These countries' campgrounds, usually run by the municipality or a park commission, are scattered about, operate unpredictably, and are usually primitive.

Other countries in Latin America lack designated campgrounds. If you travel into any of these countries or other remote areas, you need to find a secure camping site. These are eleven essential principles to staying secure while wild camping:

1. Ask permission. Unless the area is deserted, get permission first. Your communication lessens suspicion and the possibility of threats, although you could find yourself engaged in unwanted attention and hospitality.

2. Camp out of sight of the road. Attract as little attention as possible unless you are in a small village, in which case the more people who know the better. Ask the local police to recommend a site; they are never fussy about local laws, and they add security.

3. Start looking for a site before you plan to stop. By paying attention to your surroundings, you'll have an idea of how long it will take to find a suitable spot. For example, in Baja you can choose almost anywhere to camp. Pick a time, pull off the road, and pitch your tent. However, farther into Mexico's mountainous interior, finding a flat, rock-free area is challenging.

4. Pick a spot carefully. How does the site feel? Will you attract a lot of attention? Are there weather factors to consider? How secure will you be? Try to find a place that's level and obstruction-free. Avoid damp ground and watch for hazards like branches that could poke through you or your

tent, cliffs that could fall on top of you or you could fall off of, and dry washes that in a storm could become raging rivers.

5. In desert and jungle areas, keep food out of your tent, as edibles attract insects and animals. Swarms of ants can chew through nylon easily and then enter through the small holes.

6. In fields be aware that at night farmers drive through their fields without their lights on.

7. In the sierra use cold-weather camping gear. Frost and below-zero temperatures are common at high altitudes, so tuck in your water bottles, cuddle into your cozy mummy bag, and listen to the wind howl across the mountain plateaus.

8. In the lowlands you need waterproof camping gear. Forget the insulated sleeping bags used in the sierra; instead, experience the challenge of staying dry through a tropical storm. You'll learn that there aren't many worse feelings than waking up inside a wet sleeping bag and then finding all your clothes and gear saturated. The easiest prevention: seal all the tent's seams and place your gear in leak-proof plastic bags.

9. With extensive cultivation or thick jungle overgrowth, finding a quiet, clear camping site can be tough. Look ahead on your route maps and find a spot beside a riverbank, because farmers will usually have cleared that area to give their cattle access to water.

10. Avoid camping in military zones, because the military never takes kindly to strangers. Ironically, these secret, restricted zones are one of the few things that are consistently signaled on the road, either with obvious signs or with ominous soldiers enforcing roadblocks. Deal with roadblocks as you would with border crossings. Stay calm, polite, and patient.

11. No matter where you camp, at night put your valuables in the bottom of your sleeping bag or inside your pillow. In Peru mountaineers camping on a glacier at 6,000 meters during a snowstorm have had their packs stolen.

For the four years I've camped on the road, I have never had problems with security. I've had weather problems, equipment problems, and problems with comfort, but I've never faced a threatening situation. By carefully selecting a spot, you should not have problems wild camping.

DRINKS. Cyclists require water to keep them going. Because you must maintain your liquid intake, you need a reliable source of pure water.

One way is to buy only bottled water. The main advantage to this method, as long as you ensure the top seal has not been broken, is knowing the water is safe. The disadvantage, of course, is the cost. Also, you can't depend on being able to buy bottled water, as some countries don't have it at all, some sell it only in tourist areas, and every country has areas where bottled water is uncommon.

Another way of getting drinking water is through a city's water supply. If you can smell high levels of chlorine, the water should be safe, but if you are ever in doubt, treat the water.

One way of decontaminating is to boil the water for ten minutes at sea level and longer at higher altitudes. The disadvantages of this chemical-free method are the amounts of fuel and time you need to sterilize a day's cycling needs.

A second method of treating water is through manufactured filters, which come in two styles. Ceramic filters extract the water's organisms. A porousness of 0.2 microns should eliminate all the organisms. The filter, fragile and heavy, must be handled carefully and kept clean.

Another filter style allows the water to seep through a chemical-laden filter, killing the microorganisms. The disadvantage to this otherwise simple system is the uncertain effectiveness after reaching the filter's limit.

Or you can manually add a chemical water treatment, most commonly iodine, in small doses for a long period without causing any bodily harm. To sterilize the water, add three drops of iodine per liter of water and wait thirty minutes. Iodine makes the water taste terrible, but it is effective. You can use chlorine bleach in the same way as iodine, but because of the caustic effects you should minimize your intake of bleach. Use bleach only in drastic circumstances.

Although you must take care with your drinking water, finding other safe drinks is easy. You can buy soft drinks at every store, restaurant, and roadside stop in any country. International brands of drinks are common throughout Latin America, but each country also has its local brands and flavors of pop.

Diet soft drinks, purely a Western ideal, are almost impossible to find. The idea that someone would buy something that didn't contain any calories, spending more to get less, is considered a sinful waste of money in a malnourished society.

Beer, safe and widespread, displaces water as the prime beverage. Regional brands are common in every country, and men everywhere in Latin America seem to drink beer constantly.

Alcohol has become the region's anesthetic. With the region's poverty and despair, many Latin Americans use alcohol to forget and escape. Cheap national alcohol is drunk in despairing amounts, making alcoholism an acute problem. Sundays are the time for heaviest drinking, so be careful while bicycling.

Markets and restaurants offer a dazzling array of exotic juices, mixing combinations of fruits, eggs, milk, pop, and beer. Each region specializes in its native fruits, so go ahead and try the different fruit juices and experiment with their combinations as you travel between regions. Remember, diluted juices have tap water added and could be contaminated.

Tea and coffee, regional specialties, vary between countries. For example, Colombia has some of the world's best coffee, while its neighbor, Ecuador, serves a boiled, wretched-tasting extract that you add to hot water.

FOOD. Throughout Latin America, meal routines are the same. Breakfast consists of bread, butter, fruit, and coffee. If you want anything more substantial, either find a more expensive restaurant catering to tourists or prepare the meal for yourself.

The main meal, lunch, is the "plate of the day." Although the names differ throughout Latin America, it's always the same three courses. The first course, *la sopa,* is made from a broth of beef bones and has a small amount of pasta or rice thrown into it. *La segunda,* the second course, is made up of a slice of tough, fried beef with enough fat to give you a feeling of fulfillment. This bit of meat complements a serving of carbohydrates, usually rice or pasta, but you may receive exotic tubers, such as *oca* or *chuno*, two small vegetables freeze-dried for storage and then rehydrated when cooked. Occasionally added to the meal is a scrap of salad that is probably crawling with harmful amoeba and bacteria, which I hope you don't dare eat. If you are in luck, you may also get bread, a drink, or dessert.

Finding the final meal of the day is toilsome. Normally, you order from a menu or whatever the cook has available. At night, prices rise and service slows. Evening meals lack popularity among the locals because most of them eat supper at home. Thankfully, at this time of day restaurants serve their regional dishes. If you can't identify something on the menu, ask first. When you've finished a long day of cycling, it's frustrating to be served a plate of steamed tripe.

Finding restaurants is similar to finding a room for the night. You find the best values on the main square, at transportation terminals, or local markets. (For more on markets, see the "Shopping" section later in this chapter.) When you find a restaurant, get a feel for its cleanliness and popularity. The locals know where to find the best value and freshest food. Ask about the prices, including taxes and service charges, before ordering. This isn't necessary if you are in a market or small stall, but in more expensive restaurants hidden taxes can increase your final bill enormously.

Search, inspect, ask—finding a decent restaurant involves diligence.

EXCHANGING MONEY. Money issues remain the most unpredictable facet of Latin American traveling. Economic situations throughout the region change rapidly and unpredictably. In Brazil the president begins a new economic policy and the exchange rate compresses to a fraction of its original. In Bolivia inflation balloons and recedes, depending on the political leanings of the party in power. No matter where or how long you travel, you must endure the governments' financial policies.

If you are on a short trip, the economic fluctuations won't impact you in the same way that they will if you are planning an extended stay, when every dollar counts. Keep your eyes and ears open for these economic developments, remembering the most volatile event is a new government taking power. Ultimately, you are at the whim of circumstance, an inescapable fact of Latin America traveling.

Each country sanctions certain methods of changing currency. As a rule, when you first enter the country, change the least amount of money you can get away with so that you can compare rates elsewhere in the country. If you arrive by air, the international airport's exchange facilities will have worse rates and higher commissions than in the city. Arriving overland, most major border crossings have exchange facilities, formal and parallel. If you use the parallel market, shop around for the best rates.

When using any form of the parallel market—legal, illegal, or tolerated—you have to be careful. First, learn if the market is legal. Second, money changers will attempt various deceptions. Before starting a transaction on the street, have the exact cash you want to change easily available. Don't show where you have your money cached. Once you have negotiated the rate, make sure the amount you should receive is correct. Take the liberty of using the changer's calculator and double-check the figures yourself. It's easy in the heat of the exchange to err in your multiplication, leaving you on the short end of the transaction. Lastly, take their money and count it before handing over your cash. If cash is short, double-check again, as changers may try to peel off extra bills or through sleight-of-hand exchange the bills with smaller denominations. Only when you are fully satisfied should you give a changer your money.

How often you need to change money is contingent on the inflation rate. In some countries the country's inflation rate is low enough that you don't worry about rapid devaluation; you can cash larger sums of money at once. In countries where inflation causes the rate to change hourly, exchanging money becomes a ritual. Always be aware of your local cash supply, as only large cities have check- and cash-changing facilities. In Guatemala's highlands or Bolivia's lowlands, you'll run into problems if all you have is traveler's checks or American cash. Awareness of your cash supply applies to weekends and holidays as well, so don't allow your local currency to drop to less than a few days' needs.

Your supply of local currency should have a stock of small denominations, since you will hear *"No cambio"* frequently. When shopping in smaller villages, in markets, and during any bus or train trip, finding change is difficult because of vendors' small supplies of cash.

The best advice for carrying your money is to keep small stashes in various places (for example, in money belts around your waist and leg, in the seat tube of your bike, and in a corner of your pannier). Be creative so if you do get robbed, the chance of being left penniless is remote.

SECURITY. Security is exploding into a major issue for travelers everywhere. When you scan the potential hazards that could befall a traveler, it's a wonder anybody is traveling. The risk list seems endless: civil war, theft, accidents, disease, hurricanes, and radiation poisoning. Anytime you travel you expose yourself to risks, whether visiting New York, New Delhi, or Nuevo Laredo. Latin America is no different. Certain areas pose extreme danger, while other areas are safer than parts of North America. The first step in keeping safe is research.

When you start pondering the possibility of bicycle touring in a certain region, examine the country's perils and security rating in the "Security" section of the relevant chapter. With the information, evaluate the probability of an incident occurring. Then assess your ability and willingness to cope with the hazards. After you realize the risks involved and assess your ability to handle an incident, decide if the area is appropriate.

Personal safety tops the list of threats. You can replace money and possessions, but you cannot compromise on your well-being.

No security devices will keep you safe if you don't have a positive outlook. It's the best trait to pack. Displaying an open nature allows the locals to perceive you as friendly and honest. They start relating to you as a person and not as bounty.

Part of your self-assurance comes from your familiarity with your surroundings. Become comfortable with the area's customs as quickly as possible. Another part of a successful attitude is a natural and confident bearing—stand tall and walk with authority. By maintaining a positive and self-respecting attitude, you ensure that criminals see someone who is not easily intimidated and, therefore, a high-risk target. Don't act threatening, loud, condescending, or rich.

A good attitude reduces your chances of confronting a dangerous situation, and awareness of your daily state of mind also reduces your vulnerability. A grueling day of cycling, a tedious bus trip, an exchange of money, or a first day in a new city all could make you a more attractive target to thieves. Prepare yourself. When you arrive in a large city, carrying all your gear, do not stop to talk with anyone who approaches you. This may seem rude, but even children and women steal. If you need advice or directions, choose a trustworthy-looking person to approach.

If you are threatened, remember that your first goal is surviving unharmed. Give up your property. In some areas (Rio's a good example) muggers work in gangs, and at the first sign of trouble, they'll all swarm on you like piranhas. Always carry a small amount of cash to surrender to an attacker because if you have nothing, they could become frustrated and strike in anger. During any incident, stay calm and concentrate on getting a physical description of the attacker. If there are people nearby, try to attract attention by breaking the nearest window or yelling "fire." Yelling "help" is usually not a good idea because many people, hesitant to get involved in a potentially violent situation, may ignore the cries.

Hopefully, an attacker will not try to harm you. Most thieves are cowards who want as little trouble as possible, so most incidents are the grab-and-run type. But if an armed attacker does try to hurt you and you have to defend yourself, commit yourself to an all-out effort: shout, scream, hit, bite, gouge. Often a show of defiance scares attackers away because they don't expect problems from a meek traveler. Afterward, go to the police as soon as possible to report the incident.

The right attitude is also critical in securing your property. Always be alert for suspicious individuals and dangerous situations. When in public, act like you know where you are going and watch for blind spots or opportune areas for a criminal.

Minimize the bait. Jewelry and expensive watches lure thieves. Expose other valuables, especially cameras, as little as possible. Take your photos and put your camera away, keeping your gear secure to your body rather than slinging it over your shoulder. Locals have become adept at slicing and emptying all types of packs, so hug your bag in front of you.

Another popular trick is for the criminal to smear something on your bag or back, point it out, then help you wipe away the substance. The idea is to separate you from your pack. Once you put down your bag, it's gone.

Bicyclists are perceived differently than other tourists. Since only the poor ride bikes in Latin America, most locals don't see foreign cyclists as rich targets. As more cyclists are touring through Latin America, however, perceptions are changing.

Perceptions aside, bicycling makes you less vulnerable for two reasons. First, most crimes occur on crowded public transport, particularly during the chaos of boarding. Secondly, most crimes are committed in large cities, where the desperate try to survive. Cyclists spend most of their time along deserted roads and small villages, where the people are more honorable.

Before you start traveling on idyllic roads among virtuous villagers, take security precautions for your bike. First, keep a photo and the serial number of the bike. If your bike does go missing, you can show the police your photo. Hide a photocopy of your proof of ownership in the seat post or handlebar ends. If there is a dispute over the ownership or when a stolen bicycle is recovered, magically pulling out a piece of identification from the bike is a moment of triumph.

Criminals are unlikely to target your bike because specialized touring bikes are conspicuous. In cities, however, always lock your bike. In smaller towns and villages, if you plan on leaving your bike unattended for more than a few hours, either lock it or ask a waiter or storekeeper to watch it for you. Most museums, hotels, stores, and restaurants allow you to take your bicycle inside.

Some cyclists try another way of minimizing the risk of having their bikes stolen: using duct tape they wrap the bike's frame to reduce attention. Although this is probably true, it might not be the best approach. The more flashy your bike, the more curious and friendly the locals are toward you. People pay attention and keep an eye out for you. The more special you look, the more special you are treated.

Thieves are more likely to target your panniers. Use bags that attach to the bike rack securely. In cities stow everything. Don't leave anything hanging loose off your bike, even laundry or food.

Anti-government activities, such as coups, demonstrations, and insurgencies, are another security concern. Political groups seldom target travelers, so most incidents are a result of being in the wrong place at the wrong time. Terrorism is a definite threat in some countries. Before entering these risky areas, gather as much information as possible on the frequency and intensity of the terrorist activity and on terrorists' attitude toward travelers. Once you have the facts, rationally weigh the decision to enter that area.

Areas with intense terrorist activity include Guatemala, El Salvador, Colombia, Peru, parts of Brazil, and to a lesser extent, Honduras, Nicaragua, and Venezuela.

Another problem area is drugs. Travelers who get involved with drugs are stupid. Officials hunt for drug-carrying travelers. If the government can find a foreign scapegoat, they can absolve themselves of responsibility and blame the drug problem on the First World. If you try to smuggle drugs, you deserve what you get—a long sentence in a decrepit jail.

Different countries have different attitudes about drugs. Belize seems to have a relaxed attitude toward marijuana. Dealers deal and smokers smoke openly, but the drug is still illegal and if you are in possession, they'll probably deport you. Drug searches when you leave Belize are common. Bolivians and Peruvians legally harvest the coca plant. The locals use its leaves as a mild stimulant, and anyone can indulge by buying coca leaves and lime, a necessary catalyst. Coca paste and cocaine are illegal, with stiff penalties for possession. It is also illegal to export coca leaves.

Don't carry parcels for anyone. If you are in possession of drugs, you are just as guilty as whoever gave them to you. The courts don't care if you are an ignorant *gringo*.

Women traveling in Latin America have another set of security concerns. For various reasons, men in undeveloped countries often view Western women as sluts, ready to jump into bed at any whistle or show of attention. Maybe this perception comes about from the exported North American culture, or maybe Latinos believe foreign females are inherently vulnerable. Either way, all females are viewed as second-class citizens. The *machismo* that predominates in Latin American society causes women to be subject to whistles, leers, sexist remarks, and fondling.

To minimize problems, female travelers should try not to dress or act provocatively. Act confident and ignore the men's provocations. The harassment also decreases if a male accompanies a woman.

All this discussion about risk, security, and trouble should not scare you away from traveling. The rewards of traveling greatly outweigh its dangers, and you can reduce the dangers with two key attributes, attitude and awareness. Both will offer you more security than the strongest lock.

See Appendix D for a rating of security concerns (personal safety, security of property, political problems, and drugs) for each country.

LANGUAGE AND PEOPLE. In general, Latin Americans exhibit friendliness, curiosity, and helpfulness, but they lack a sense of personal space and privacy. This is particularly true in smaller villages, where you arrive not only as a foreigner but as a foreigner on a bike. You would attract as much attention if you had come from the moon. I remember the times I would set up our tent and start cooking. Soon the entire village surrounded us and became our audience. We entertained them with our modern technology, and it wasn't long before their questions about how things worked and how much they cost demanded much of our time and attention. As you go through your routines, they'll stare, question you, and talk among themselves. Bearing in mind this inevitable onslaught of curiosity, it's important that you stay friendly to them. If they sense your respect and patience, they'll treat you as a guest and keep an eye out for you and your belongings.

With this boundless attention and questioning, knowing as much Spanish as possible helps in understanding, communicating, and surviving. Finding a room, ordering at a restaurant, or getting directions becomes easier if you know the language. Don't go to Latin America thinking everyone knows some English. In tourist areas you can find English-speaking locals, but in remote areas it's rare; and in some regions of Latin America, the locals don't even speak Spanish, preferring to retain their local dialects of Maya, Quechua, or Ayamara.

Spanish itself is regional. The people may use different words for almost the same thing. For example, locals may call a hotel a *hotel, hotelito, hospedaje, pension,* or *casa de huéspedes*.

Different pronunciations merge into dialects. You may find Mexican

Spanish easier to understand than Argentine Spanish that clips its words, drops its vowels, and treats consonants lazily. You'll develop an ear for the differences as you travel through the region.

Differing from the rest of Latin America, Brazilians speak Portuguese. Brazilians will understand your Spanish, but you won't understand their Portuguese replies. Although many words and grammar structures retain similarities to Spanish, letters are pronounced differently.

Therefore, learn as much Spanish as possible before starting your trip. Rent cassettes, read books, take lessons, practice with Spanish speakers—do what you can beforehand to make your trip more gratifying and to minimize the culture shock.

Culture shock is the confusion you suffer when entering an alien environment. Suddenly, the unknown surroundings upset your morals, values, routines, language, and lifestyle. Prepare by reading and learning about the culture, gaining a clearer idea of what to expect. Once in the country, an open mind and attitude help to reduce your anxiety. When you impose your values on another culture, it increases your resistance. The process of feeling comfortable takes longer.

See Appendix E for a guide to pronouncing Spanish and Appendix F for a list of bicycling terms in Spanish.

CLIMATE AND ALTITUDE. Cycling puts you into the open; that's its primary joy. To exult in the heat and cold on a daily basis, to defy the wind and rain on your face intensifies the here and now of traveling. It helps if you know how to manage the weather conditions you might encounter. Climatic factors can mentally drain, emotionally depress, and physically challenge you.

Check the appropriate climate chart in Appendix H. What are the high,

Enjoying the mercado de dulce, *the sweet market, in Morelia, Mexico*

low, and average temperatures, and when is the rainy season? If you know that the 80-kph winds of the Argentine Patagonia peak in spring, you'll anticipate the work of pedaling. If you know that the Bolivian *altiplano* temperatures drop to sub-zero, you'll bring appropriate gear.

Cyclists can easily tolerate cold. Start by dressing in layers, paying attention to the most vulnerable areas, your feet and hands. While cycling, your activity should warm you through the coldest weather. When you stop, hoard your heat. Change from your wet, sweaty clothes and bundle yourself in dry layers. Wet clothes of any kind strip you of your body heat.

Rain depresses every cycle tourist, and during every journey, no matter how well planned, rain will fall. Check when the rainy season occurs in the area you want to travel. This lone fact should play a major part in your choice of destination. No one wants to slog through gray, rain-soaked days. If your schedule or stubbornness forces you to continue, the best way to tackle the situation is to arm yourself with appropriate gear: a water-repellent jacket, a hat, fenders, and plastic bags for all your gear.

Bicycling in the rain, you risk saturated gear, but with a combination of cold and rain, you risk hypothermia. Hypothermia must be taken seriously—it kills. In extreme hypothermia the temperature of your vital organs drops below functioning levels. The first signs are convulsive, dramatic shivering. As it progresses, the shivering decreases and the muscles turn rigid. The victim starts becoming incoherent. This is a critical time; if you do nothing, the victim will fall into a coma and die.

Prevention against severe hypothermia requires stopping the heat loss and warming the victim. At the onset, shelter him or her from the wind and feed something sweet to the victim. If the hypothermia escalates, you must slowly warm the victim with direct body contact. You should never reach this severe stage if you continually monitor your physical state in cold, wet conditions.

Maybe you decide to avoid cold, wet areas and to travel in a hot, sunny area instead. But high temperatures combined with intense cycling are also potentially harmful. If your core body temperature starts to rise faster than your system can moderate it, you start suffering from hyperthermia. At the onset the victim feels nauseous and faint, and his or her skin turns clammy. Heat exhaustion is when the victim grows slightly confused. When there is disorientation and feverlike temperatures, the condition is classified as heatstroke. Beyond this phase, hyperthermia has the potential to kill. Move the victim into the shade and keep him or her cool. Dip the person in a stream or use wet cloths while fanning him or her.

Before starting a long tour in hot weather, spend a day or two getting used to the heat before exerting yourself. While cycling, drink as much water as possible and keep your shirt and hat on so that your perspiration will keep you cooler. Finally, do what almost every Latin American does: avoid the hottest part of the day by taking a siesta.

Sunburn can be another problem. To avoid being burned, you should stay covered with a hat and shirt, exposing your skin gradually. Always bring and use sunscreen, a tourist luxury that is expensive everywhere. The sun is most blistering at high altitudes. The thinner atmosphere combined with the concentrated sunlight of the middle latitudes is a recipe for barbecued skin.

High altitudes can cause another problem. As you climb into the Andes, slowly pedaling and gasping for breath, it's hard to believe that the Amazon rainforest, neighboring the Andes, produces a third of the world's oxygen. Not much of it seems to rise to the sierra! In this thin air you'll find yourself panting and becoming dizzy as you climb higher into the mountains. The altitude starts affecting each cyclist at different heights. I didn't start feeling short of breath until 4,000 meters, but other cyclists have had difficulty at only 3,500, while others aren't affected until 5,000 meters.

You can ease ordinary altitude symptoms with proper physical conditioning and slow ascents. For instance, if you fly into Quito, it's a good idea to relax the first couple of days and reduce activities causing shortness of breath: alcohol, smoking, and rigorous exercise.

Acute, or ordinary, mountain sickness begins with a headache, a feeling of exhaustion, and shortness of breath. Severe cases develop into vomiting. These conditions diminish over a few days for most people. But do not ignore these early symptoms—if the condition advances, the victim could develop high-altitude pulmonary edema, in which fluid builds up in the lungs. The victim experiences symptoms like pneumonia: coughing and shortness of breath. If the condition gets worse, the coughing generates a pink foam. Soon, the victim could die.

In cerebral edema, an even more serious high-altitude condition, fluid builds up in the brain. Rare but deadly, the condition causes violent headaches and hallucinations. If acute mountain sickness symptoms persist after a few days, you must return the victim to lower elevations, or a coma or death could occur.

Rain, heat, and altitude can be serious, but the wind is psychologically the worst element facing a cyclist. A strong headwind can be frustrating and discouraging. A crosswind can blow you off the road or into traffic, and debris and dirt can be whipped into your eyes.

Most winds decrease in the early morning and at twilight—the best times for avoiding windy conditions. Pressure systems also factor into shifting winds. Usually, low-pressure systems arrive from one direction and high-pressure systems from another. If you are having great weather and you notice an opposing wind shift, you can expect a change in the weather.

To lessen the effect of wind, stay tucked in an aerodynamic position on your bike. Pace yourself and try staying in a comfortable rhythm, no matter how slow. Fighting the wind tires you more quickly and adds to your frustration, so take breaks regularly.

HEALTH AND HYGIENE. A major concern for every tourist in Latin America is health. The cyclist is even more exposed than most travelers to contaminated water supplies, suspect food, and rustic sleeping conditions. With proper precautions, however, you can turn these liabilities into advantages. When bicycling, you control precisely where you eat and sleep, and your conditioning gives you greater resistance to diseases than travelers who spend most of their time on buses.

The greatest cause of most diseases is unsanitary drinking, eating, and sleeping conditions. Amoebiasis and intestinal parasites can be contracted through impure water supplies, cholera and hepatitis from poorly handled food, and malaria and lice from unprotected sleeping arrangements. If you remain meticulous about these three factors—water, food, and sleep—your risks will decrease.

Water may be the easiest to control if you disinfect all drinking water. Also avoid ice (because freezing does not kill disease-causing organisms), diluted juices, and food contaminated with tap water.

Carefully select where you eat, opting for busy restaurants with well-cooked food. The hygienic standards of fast-food vendors on the street are atrocious: they're the major cause of cholera in travelers.

If you decide to cook, ensure you thoroughly cook meat and vegetables; peel all fruit and wash vegetables with treated water.

As you drink, eat, and sleep in Latin America, you develop an immunity to the local bugs. If you are on a short trip, you should be extra careful of what you ingest, but as you spend more time in the region, your digestive tract will adapt and you'll become less susceptible to minor ailments.

When you are looking for a hotel, consider its cleanliness. If the room, bathroom, and sheets look clean, there's less chance of contracting a pest. The most serious risk is malaria. In malaria-prone areas, check whether the fan in the room works and whether they provide a mosquito net.

If you do catch a suspicious ailment, or symptoms are lingering and minor medications haven't helped, you should find a medical professional. You can find a reputable English-speaking doctor who is an expert on the region's illnesses either through your embassy, which should maintain an updated list of doctors and pharmacies, or through the International Association of Medical Assistance to Travelers, IAMAT. (See the "Health" section earlier in this chapter.)

Most travelers are stunned when they see a Latin American pharmacy. Operated by staff in authoritative lab coats, the pharmacies' shelves are filled with any pharmaceutical you could want, from aspirin to morphine—all without prescription. You can use pharmacies safely if you know what you want and can understand enough Spanish to realize what you're taking. Be aware, however, of how enticing it can be to prescribe yourself medications for every little problem that you have. Pharmacists, ignorant of the problem or just unscrupulous, may sell you expired, inappropriate, or dangerous drugs.

Doctors are the best authorities for dealing with health problems. They can be cheap and reliable, and have plentiful experience dealing with local health problems.

Keep a basic supply of medications with you while bicycling. If you travel through an isolated area and you get hit with an incapacitating bout of diarrhea, a dose of Lomotil will calm your system and get you to an area where you can rest and let the bug run its course. More serious, if you are hit with what you think is a case of malaria (abrupt onset of fever, chills, headache, and possibly nausea), you need to act quickly. You can't allow the virus to do its damage or it could be fatal. If you cannot see a doctor who can take a blood smear, take a regime of Fansidar and then seek medical attention.

CYCLING PROBLEMS. When you start logging kilometers on a bike, your body may eventually suffer different types of distress, from the preventable to the unavoidable.

The biggest unavoidable cycling problem is the accident. No matter how cautious you are, an accident can happen to anyone. Start with prevention and caution. Wear a helmet; most serious head injuries are the result of not using one. Stay alert for possible dangers when you are cycling. On descents and in cities, maintain a safe speed. When you start feeling reckless, you're going too fast.

If you take a spill, use the tuck-and-roll method. The best response is to quickly flex your neck, forearms, and shoulders in a curled position to prevent your extremities from taking the brunt of the fall. Unfortunately, most cyclists who crash find themselves landing on their hands or shoulders. If you keep your arms stretched above you, you may lose a bit more skin (wear your shirt), but you'll prevent breaking an arm or collarbone, separating your shoulder, or striking your head.

Learn basic first aid, particularly for managing cuts, scrapes, "road-rash," broken limbs, and blows to the head.

You'll also need to know how to counteract the continuous stress on your joints. On an average cycling day, your legs rotate 28,000 times. If your joints start bothering you, especially at the beginning of a tour, take a day off and restart using lower gears to lessen the stress. If you are an experienced cyclist, examine your pedaling, particularly if you've changed any elements. A new pair of shoes may cause a new leg alignment on your rotation, and your joints will need to adjust to the change.

Your feet can become numb because the pressure of your feet on the pedals restricts the blood flow. Shift your feet slightly on the pedals to increase circulation.

Most alarming may be your crotch area going numb. The nerves between your pelvis and saddle compress and constrict the circulation. If you lose the feeling in your crotch, stop riding until the feeling returns. To prevent the condition, tilt the saddle forward (downward) or raise the handlebars a bit. All these actions shift more weight onto your wrists and hands.

After placing more of your body weight on your wrists, you may get a pinched nerve, which can cause your hands to go numb. Adding extra padding on your bars, wearing gloves, and shifting your hand position on the bars reduces the pinching.

Shifting positions on the bike also reduces the strain in your neck. The best remedy is to stretch your neck frequently and to stop and rest.

Another common cycling problem is saddle sores. As your pelvic area slides over the seat, the friction and sweat causes burning and then a sore to develop.

The best prevention for saddle sores is a good pair of shorts with a crotch of seamless cotton or chamois. Whatever the material, it must absorb sweat. Keep your shorts as clean as possible. Ideally, you will have two pairs, one to wear while the second is drying from the previous day's wash. If irritation does develop, use petroleum jelly to reduce the friction. Clean the area after you're finished cycling and keep it dry to prevent the sore from becoming infected. Overall, cleanliness is an important factor in staying healthy on the road.

SHOPPING. Shopping for market foods is a way of sharing in the common public experience of Latin America. In the markets you can experience a lifestyle underpinned by community reliance and responsibility. The experience of shopping for your onions and canned tuna, haggling over a few cents, will reap rewards. Cross-cultural barriers will dissolve and you'll learn humility. These simple efforts will promote a greater understanding of a culturally fragile region and allow you to feel greater empathy for its people, long subjugated by events beyond their control.

There was a period when the universal market day was Sunday. The Catholic church wanted market day to increase attendance at Sunday Mass. Today, the mobile general store has changed this tradition. Drivers selling a variety of merchandise from other parts of the country rotate weekly among an area's markets.

When you explore the market, your senses will reel. Indian women in their rainbow-embroidered shawls sell eerie tubers. A group of dusty men, bedraggled from the pre-market debauchery, check a frightened llama's teeth. Will the buyer use the animal for wool or for tomorrow's meal? Despite the market's intensity, show respect. The people of the Andes, for example, remain inward and stoic and are offended easily. So don't become another tourist whose only interest is to take photos as you would of animals in a zoo. The people will accept you more easily if you delve in, bargain, and interact. Learn to laugh over ridiculous prices, play the bargaining game, and don't be insulted if they treat you as a *gringo*.

At the market there are some ground rules. First, learn what's acceptable to bargain for. Some food vendors stick to their standard prices; others bargain for any and everything. If you're shy and don't bargain for staples, everyone suffers the consequences. Bargaining for folk art is different. Artisans produce folk art to sell to tourists, not to locals. Tourists can be expected to pay a higher price. However, everyone has to buy food. If the vendors think they will get a higher price from tourists than from locals, prices may rise for everyone.

As a *turista* you should expect to pay more than the locals for things, but how readily you accept this depends on how desperately you need the item. For example, you may not be bothered over an extra five cents for a soft drink in one instance, but in another circumstance you may squabble and storm away frustrated. I recall the times I argued over only a cent or two, then felt angry over the incident. Keep your perspective. Latin Americans see Westerners as having enormous riches (relatively, we do), and you should remember the amount you choose to quibble about.

When you start bargaining for something you "just have to have," try acting indifferent, muting your initial enthusiasm. Decide on a fair price, based on the local standard of living and the amount of effort needed to make the item. Determine beforehand the item's worth and the maximum you're willing to pay for it.

A mask-wearing campesino *enjoys the pre-market festivities in Zumbahua, Ecuador.*

A common complaint from tourists is that the quality of Latin American folk art has decreased in recent years. What travelers don't realize is how their stinginess has caused this to happen. If you're unwilling to pay a fair price for an item, you force the local artisan to sell something so he can feed his family. He can't afford to labor for a month to produce a high-quality piece if tourists refuse to pay a fair price. Consequently, the artisan begins to use cheaper materials and skimps on workmanship so he can get the same stingy price from a tourist. So, don't dread paying a fair price for quality. Most artisans take pride in their work and just try to get what they feel the tourist can afford; they're not trying to swindle you.

Markets, whether in crowded plazas or on the main streets, are prime districts for thieves. When shopping, carry your cash in small denominations; that way merchants can make change and you won't telegraph to thieves how much money you have and where you are carrying it.

Another frustrating aspect of shopping in Latin America is managing the siesta, the routine of closing shop and sleeping away the afternoon heat. Each country and each region within a country observes the siesta with varying degrees of rigidity. When you enter a region, find out what opens when. This information will help when you need to buy provisions where towns are far apart. Your day's progress ends when you have to wait two hours for the only store in town to open.

Like siestas, Sundays and holidays create problems with store closures. An unannounced holiday will have you scrambling for food supplies. Check the "Money" sections for respective holidays and how the people regard siesta and Sundays in each country.

COMMUNICATIONS. You start feeling homesick, you get lonely, and you wonder why you even started traveling. Every traveler has these feelings, and the longer you travel the more acute they become. But what better way to reduce the gloom than by receiving a letter from a friend, or phoning home and hearing your family's voices? Communication is the salve to a wounded traveler's spirit.

The most common form of keeping in touch is through the mail. Send all mail first-class and register all parcels. If any items, such as film and journals, are important, use the international couriers found in every country.

You can receive mail through the *Lista de Correos* at major post offices. Companies you buy your traveler's checks from usually have a mail service for their customers; get a list of offices and forward them to your contacts. Instruct your contacts to underline and capitalize your last name and use lowercase letters for your given name after your surname (for example, "SIENKO, Walter"). Do not use any titles, such as Mr. or Ms. If you are expecting a letter and it hasn't arrived, ask the staff to check under any combination of your name.

Every country operates a telex and telephone system with varying abilities to handle long-distance and collect calls. Telex operations are usually at the same offices as telephones.

It's possible to keep up with world events. Countries with a hefty English population or ones that experience a large influx of tourists carry English-language newspapers, either published in the country or imported from the United States. Weekly newsmagazines from abroad are distributed throughout capital cities.

HOBBIES. Insect collecting, writing, stamp collecting, shortwave radios, and photography are only a few of the hobbies that travelers continue to pursue while traveling. You can partake in any type of hobby that you are willing to pack on your bike.

Photography is the most popular pastime of travelers. The major risk is that your camera will attract thieves, so don't wear it hanging off your chest while you wander; take your picture and put your camera away.

The key to combining photography and bicycle touring is to be adaptable. If you want good photographs, the minimum equipment includes a solid 35mm camera body with a minimum of electronics because dust and humidity will eat away at the circuitry. A 35–105mm zoom lens will cover most shooting situations, but to expand your range, two lenses, a 28–85mm and a 75–300mm, are excellent. I use a waist pack to carry my camera so it stays available and secure and my body can absorb most of the road shock. A small flash is helpful to fill dark areas, but a tripod isn't necessary because you can find something to rest your camera against while you take a picture. An autofocus system is excellent, but you sacrifice f-stops and creativity for convenience.

Discretion is important if you don't want formal, stiff poses from your subjects. Anytime people object to your taking pictures, respect their rights. Avoid photographing military installations, border posts, and scenes of poverty. Latin Americans maintain a strong sense of pride and do not appreciate wealthy *gringos* documenting their shortcomings.

After you've taken your pictures, I generally recommend avoiding the film processing in Latin America. Its quality is unpredictable. However, each country offers different prices and availability for photography supplies and film. Consult the "Photography" sections.

CONTENTMENT. The three keys to contentment are having a positive attitude, keeping your travel expectations realistic, and staying in shape. A positive attitude can keep you going in a difficult situation—through Ecuador's inundated markets or Patagonia's debilitating winds, for example. A mature traveler realizes that engaging areas don't last forever and that rainy days and climbs don't last forever either.

Another key for relaxing on the road is to keep your expectations realistic. Understanding that every area and every day won't be perfect, you keep situations in perspective. Enjoying being there is what traveling is about. Pamper yourself sometimes. Eating in a fancy restaurant, taking a day off, or hopping on a bus to skip an uninteresting area will help you to enjoy the adventures and misadventures.

These mental parts of touring are half the effort; the other half combines physical conditioning and health. When cycling is a preference rather than a means to an end, bicycle touring is magic. Combine the mental and physical ingredients and staying strong and happy comes effortlessly.

CHOOSING YOUR ROUTE. Choosing the right route is critical to your cycling enjoyment. You can choose a route and area for its challenge, for its scenery and sights, or simply because it's the shortest distance between two points.

Decide your priorities for a given area. For example, bouncing around on large rocks and swerving constantly to avoid potholes requires all your concentration, so scenery and wildlife become secondary to accepting the route's challenges.

Some countries have excellent roads that are well maintained and have little traffic, while other countries' roads are a cyclist's nightmare of diesel-spewing buses and broken asphalt. Road conditions continually deteriorate and improve. Advance knowledge of road conditions helps in choosing a route. You can judge the amount of traffic by the number of alternate routes between major cities. For example, in Brazil between Rio de Janeiro and São Paulo lies a multilane expressway carrying immense volumes of traffic, but the stupendous coast holds a quiet, well-maintained road—a cycling treasure unknown to most travelers.

You can also find out about current road conditions by asking the truckers and bus drivers who drive the route continuously. Good maps that detail surfaces and types of road also help your advance knowledge and planning.

Cycling through the Andes Mountains takes more courage and better conditioning. Whether you ride on the heavily traveled roads of the Pan-American Highway or strike out onto the isolated tributary roads, prepare for the length of grades and the condition of the road surfaces. The average length of climbs in the mountains is between 20 and 40 kilometers. On the Pan-Am, the grades are usually more manageable and the road better engineered, but other roads through the mountains can be exhaustingly steep and frustratingly endless. At times, the road is a roller coaster, chasing ridges but never reaching one decisive pass. Other times, a climb may embrace your full day's effort, starting from the floor of the jungle and peaking in the half-frozen *paramó*. Carefully plan lengthy ascents by studying your map's topography lines and collecting needed provisions at available stops.

As opposed to the slow mental preparations of Andean ascents, descents require a different sort of planning. Before submitting to the exhilaration of a long descent, check your bike's brakes, tire pressure, and all nuts and bolts. A rack's shaking loose into a front wheel during an 80-kph descent should be left for nightmares. As you descend, keep your head up and concentrate on what lies ahead. No one will hear you coming; people, dogs, and sheep may wander out into the road unexpectedly.

When you are thousands of miles from home, you need to use more caution than if you were cycling to your local corner store. Certain hazards you should watch out for are car doors opening in front of you (watch for drivers in parked cars), people and animals suddenly running in front of you (both in cities and in the country), Saturday and Sunday drunk drivers, cars that want to turn right, sewer grates and potholes beside the curb (they can flip you, throw you into traffic, or damage your wheel), bridge expansion joints and railway crossings (cross them laterally), and finally, dogs.

Use trial and error to find a method for repelling dogs intending to take a chunk out of your leg. Try stopping and pretending to throw a rock. If that doesn't work, you may need a more aggressive tactic to deter a vicious dog.

For various reasons you may want to take another form of transportation instead of bicycling: your time is running short; the weather is depressing; you want to avoid a bad stretch of road, traffic, or an unsafe area; you suffer from burnout; or you're ill. Any of these reasons may lead you to take planes, buses, trains, taxis, or boats. Unless you are trying to break a record, there's no need to embrace unnecessary suffering.

The definite advantage in flying is its speed. The disadvantages are the extra fares, which can total 50 to 100 percent more per bicycle. You may also need to do some quick talking to take a bike with you, so prepare for a debate. Before you buy your ticket, ask about packing and additional costs and try to obtain something in writing.

Trains are more laborious because of the extra procedures and costs in checking your bike. Also, on a long journey you may have a nagging fear that your bike won't arrive when you do, or won't arrive at all.

Buses offer the best value in almost every country. Fares vary, depending on how badly the driver needs passengers and how strongly you persist. You can also increase your chances for getting bus transport by disassembling your bike beforehand. For security, take your bike bags inside with you.

Hitchhiking is an alternative for the desperate. Don't rely on hitchhiking as alternate transport because the idea of a free ride is unheard of in most of Latin America. Out of kindness, people may stop and ask if you want a ride, but this is usually when you least want one.

Certain countries, most notably those in the Andes, operate cargo trucks, designating people and baggage as extra cargo (and supplementary income). Expect to pay for the ride and always ask the price beforehand. Cargo trucks are great for meeting people, and it's rare for a driver not to have room for a bike.

As a rule, getting a lift at the point of departure is much easier than trying to flag down a moving vehicle en route. With all types of transport, try to load the bike yourself. Keep an eye on it at all stops, ask the fare for the bike beforehand, and arrive well before the departure time.

THE BIKE AND EQUIPMENT

Begin by reviewing your existing equipment and then, armed with the following recommendations, decide if the equipment is appropriate for the type of bicycle touring that you are planning. In Latin America, bicycle touring is unknown; therefore, you can't depend on being able to buy spare parts. This means that your initial decisions about equipment will decide your success.

The first premise to buying equipment is to get the optimum affordable equipment that best meets your needs. You might feel that the more money you spend on gear, the better your trip. But realistically you have to compromise your wishes with your budget. We would all love to lavish $800 on a tent, but as the price tags of equipment get higher, the differences in quality start to shrink. Many hazards of traveling in Latin America, from harsh terrain to your bike's journey in the luggage compartment, abuse your equipment. It's worth buying quality equipment—you'll reap the benefits of comfort and worry-free traveling.

Because the latest developments in bicycles don't exist in Latin America, you can't replace or modify the latest design in frames, brakes, and gearing systems if you need to. For example, you can find standard freewheels in most countries, but a cassette-style freewheel won't be available once the chain has worn out. Consequently, changing this freewheel requires either trying to get the part from home or replacing the entire wheel.

The final premise is to watch the total weight of your equipment. The less weight you carry, the more you'll enjoy yourself. Take along a few of the accessories that add extra enjoyment to a trip, but be careful in deciding between the essential and the superfluous.

So before leaving, survey your equipment. What do you need? What's new and what should be replaced? Can you replace and repair the equipment yourself? Ultimately, what do you feel most comfortable and confident with?

BICYCLE TYPES. You can tour anywhere on any type of bike, but you'll get maximum enjoyment when your bike is well suited to where you want to go. If you plan on traveling for a long period, you will want the most versatile bike style. The type of bike is less of a concern if you have a definite itinerary, if you are on a short trip, or if you already own an adequate bike. I have divided potential touring bikes into four classes: the mountain bike, the touring bike, the hybrid, and the ten-speed.

The mountain bike, or all-terrain bike (ATB), remains the most versatile of all styles. Its larger tires, frame strength, wide handlebars, and ample gearing ratio allow the bike to handle any condition. The major disadvantages to ATBs are their weight (they're usually heavier than other bikes), their restricted riding positions that cause discomfort, and their slower speeds (ATBs' larger tires increase rolling resistance). If you're thinking about touring with a mountain bike, consider whether its durability and versatility offset its weight and discomfort.

Designed for comfort over long distances, the touring bike comes equipped with dropped handlebars, thinner tires, numerous frame eyelets, and relaxed frame angles. The bike is ideal if you plan tours with minor rough sections. With a touring bike, you may have to walk over sand, mud, and rocks because the riding is impossible or dangerous. Deep sand can grab and twist your front wheel; a steep, stony downhill can lead to a crash.

The commuter bike is a hybrid between the touring bike and the ATB. Its predominant characteristics are slightly curved, upright handlebars and wider tires than the touring bike. You choose a commuter bike for safety and short-range comfort. The gear ratio is usually insufficient for extensive touring unless you ride in flatter areas and are not carrying much gear. Commuter bikes are also not designed for strength and durability. Because they're cheaper, the components are of poorer quality and therefore won't withstand rugged or intensive use. Unless you are on a limited trip, do not take a commuter bike.

The ten-speed is probably the worst choice you could make. Designed for either casual bicycling or racing efficiency, you can expect problems with its reliability, strength, and gear ratio. All these factors severely restrict your touring options.

COMPONENTS. The frame, the backbone of the bike, stands out as the bike's most important part. If there are faults in the frame's design or manufacturing, they will magnify the poor performance of other components. If the frame breaks or cracks, it's not only dangerous to ride, it's also impossible to repair properly in Latin America.

The best frame material remains chrome-molybdenum, stronger than steel and more durable than aluminum. Try to get as many tubes fitted with "cro-moly" as possible, including all the stays and the forks. The average-quality frames are double-butted, which means the tubes' diameters are double thickness at the joints. You can get triple-butted tubes if you customize, but double-butted is sufficient.

When you choose a frame, you can get caught up in angles, wheelbases, and fork rakes, but the most important measurement is the seat-tube length. Everyone refers to seat-tube length when fitting a bike. The right frame size, critical for comfort and safety, is measured by straddling the bike. On a touring bike you should have at least 6 centimeters clearance between the top tube and your crotch, and 12 centimeters clearance for a mountain bike. Seat-tube length defines the rest of the frame's geometry.

A last point in selecting a frame: Look for proper braze-ons. Eyelets on the forks and stays avoid the problem of additional hardware for the racks and fenders. Make sure you have eyelets on the front forks, seat-stays, and the rear dropouts where the wheel sits.

Most bicycle problems occur with the wheels, the link between you and the road. The key to good wheels is strength. If you have a choice between lighter and stronger, choose the stronger wheel.

You can replace 26- and 27-inch tires easily anywhere in Latin America; these are the best choices for wheel sizes. Seven-hundred centimeter tires are nearly impossible to find anywhere, so unless you plan on carrying extra tires and tubes with you, do not use metric wheels. The ideal mountain bike rims are lightweight aluminum with a concave box construction, size 26 inches by 1.75 inches so you can use them with a variety of tire widths.

With tires you buy in Latin America, be wary of the printed sizing because sometimes it's incorrect. Try the tire on before you buy it. Always keep a spare tire with you. Try to keep your tires in impeccable shape; some road conditions can easily rip apart a tire.

Tubes may come with one of three types of valves: Schrader, Presta, or Woods. If you are on a short trip, bring a couple of spare tubes and your patch kit. If you are going on a longer trip, bring a pump you can modify for different valve types. In Latin America, Woods valves, with their inherent problems, are the most common. Schrader valves, the type used on cars, are the second most common form of valve, and Presta valves only come on tubular tires.

The hub keeps the wheels turning smoothly. High-flange hubs, which are larger and stronger, need shorter spokes, creating a more rigid ride. Small-flange hubs, more common in Latin America, offer a smoother ride. Stay with a thirty-six-spoke lacing system for both wheels because replacing forty-spoke hubs and rims is impossible.

Good-quality sealed bearings are ideal. If you can't afford them, go with

Being inventive and being independent are two necessary ingredients of life on the road: a cyclist fixes a flat outside Jujuy, Argentina.

simple hubs for easy maintenance and replacement.

A final word about wheels: Try to get quick-release hubs. This will save time when you change inevitable flats, but more importantly, when you use public transport, being able to quickly remove the wheels helps persuade drivers to carry your bike.

You and your bike, a combined 90 kilos, are traveling at 70 kph down a twisting road slick from rain. From out of nowhere, a pack of sheep appears on the road. You need to stop right away! Brakes, effective and well adjusted, are critical for your safety. Cantilever brakes, attached by brazeons at the seat stay and forks, are the strongest and most reliable. Their only disadvantage is their replacement difficulty, so if you plan to go through mountainous terrain or wet or dusty conditions, bring an extra pair. If you have a different type of brake on the front and rear, bring a replacement for both sets of brakes. Caliper brakes and their shoes are easier to replace, but this type of brake gets mushy faster and doesn't have the same stopping power.

You must demand safety from your brakes and comfort from your saddle, the stress point between you and the road. Your saddle absorbs most of the road's vibrations and shocks. Surprisingly, comfort is not a big, comfy seat with a suspension system the size of bedsprings. Get a seat that is comfortably wide and make sure the insides of your thighs don't chafe on the saddle. It should be firm enough that you do not shift unnecessarily. If you plan on rough riding conditions, forget hard leather seats. No matter how broken in they are, a leather saddle is unforgiving on rough terrain.

If your behind isn't broken in before you leave, you might want to invest in a gel covering for your saddle. Gel, however, shifts over time, eventually making you uncomfortable and prone to saddle sores. Gel also adds to your leg extension so you may need to adjust the saddle height.

Saddle adjustment plays a major role in knee, hip, and tendon problems. The ideal seat height, from the top of the saddle to the top of the lowest pedal, is 109 percent of your inseam, measured from the sole of your foot to the inside crotch. But if joint problems occur, adjust the height incrementally. The seat should have a downward tilt of about 10 degrees so that your arms bear some body weight. You should also adjust the seat to be about 6 centimeters behind the center line of the bottom bracket. Whatever the saddle adjustment, you should always ensure you keep at least 7 centimeters of the seat post in the seat tube.

Finally, if you are planning to use public transport, a quick release for your saddle is convenient.

Pedals take a tremendous pounding. Situated close to the road's grime, water, and dirt, pedals also take the grinding power of your legs. Luckily, pedals are easy to maintain. Sealed pedals exist, but if they start to fail they are difficult to repair and their parts impossible to replace.

Attached to the pedals are a safety feature novice cyclists fear—toe clips. Toe clips keep your feet in proper alignment to the pedals, and they also prevent your feet from slipping off the pedals on rough or wet roads. Additionally, toe clips increase your pedaling efficiency. For safety reasons, in heavy traffic don't strap your feet tightly into the clips.

If your legs are the pistons, the bike's gearing system is the transmission. The gearing system, which includes the derailleurs, chainrings, cranks, chain, freewheel, cables, and gearshifters, is designed to match the rider's strength to the terrain, weather, and road conditions. Learn how to use your gear systems to match your ability; remember that an ideal touring cadence is 70–90 rpm.

Most derailleurs now use the shifting index system, but the prime concern for your derailleurs is ensuring they have the capacity to handle the gears you need. The ideal would be 28–38–48 chainrings with a 15–34 freewheel. A thirty-four-tooth rear cog may seem excessive, but when you start cycling over rocky 4,500-meter passes, gasping for oxygen, you'll be thankful you have that number thirty-four.

Of all the components, your chain and freewheel will wear out the fastest. Depending on the riding conditions, you can expect a 5,000- to 10,000-kilometer lifespan for your chain. When you have to replace it, you should change the freewheel; the complimentary wear makes replacing both a necessity. You can increase the life of a chain by keeping it well lubricated. Getting both a replacement freewheel with an adequate sprocket range and a narrow-profile chain is a problem. If you plan a long trip, check the country's "Bicycles" section for availability of parts.

As an alternative to carrying a few kilos of spare parts, you could use prearranged mail drops. Send your equipment to a post office in care of the *Lista de Correos,* or send them to whatever other mail service you are using.

The location of gearshifters is a matter of personal preference. On touring bikes, you can either place the shifters on the ends of the handlebars, a system that will be difficult to find parts for, or you can keep the shifters on the down tube, which is more common in Latin America. Avoid placing the shifters on the handlebar stem: if you are propelled forward and the shifter is pointing horizontally, you could injure yourself.

Your bottom bracket, consisting of the axle, bearings, cups, and rings, is the heart of the drive train. If you adjust the bottom bracket with the proper tools, you should have few problems. Again, use sealed bearings only if you can afford the best quality. If traveling on a long trip, carry a spare axle; if you need to replace it, you'll need the proper length to clear the chainrings on the chainstays. Bearings and races are easy to find almost everywhere.

The steering system consists of the fork, handlebars, stem, and headset. Handlebars are a major factor in keeping you comfortable. Well-padded, dropped bars offer a variety of positions. With dropped bars you can change your hand position, and, subsequently, body position. Flat bars with bar ends also allow a variety of hand positions.

The top of the handlebar stem should be level with the seat and extend at least 5 centimeters into the head tube. The stem's length should prevent overextension of the body.

Taking a constant pummeling, the small bearings of the headset maintain your steering control. Your forks and steering column connect through the headset. You can use high-quality sealed bearings or simple races in the cups. Check the headset adjustment by feeling for binding when you twist the handlebars with the front wheel off the floor, or by applying the front brake and pushing the bike forward. If you feel looseness, then it's time for adjustment. Use the proper tools because gross adjustments can destroy a headset.

BIKE ACCESSORIES. Strong, reliable racks are worth every cent you invest, for both convenience and safety. Rack failure will jam the struts into the wheels, destroying them and guaranteeing a spill. The best rack systems, made from strengthened aluminum, are four-point attachments that connect to the frame's eyelet braze-ons.

The ideal system is one rear rack and a "low-rider" rack on the front. "Low-riders" are racks with the center of gravity at the front hub. Look for the newer design that is thicker at the connections to the fork's dropouts.

You'll also need panniers. A pannier set is an area where you can compromise. Satisfactory panniers for Latin American touring need to strap onto the bike securely to prevent them from being jarred loose and landing on the road. Don't settle for shock-cord systems because they lack roadworthiness and allow the bags to be stolen easily. Pannier material should be coarse, heavy nylon of darker colors that won't show the dirt. All seams should be double stitched with few frayed edges. Look for stiffness in the panniers' back corners because if they're sloppy, the edges will sag into the wheels.

The more pockets you have on your panniers the better organized you can be. All the zippers should be nylon and self-repairing.

The ideal pannier system has a rear-to-front weight-distribution ratio of sixty-forty. The best arrangement I've found is two medium front panniers, two medium rear panniers, a small internal frame backpack to place atop the rack, and a handlebar bag for a camera, food, and maps. You can access areas of Latin America that offer incredible hiking trails if you carry a backpack with the capacity to hold three to five days' worth of supplies.

Remember that the fewer bags you carry the fewer pieces you have to worry about when using public transport or leaving your bike outside your hotel room. Seat bags are unnecessary if you have pockets in your panniers. Frame bags are extraneous because they crowd the space on your frame and get in the way if you need to lift or carry your bike.

You need to carry a good lock, but it doesn't have to be elaborate or extra strong. If two or more of you travel together, one could carry a strong U-shaped lock, the other a long cable and padlock. With two locks you can secure your bikes in any situation. If you cycle alone, a cable with a reliable, difficult-to-pick padlock suffices. Always lock your bike in cities and at night, but if you stop in small towns, you only need to lock your bicycle if you leave it for a long time.

Each cyclist should carry a pump. If you get separated on a descent, it's always the person in front who has the pump when the person in the rear gets the flat. Take along a pump that you can adapt to the three kinds of valves. Strap your pump to your frame or pack it away; otherwise, in cities someone could steal it, and on rough roads it could bounce off—either unnoticeably on the road or noticeably into your wheel.

No matter where you bicycle tour, equip your bike with fenders. In the desert they will keep dust off your components; in rain, mud off your gear; and in rural areas, animal droppings off your face.

Water bottles are a necessity, and you should always carry two oversized bottles. Have the capability to carry more if you plan on camping. If you go to remote areas, you can always use 2-liter plastic pop bottles, which are easy to find, carry, and then dispose of at the end of the journey. You should secure good-quality water-bottle cages to braze-ons.

Neither lights nor horns are necessary. You should never ride at night unless it is an emergency, and in that case you can use a small flashlight to warn other traffic. A loud yell gets a quicker response from people and animals than horns or bells.

TOOLS AND MAINTENANCE. Latin American parts are generally shoddy and difficult to find, so you must have the knowledge, ability, and resourcefulness to handle most situations. The first step is prevention. By keeping your bike maintained, you can correct small problems early and continue happily on your way.

Keep a routine for checking your bike. Daily you should check tires for pressure, cuts, and bulges; check your saddle and handlebars for tightness; and check your brakes to make sure they work effectively. Every week you should check the wheels for trueness and broken spokes and check all nuts and bolts, bearings, the headset, bottom bracket, and hubs for looseness. Finally, check that all the parts run smoothly and lubricate when necessary.

Bicycles are simple machines, so with a small amount of study and experience you can do most repairs. Compact books that explain roadside repairs are helpful if you are uncertain about certain procedures.

You cannot rely on Latin Americans to have the proper tools to fix your bike. Appendix G, which lists recommendations on what to pack, includes a section on which tools and parts to carry along and know how to use. A freewheel remover isn't useful if you don't know how to use it. As well as being lightweight and of good quality, your tools should be compatible with the components on your bike (crank-pullers and freewheel removers come in different sizes).

You should know how to adjust cables, handlebars, headset, seat, bottom bracket, pedals, derailleurs, hubs, and brakes. You should also know how to replace a chain, freewheel, broken spokes, and cables. Finally, you should know how to true a wheel and how to fix a flat. When you replace a part, make sure it is what you need before leaving the city.

If you rely on mechanics to fix your bicycle, try to watch their work. When they bring out the pipe wrench or ball-peen hammer, stop them.

CLOTHING. First, bring appropriate clothes based on the conditions you are likely to experience. There's no point in bringing extensive raingear to Baja California or cold-weather gear to the Amazon. Secondly, bring functional, adjustable layers that fulfill a variety of needs. Forget the down vest; instead, pack a polypropylene undershirt, fleece shirt, and windproof jacket. Appendix G is a checklist of items to pack.

We'll start from the bottom and work upward. I've found the ideal cycle-touring shoe is a lightweight, well-constructed walking boot. They are versatile, breathable, and rugged and have a reinforced sole. Look for a sole made from ethyl vinyl acetate (EVA); it's the most durable and its stiffness reduces foot fatigue. Full hiking boots are too heavy and take too long to dry. Bicycle touring shoes are not rugged enough if you plan to do much walking. Running shoes are abysmal for touring because they have no foot support, wear poorly on toe-clip stress points, and lack support when walking long distances. Don't wear cleated cycling shoes; over rough terrain and during forays for food, they'll be impossible to walk in.

Bring socks that are a blend of wool and nylon. In cold weather your feet are the most vulnerable part of your body. Throw in a good pair of wool socks if you expect cold weather.

Touring cyclists have strong opinions about what kinds of shorts work best. Look for pairs that don't constrict your legs and have a chamois padding between your seat and the saddle. Some cyclists prefer racing shorts with machine-washable chamois because they are easy to clean and you can wipe your dirty hands on them without making a mess. Racing shorts attract more attention than touring shorts in Latin America, but are more comfortable to ride in. Touring shorts, on the other hand, look similar to walking shorts. They usually have side pockets and a terry-cloth liner. Take what you feel most comfortable in.

During cold weather or for strolling the town, you will want a leg covering. I find that while I am cycling my legs rarely get cold, even in temperatures below 5 degrees Celsius. My legs do get cold when I've stopped cycling, so I carry a pair of tights and a pair of light pants. If you stay in freezing areas, such as Potosí in Bolivia, you can wear your tights under your lighter pants.

As well as looking fashionable, cycling gloves allow you to brush debris from your tires, keep a better grip on your handlebars, and save skin in a crash. They also make great potholders! Unfortunately, cycling gloves tend to wear out quickly. If you are keen on using them, treat them like any other piece of replacement equipment. Ask yourself how long your trip is, if they'll hold out that long, and if you want to carry replacements (buying them in Latin America will be difficult). If you are cycling in cold weather, carry a pair of wool gloves, too.

When you are choosing your shirts, look for unobtrusive colors that don't show the dirt and that open down the front for ventilation. For cooler weather, a long-sleeve fleece top is ideal because it is an excellent compromise between bulk and insulation. Layers with zippers are the best method of keeping warm without overheating.

Bicycle touring requires a good jacket, preferably one designed for cycling. A good jacket will be brightly colored, water repellent, ventilated, and windproof and will be cut longer in the arms and back to fit the cyclist's riding position. A good jacket is expensive but invaluable.

Eyewear to keep bugs, dirt, and ultraviolet rays out of your eyes is essential. It can be painful and dangerous to get a bug in your eye when flying down a hill at 70 kph.

For weather protection and insulation, you should carry some type of hat. Wear something that stays on your head during speedy descents. I've always liked cycling hats.

On top of the hat sits your helmet. Most riders leave home with the intention of always wearing a helmet. Yet once they ride in a quiet, flat area with the sun blazing, good intentions tend to get packed away with the helmet. You should definitely wear a helmet in cities and intense traffic areas because Latin American motorists are reckless, particularly on highways, where they get competitive with their fellow drivers.

In these dangerous situations, a rear-view mirror, either attached to your handlebars or to your helmet, makes bicycling safer. When you see potential hazards as they bear down on you, you can bail out and hit the shoulder.

Bicycling in the rain presents its dangers. Roads become more slippery and drivers have a harder time seeing you. The first requirement of rainwear should be visibility, not how well it repels moisture.

Ponchos are heavy and bulky, increase wind resistance, and don't protect you from water splashing up from below. The most effective material for repelling water is a heavy rubberized cloth. This hefty item is suffocating because it doesn't allow sweat to wick away from your body. Now there are materials that are designed to repel rain but allow sweat to evaporate. Users have given mixed reviews to this kind of fabric. Some people rave that the fabric has revolutionized the outdoors; others feel the material's virtues are exaggerated. The biggest complaint comes from those who extensively expose the material to rugged conditions. With rough use, the impermeability can break down quickly. Realize the limitations of this kind of fabric before you buy it.

CAMPING EQUIPMENT. All your equipment should be light, versatile, and durable. The lighter your gear, the more enjoyable your trip. With more versatile gear, the less you need to take and fear losing. The more durable the gear, the less concern you have for the abuse it will take along the way.

Before purchasing a tent, sort out where you plan to travel, the number of people in your group, and how much you have to spend. A good, functional tent should contain a full bathtub-style floor with nylon walls 5 centimeters off the floor. It should also have mesh windows that open from the inside, both to let air circulate and to keep bugs out. The windows should also have inside moisture coverings for cold weather. A good tent can be erected easily and quickly in the dark or in cold weather, with a minimum of poles. Wind design is an important factor to consider because poorly designed tents can collapse in high winds. A vestibule is perfect for storing gear or even a bike with the wheels removed. Finally, I recommend getting a neutral color for your tent. You want to blend into the landscape. Bright colors, such as blues and yellows, will have every passerby stopping to examine you.

Spend some time deciding what you want, factoring in your need for comfort, durability, permeability, and versatility, and then start examining many types of tents.

Some cyclists prefer to keep their baggage weight to a minimum, and instead of lugging a full tent, they use tarps, ponchos, or tube tents. Although these methods work, I like the sense of security and comfort I get from a tent.

After you've chosen your destination, examine the area's weather conditions, finding out what you can expect for precipitation and temperature, and then decide what you need in a sleeping bag. The factors in choosing an appropriate bag are its price, weight, loft, stuff-ability, washability, and durability.

The biggest factor is the type of fill the bag uses. A down fill, with a high loft, insulates you better for its weight and stuffs well. The disadvantages to down are that it's useless when wet and it's expensive.

Synthetic fills provide adequate insulation for their weight, are less expensive, are washable, and are usable when wet. Disadvantages of synthetics are that they stuff poorly and are bulky and heavy. Solid polyester bags, whose insides are usually printed with hunting dogs or cartoon characters, are not worth bringing along. Instead, buy a blanket when you get to Latin America.

Sleeping bags come in three designs: the confining mummy bag, tapering down to the feet and providing excellent insulation; the semi-mummy, or taper design, which narrows toward the feet and provides good insulation without the confinement; and the rectangle, which provides less insulation but more room. I prefer the semi-mummy; it eliminates most dead, cold spots but still provides enough room to move around.

If you plan to camp in cool weather, look for a head covering and choose a nylon double-sided zipper. You'll wake up quickly if your bare skin touches a metal zipper. Finally, if you plan to camp with a loved one, choose bags with opposite zippers so you can stay cozy.

Some travelers consider sleeping pads an accessory, but most bicycle campers know pads are a necessity. They level uneven ground and insulate you from the cold and dampness. For the weight and bulk, there's little point in acting like a Spartan, sleeping on chilly, wet ground. The best pad for bicycle camping is the self-inflating style, providing excellent insulation and comfort. If you've never slept on one, you'll be amazed at how comfortable they are. Don't even consider anything else.

Nothing satisfies the cyclist more than a hot, fulfilling meal at the end of a long, tiring day. A good stove gives you the satisfaction of being able to cook a tasty, cheap meal anywhere. As with other equipment, examine where you plan to go, because temperatures, elevations, and fuel availability affect your stove's effectiveness. When you shop for a stove, examine the boiling time, simmering ability, weight, price, stability, and size. Multifuel stoves are the best for travelers, because white gas, alcohol, and Sterno are difficult to find in Latin America. In Brazil, for example, the altitudes are low, temperatures are moderate, and butane (GAZ) cartridges are readily available. I wouldn't recommend butane anywhere else because it functions miserably at high altitudes and in cold weather. Kerosene, easy to find and the safest of all stove fuels, burns apathetically and dirtier. Gasoline, the universal fuel, burns well but you must transport it in the stove's carefully designed bottle, and you have to be extremely careful using it.

Carry spares for the parts susceptible to failure, an extra fuel bottle, a fuel filter for the notoriously dirty fuel, and don't forget matches or a lighter.

I recommend packing one 2-liter pot and one 1-liter pot. If you have lids, you can use them as frying pans. A spoon and utility knife are all you need for utensils, because anything you can eat with a fork, you can eat with a spoon. A good knife has indispensable extras such as a can opener and corkscrew. Finally, don't forget the pot-lifter and pot-scrubber.

MISCELLANEOUS. When you buy personal items, buy the smallest amount possible. Items such as shampoo, toothpaste, and soap are easy to find everywhere. Always carry toilet paper with you because hotels and restaurants rarely supply it. An essential item for the days you are cycling on dirt or heavily traveled roads is a dust filter. Imagine struggling over a dusty mountain pass, lungs screaming for every available molecule of air, and a bus comes speeding past, leaving a cloud of dust and exhaust in its wake. You can buy special cycling filters or a simpler dust filter or improvise one out of a simple bandanna.

A final word on gifts. Some travelers advocate carrying small gifts, such as balloons or pens, for handing out to children. I don't think it's a good idea, because gifts start an attitude of expectation. Soon every traveler has to carry a box of pens to dispense to the infinite number of surrounding children. In larger cities I tend to ignore the children; they mark a traveler's gullibility and guilt. In smaller villages, where I want to make an impression, I give my time and energy—a ride on the back of my bike. Kids love getting a ride around a main square, and they line up, laughing gleefully, while the adults see me as someone willing to spend some time with their children. Some of my most rewarding afternoons touring were spent riding around main squares with kids in tow. I didn't make any great distance on the road those days, but I won a lot of people's hearts.

A NOTE ABOUT SAFETY

Safety is an important concern in all outdoor activities. No guidebook can alert you to every hazard or anticipate the limitations of every reader. Therefore, the descriptions of roads, trails, routes, and natural features in this book are not representations that a particular place or excursion will be safe for your party. When you follow any of the routes described in this book, you assume responsibility for your own safety. Under normal conditions, such excursions require the usual attention to traffic, road and trail conditions, weather, terrain, the capabilities of your party, and other factors. Keeping informed on current conditions and exercising common sense are the keys to a safe, enjoyable outing.

Political conditions may add to the risks of travel in Latin America in ways that this book cannot predict. When you travel, you assume this risk, and should keep informed of political developments that may make safe travel difficult or impossible.

The Mountaineers

Legend

	National Highway		Airport
	State Highway		Colonial Architecture
	Main Highway Paved - Unpaved		Archeological Site
	Secondary Road Paved - Unpaved		Market
	Trunk Road Paved - Unpaved		Camping
	Urban Area		Spa
	Population Centre with Full Provisions		Refuge
	Population Center With Only Food		Pass
	Landmark With No Provisions		Mountain Summit
	International Border		Tunnel
	National Park Boundary		Mountainous Area
	Shoreline with Ferry Crossing		Hilly Area
BOLIVIA	Country	**N**	North
SALTA	Tour Start		To

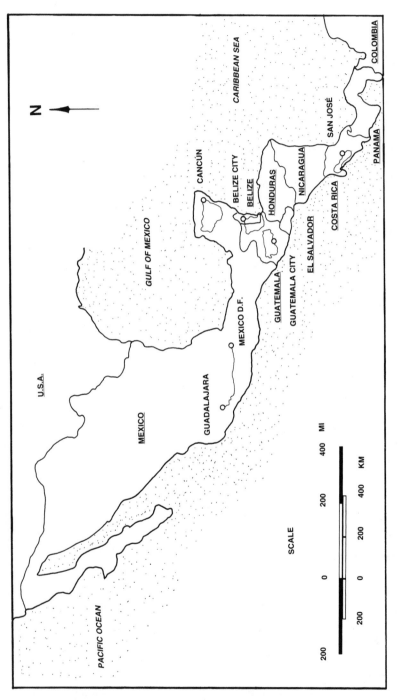

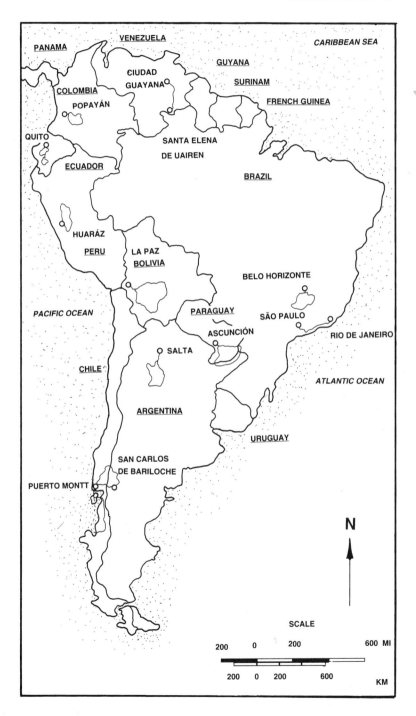

PART II

A campesino *carries his goods into the town of Sangolquí, Ecuador; Cotopaxi Volcano rises in the background.*

ARGENTINA

When I remember Argentina I recall most of all its people. Generous and genial, the Argentine character lingers with the traveler. From the Buenos Aires city-dweller to the lonely rancher of Patagonia, everyone desires to display their hospitality and lend an ear to your adventures.

When traveling in Argentina, you discover a degree of recognition and comfort. Since 85 percent of Argentines originate in Europe, you feel you are in a European country. Adding to these familiar feelings, the land has parallels with North America. *Gauchos* ranch on the vast plains like American cowboys of the Wild West, intensive farming covers the large central area, and in the far south natural resources compete with natural beauty.

In Argentina you experience moments of sublime beauty and grandeur. You can see South America's two most spectacular sights, the Perito Moreno glacier and Iguazú Falls. Both are stunning and worth every effort to visit. Argentina also has excellent cycling areas, particularly in the Lake District around Bariloche and the Andean northwest.

Travelers don't often visit Argentina. They are usually more intent on seeing the Andean *Quechua* culture or indulging in Brazil's hedonism. Those travelers neglecting Argentina miss something special, though. Argentina—least visited but last forgotten.

CYCLE ZONES

The Andes

TERRAIN. The mountainous area of northwest Argentina is a continuation of Bolivia's *altiplano*. Argentines label this extreme northern area the *puna*, a high, dusty, uninhabited area, useless except for llama herding.

Farther south, the land dips and altitudes become less severe. Most roads in this district follow long, narrow valleys known as *quebradas*. The prominent valley throughout the region, the narrow Quebrada de Humahuaca, gradually descends in 160 kilometers from 4,000 meters to 1,200 meters. Major climbs rise between the valleys, but often the passes offer gentler and shorter climbs than you would expect.

SCENERY. The *puna*, in the extreme north, presents a desolate, flat area of little beauty. As you travel farther south into the valleys, the mountainous scenery bands into colorful mountain walls, glistening rivers, and intriguing rock formations. Along some roads, rock formations boast nicknames such as the Amphitheater, the Obelisk, and the Castle. The northwest shines with brilliant luster.

CULTURAL INTEREST. The Incas' farthest southerly expansion reached Quilmes in the Tucuman province. Today you can explore the settlement's dusty foundations. Other lesser-known indigenous tribes settled in the area as well.

In the colonial era, vagabonds from Europe accessed the northwest, using the Buenos Aires–Jujuy–Potosí route to plunder Peru and Bolivia's silver and gold. Along the key trails, churches sprang up and priests pressed their beliefs on the colonists and natives. Maintained diligently, these charming churches repose throughout the valleys.

The present-day northwesterners worship their proclaimed saint, the Diffunta Correa. The local legend tells of a mother and her young child who were stranded in the desert. Eventually, the woman died of exposure, but her milk sustained the child for another three days until they were found, the child still suckling on the remaining maternal nourishment. Along the roads the devoted believers erect shrines to the sacrifice of motherhood, reminding the inhabitants of their vulnerability in this harsh land.

WEATHER. Altitude is a major influence on weather conditions. The *puna*, the high plateau, stays moderate during the day and turns frigid overnight. As you drop in altitude, daily extremes decrease but seasonal variations occur. Average winter temperatures in the valley moderate at 10 degrees Celsius, and summer temperatures reach a comfortable 21.

Summer is usually when the least amount of rain falls, while the greatest amount falls in January. Even during the rainy season, precipitation only occurs in short thunderstorms. The main concern is avoiding flash floods, so don't camp in dry riverbeds. Despite the area's desert conditions, winter snow squalls occur higher in the mountains.

Winds signaling good weather blow from the northeast, while low-pressure systems and poor weather ride on a south wind.

Water thunders down a small section of Iguazú Falls

TOUR OF ARGENTINA

SALTA

Distance: 509 km
Start/Finish: Salta/Salta
Season: April–November
Terrain: Hilly to mountainous
Scenery: ***
Interest: **
Difficulty: Moderate

Km	Location	Scenery	Interest	Comments
00	**Salta**	**	***	
17	Cerrillos	**		
20	El Carril	**		
22	**Coronel Moldes**	**		
(26)	Excursion to Cabra Corral on Hwy. 47	***		
10	Ampascachi	**		
14	La Viña	**		
21	**Alemania**	**		
81	Jct. to Cafayate	***		
02	**Cafayate**	**	**	
02	Return to Jct. 68	**		
13	**Animaná**	***		
09	**San Carlos**	***	**	
52	Jct. to Angastaco	***		
02	**Angastaco**	**	***	
02	Return to Hwy. 40	**		
38	Jct. to Molinos	***		
02	**Molinos**	**	***	
02	Return to Hwy. 40	**		
17	Seclantás	***	**	
30	**Cachi**	***	**	
11	Payogasta	***		
72	Escoipe	***		
27	Pulares	***		
07	**Chicoana**	**		
06	El Carril (Hwy. 68)	*		
20	Cerrillos	*		
17	**Salta**	**		

The Pampas

TERRAIN. The pampas, a third of Argentina's total area, adjoin the Andes' foothills in the west and extend to the Atlantic Ocean in the east.

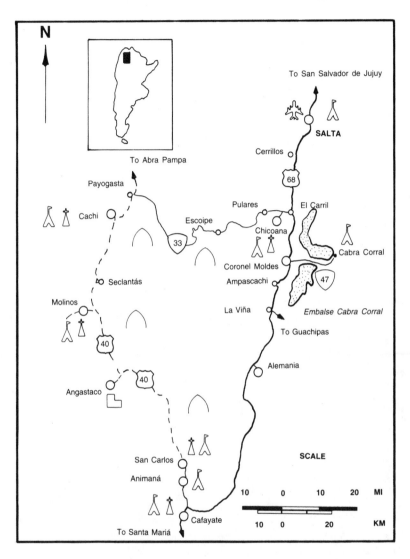

From north to south, the pampas zone ranges from the northeastern border with Paraguay to the Rio Dulce in the Rio Colorado province.

Most of the zone consists of monotonous plains, with a concentration of minuscule river basins in its hub. Hilly regions squat in Misiones, the western foothills, and there are a few minor ranges around Tandil, Bahia Blanca, and in the area near Cordoba. The zone's highest range culminates at 2,975 meters. Except for these areas, expect flat, boring cycling.

SCENERY. The pampas zone defines Argentina's agricultural heartland. Ranching and farming predominate in this land that consists of treeless savanna and scrubland. Farther westward the land becomes parched.

The scenery dulls the senses; the only highlights are the seaside resorts around Mar del Plata and in the far northeastern corner, the phenomenal Iguazú Falls. Distances in the area are vast, while the rewards are few.

CULTURAL INTEREST. In the late 1700s, Argentine *gauchos* and Brazilian *bandeirantes* combined to decimate the native population, leaving only the *gaucho*'s nomadic tradition. Foreseeing the fate of the Guaraní Indians, the Jesuit missionaries attempted to teach the Indians survival skills so they could adapt to this inevitable change. The Society of Jesus was highly successful until Pope Clement XIV, under pressure from the Bourbon monarchs, suppressed the order. The Jesuits were forced to abandon their missions and leave the Guaraní in the hands of the new landowners. All that remains of the Indians' artistic achievements are the magnificent ruins in the Misiones province. The tragic end of this noble experiment lingers in your mind as you tour the hauntingly beautiful Misiones area.

A detail of the San Ignacio Miní ruins, in Misiones

Today the pampas contain two-thirds of Argentina's population. The zone's major population centers, founded as agricultural entities, connect through excellent road networks.

In summary, little exists to interest the traveler.

WEATHER. The heaviest rainfall in the zone falls in the northeast. Moving farther south and west, precipitation diminishes, and what does fall is concentrated in the summer months of October through March. In the western foothills, droughts commonly occur, but winters hold dry and mild weather.

The pampas carry the record for South America's highest temperatures. Daily averages are extremely high, the humidity varying from desert to semitropical, depending on the rainfall. Winters remain mild, but farther south temperatures drop, producing infrequent snowfalls.

Winds are generally from the west.

Patagonia

TERRAIN. Patagonia, the last third of Argentina, comprises the area from the Rio Colorado south to the final territory, Tierra del Fuego.

Patagonia's western section holds the Andes, peaking in Aconcagua at 6,960 meters, the highest point in the Western Hemisphere. The Andes diminish quickly as the continent fades into the Antarctic Ocean at Cape Horn. Eastward from the Andean foothills, the land is made up of a series of plateaus made of lava rock and then cut by small surface rivers. Most of the plateaus roll in a north–south orientation except along the flat coastal section.

SCENERY. Patagonia has a postapocalyptic feel. As you cycle along the monochrome plains and barren mountains, the unfettered wind howls in your face and loneliness slams into your bones. The world has deserted you, and nothing exists but desolation. Uninhabited buildings and blank crumbling walls persist as the final remnants of society. Yet this dull feeling of isolation focuses you inward. As you battle the loneliness and weather, you intensify your contact with nature's harshness. The area mesmerizes you. Here your greatest South American stories unfold: tales of horrific winds, ghostlike *gauchos*, and glimpses of wild guanacos on the hilltops.

Fauna abounds in Patagonia. Half-wild sheep share their ranges with the guanaco, a cross between the domestic llama and wild vicuña. Stay alert: Plenty of guanacos, armadillos, and ñandu, Patagonia ostriches, blend into the landscape.

On the coast, the Valdez Peninsula sustains colonies of sea lions, sea elephants, penguins, and, from September to October, whales. Bicycling offers by far the best way of visiting the peninsula. You can camp, slow down, and fully appreciate the area.

Inland, the Andes present the greatest beauty and wonder. South America's most scenic alpine region unfolds in the Lake District around Bariloche. Snow-covered volcanic cones rise from the shores of glacial lakes, and among the meadows and wooded hills wild flowers bloom bountifully.

Slightly farther south, Las Alceres National Park, the country's virginal park, holds South America's greatest glaciers.

Still farther south, sitting in Parque Nacional Las Glaciares, is the granddaddy of Argentina's glaciers, Perito Moreno. This huge glacier, inching across the lake, is one of the few growing glaciers in the world. It isn't just a sight, it's a spectacle. The crystal-blue glacier has massive pinnacles of wind-sculpted ice. Standing at attention like a crowded battalion of soldiers, thousands of ice peaks ascend the mountain crevices into eternity. Above the glacier, condors soar silently on the thermal air currents. Suddenly, a thunderous crack breaks the serenity. The glacier calves, and a monolithic slab of ice cracks away from the glacial wall and slams into the frigid water below. In slow motion the massive slab of ice bobs back to the surface, and as it drifts slowly away, it becomes another surrealistic ice sculpture adorning the lake.

In Argentina's extreme south lies South America's final destination, Tierra del Fuego. This untouched land of mountains, marsh, and wind punctuates the end of the world. Traveling in this primal landscape, you sense finality.

CULTURAL INTEREST. I wish that Patagonia's spectacular oases of beauty and hauntingly austere conditions held ancient ruins and deep cultural roots. Yet I know if it did, the land would lose its eerie loneliness. The sole reminder that people once roamed these plains hides in the Cuevas de los Manos. In this cave, cultures left painted silhouettes of their hands in testimony of their passing.

Today the people of Patagonia living off the land are illuminated with a pioneer spirit. *Estancia* workers, maintaining a lonely vigil over the plains, wait for the shearing season, when they corral half a million wild sheep scattered over 1,000 square kilometers. The ranchers, despite their loneliness, display a strong sense of hospitality and generosity. If you need help, they won't hesitate to give what they can.

Gauchos still roam the plains of Patagonia. Keeping a sense of independence, they play the troubleshooters, the hired hands, the cowboys of Patagonia, intent on preserving a romantic tradition of freedom.

WEATHER. Patagonia stretches from 40 to 53 degrees south latitude. In North America the equivalent latitudes extend from just north of San Francisco to the Alaskan panhandle. Summer temperatures differ from the blistering heat waves of the pampas, and the farther south you travel in Patagonia, the colder the temperatures. In the far south the temperatures rarely rise above 18 degrees Celsius, while winter temperatures routinely fall below zero.

Most of the area's precipitation falls as winter snow, particularly as you travel farther west toward the mountains. The subsequent spring runoffs supply the surface streams with their yearly water supply.

Wind—the horror of the bicycle tourist. Every story you hear about the westerly Patagonian winds is true. No one needs to embellish. The wind's ferocity is unparalleled. Screaming from the mountaintops, these cold winds from the Pacific Ocean pass over the Andean peaks, hit the treeless plateaus, and mercilessly rip across the land. Generally, winds peak in the spring and summer and moderate in the autumn. In winter the land is transformed into an eerie stillness.

Bicycle touring in Patagonia requires excellent windproof gear. Few shelters exist among the open plains, so the winds will test the quality of your equipment. Also, if you travel outside the summer months, prepare for extreme weather fluctuations. Carry cold-weather gear; Patagonia is nowhere to suffer exposure.

GENERAL INFORMATION

GETTING TO THE COUNTRY. When entering from Paraguay, you can choose from two main routes, the Asunción–Clorinda route and the Posadas–Encarnación route. The road you pick depends on how long you wish to stay in either country. Both routes offer pavement, but if your goal is Uruguay, take the Encarnación route.

The main passage between Argentina and Bolivia crosses at La Quiaca–Villazón. The entire road (91 kilometers worth) lacks pavement on the Bolivian side, and the road is only upgraded sporadically on the Argentine side. To the east, another Bolivian crossing waits at Aguas Blanca, paved on the Argentine side but not the Bolivian. A minor route, Aguas Blanca holds little of interest on either side. The last route is at Yacuiba. This is the ideal track if you arrive from the Bolivian lowlands. A diagonal highway in Argentina heads southwest to Salta and Jujuy.

From Brazil, the most spectacular crossing waits at Foz do Iguaçu, the highlight of Argentina. The second, less rewarding crossing passes through Paso de los Libres and Uruguaiana. Both routes are equal in their low traffic densities and moderate road conditions, so points of interest and destination should determine your choice of route.

When crossing from Brazil and especially Bolivia, you may be targeted for intensive baggage searches. Commonly, officials view cyclists as innocent travelers, and incidents occur less frequently than with bus travelers.

From Uruguay, you can choose one of the many crossings over the Rio Uruguay to Argentina. Although most crossings have bridges, tolls and bike accessibility vary. If officials on the bridges won't allow you to cross, most towns operate ferries.

Two boats make crossings of the Rio de la Plata. The first service runs overnight between Buenos Aires and Montevideo, and the second squirts between Buenos Aires and Colonia. Prices for the two are comparable.

Please refer to the "Getting to the Country" section of the Chile chapter for details on the many Chile–Argentina crossings.

DOCUMENTS. Everyone entering the country fills out a tourist card. If you need only a card, there is no limit on the amount or number of times you may enter the country. If asked at the border, state you want the six-month maximum stay.

Because of the changing political climate, Argentine visa restrictions are changing. Check before you arrive at the border. If you need a visa, you can easily obtain one in neighboring countries. On the continent procedures slacken as your authenticity as a traveler appears more verifiable. If you apply from home, a few weeks' delay can occur. Getting visa renewals is easy, and costs vary according to nationality.

The most sensitive nationalities facing visa restrictions are England and other countries that supported the United Kingdom during the Falklands War. A few years ago, getting a visa was almost impossible for English nationals, but restrictions are lessening.

Check your plans carefully, particularly the multiple-entry requirements if you plan to travel on Tierra del Fuego or in the Lake District. Both areas require alternating between Argentina and Chile.

No one will bother checking your passport if you pop into Villazón or Foz do Iguaçu for a day trip. But if you plan to travel farther into either country, ensure you follow the proper procedures; otherwise, you'll face serious problems when the officials discover you've entered the country illegally.

You will find immigration officials at the border, but the customs and baggage inspection areas are situated as much as 30 kilometers farther down the road. Make sure you fulfill all documentation requirements before traveling farther.

You don't have to follow any special procedures to enter Argentina with a bicycle, although officials may note its entry in your passport.

ACCOMMODATIONS. The cheapest type of room is the *hospedaje*, the family-run guest house with an extra room or two to rent. You can find these rooms by asking at the town's tourist office or of any passerby. The *residencial*, the permanent hotel, offers basic services: a bed, chair, table, and shower. *Pensiones*, which are more expensive, sometimes have better services and standards, such as a private toilet and shower. Keep in mind that a good *hospedaje* may offer more comfort than a mediocre *pension*. Browse for the best value if you have the energy and inclination.

Any establishment can share the term "hotel." Officially, the authentic hotel offers rooms of the highest standards and amenities, including the use of a telephone and television.

Youth hostels exist in Buenos Aires, Mar del Plata, Cordoba, Puerto do Iguazú, Mendoza, Humahuaca, and Bariloche. The question is, with cheaper options around, why bother?

The Automovil Club Argentino, ACA, operates *hosterias* throughout the country. These deluxe accommodations are expensive, but if you become an automobile association member you can get discounts.

The ACA also operates camping facilities throughout the country. Reasonably priced and ranging from basic to luxurious, they are usually found in tourist areas.

Municipal camping and camping in the national parks are popular. Most cities and all parks manage campgrounds during the tourist season. Prices, services, and distances from the city and tourist areas vary. Paid camping is an excellent alternative in Argentina, especially during the summer months.

Preparing breakfast at a camping spot amidst a sea of cacti

At times, you must have camping capability. In the remote areas of Patagonia and the northwest, there are few opportunities to find a room. Camping wild in Argentina is safe, and the easiest way of locating a spot for the night is by asking for a recommendation at the police station. Police officers, friendly and helpful, will help keep an eye out for you. Finally, if you cross any gates, make sure you close them; *estancia* workers hate it when different herds of thousands of sheep mix.

FOOD. Restaurants in Argentina serve a different purpose than in most other South American countries. People frequent restaurants as a social occasion. Few Argentine restaurants provide basic sustenance; instead they offer clean tablecloths, matching napkins, and uniformed waiters.

Meal habits differ in Argentina as well. Starting with breakfast, restaurants and hotels offer *petit déjeuner*, made up of rolls and tea. Anything more substantial must be ordered from the menu. Argentina's big feast happens at lunch. Taking two to three hours for siesta, Argentines consume meat, salads, tea, fruit, and a couple of bottles of wine. Totally stuffed, they then go to sleep for the remaining hours of siesta. After siesta, toward 5:00 or 6:00 P.M., Argentines have *merienda*, afternoon tea, which consists of tea, bread, and honey. The day's last big meal happens about 10:00 in the evening, then they stay up until 1:00 A.M. before going to bed for a second time.

This entire routine drives cyclists crazy. Most of us want a big breakfast, light lunch, huge supper, and then to sleep around 9:00 or 10:00 P.M. This routine requires planning, as few restaurants stay open beyond an hour into siesta.

The fixed meals provide meager portions for the cyclist. An excellent alternative is the *tenedor libre*, the free fork. These limitless buffets offer meat, pasta, and salad dishes. Finding an all-you-can-eat steak house, the *parrillada*, is a quest worthy of a hungry cyclist. Waiters bring a small brazier heaped with cooked meat: steak (*bife*), sirloin (*vacio*), steak and eggs (*bife a caballo*), blood sausage (*morchilla*), and pork sausage (*milanesa*). Argentine meat ranks with the world's best.

If meat doesn't excite you, the ice cream will seduce you. A variety of vendors, from stores to youngsters on street corners, sell dozens of different flavors that multiply into hundreds of combinations.

When preparing your own food, regional items are cheaper. In Patagonia, meat is cheap and fruit expensive; in Mendoza the opposite is true. Most large cities have supermarkets and general stores, *despensas*, that stock most staples. Buying food rarely presents a problem except in remote areas. In these areas plan on carrying an extra day's food.

DRINKS. Generally, drinking city water is safe. Carbonated water in a bottle is called *soda* and is excellent if you become tired of the pop found everywhere. *Jugos*, juices, are delicious but more expensive.

Argentines drink less coffee than any other South Americans. Instead, *yerba de mate* substitutes for it. Made from a local plant, *mate* is a bitter tea Argentines drink obsessively.

The Mendoza, San Juan, and La Rioja regions produce excellent wines. *Bodegas*, or wine-cellars, schedule tours ending with free samples. The most dreadful drinking habit: Argentines mixing their wine with soda.

HEALTH. Argentina has an excellent health system, and most diseases are rare. Travelers require no vaccinations. A small malaria risk exists from October to May in the lowland strip bordering Bolivia.

The two greatest health threats are altitude sickness and conditions resulting from the extremes of weather. In the ovenlike temperatures of the pampas, heat exhaustion and sunstroke are possible, while in the cooler zones of Patagonia exposure and hypothermia threaten.

The northern desert holds its vermin and pests, such as tarantulas, snakes, and scorpions. Watch where you put your hands and feet: these surprises lodge in secluded corners.

An obnoxious pest is the gnat. Breeding in animal droppings, these inescapable hordes teem in agricultural areas. Swarming around your eyes, nose, and mouth, they try extracting as much moisture as possible. Little deters these annoying flies.

Finally, in long grass beware of ticks clinging to your clothes and then finding soft spots to burrow into your skin. Check for ticks frequently when camping in these situations.

PHOTOGRAPHY. Film and supplies are expensive, but film developing is inexpensive and of good quality.

MONEY. Once Argentina was a world economic power. The country had natural resources, a self-sufficient food base, vast areas of land, and waves of motivated immigrants. How they wasted their talent, resources, and future is an incessant debate in Argentina. Recently, inflation had topped 5,000 percent, the average worker took home $40 per month, and unemployment had soared. Waste, corruption, and union greed produced an economic catastrophe.

Today the austral is pegged to the American dollar. This has eliminated the rampant speculation on the dollar, but hasn't cured the country's other woes. Argentina has become an expensive country for visiting and shopping.

When shopping, remember Argentines take their siesta seriously. Everything closes for three to four hours in the afternoon, and then reopens until about eight in the evening. The length of siestas varies, depending on the season and region.

Banks are open from 10:00 A.M. to 4:00 P.M. and close for a midday siesta. Post offices are open from 8:00 A.M. to 8:00 P.M. In Buenos Aires ensure you check international parcels at the international office. Other cities' post offices are less strict about customs formalities.

Argentines celebrate the following holidays: January 1, New Year's Day; Holy Thursday; Good Friday; May 1, Labor Day; May 25, National Anniversary of the Cabildo Abierto; June 20, Flag Day; June, Corpus Christi; July 9, Independence Day; August 17, Anniversary of San Martín's Death; October 12, Columbus Day; December 8, Day of the Immaculate Conception; December 25, Christmas.

SECURITY. Argentina is safe. A minor scam involves a thief secretly smearing a condiment on you. While he or she is helping you clean it up, an accomplice runs off with your bag. Pickpockets also work the streets, but violent crime is rare. Argentines are proud, honest people and their geniality is refreshing. No terrorist groups operate, and although the deposed military junta is still a target for demonstrations of lingering anger, Argentines spare the tourist.

Security Rating: A.

CYCLING INFORMATION

BICYCLES. In most of Argentina bicycling has never been a necessity or even a popular sport. Disregarded as either a kid's toy or a woman's conveyance, bikes are basically ignored.

Most bicycles in Argentina are poorly made imports from Brazil. There are also low-quality Argentine bikes. Touring and mountain-bike parts are rare. Finding imported parts is difficult, but you can find 27- and 26-inch tires more easily.

The northwestern provinces of Jujuy and Salta embrace cycling. Argentina's best shops and equipment are in these provinces' capital cities, where people actively participate in races and tours.

All types of mechanics lack vitality regarding any minor repairs—they seem to think that a minor job is beneath them. The best advice is to do your own repairs.

Posadas maintains two reasonable bike shops, the first on the corner of Avenida Rademacher and Avenida Cabred, and the second at Avenida Mitre and Avenida Colon. Buenos Aires' two best shops are located at

Avenida Defensa and Avenida Caseros, and at Avenida Cordoba and Avenida Florida. The best shop in San Juan is on the corner of Avenida Rioja and Avenida Libertador General San Martín. In Mendoza the best shop is on Avenida Lavalle and Avenida Salta. Finally, Jujuy has two good shops: The first is on San Martín and Lavalle, while the best bike shop in the entire country is on Avenida Urionda 582.

ROADS. Argentina contains 140,000 kilometers of roads; 30 percent are paved. Between major destinations, most roads are asphalt-covered and well maintained. In the northwest region, the major north–south routes are paved, while the east–west routes that cross over the mountains are unimproved. In this region engineers build roads directly over riverbeds. After rainstorms the river-wash leaves its flotsam and jetsam of cacti thorns, sand, and rocks on the road. If traveling in this area, use tire savers.

Road conditions in the pampas are excellent. Most routes maintain full pavement, and occasionally roads even have shoulders. Most traffic in both regions travels in the late evening and at night. If you can endure the heat, the afternoon makes the best time for cycling.

In Patagonia traffic rarely poses a problem. Traffic in the winter season is nonexistent, while in summer only one vehicle a day may pass. Two routes head southward through Patagonia. The main one, Ruta 3, follows the coast and carries almost all the traffic. On certain stretches, only one lane of the road remains paved, allowing traffic the benefit of traveling on pavement and yielding to gravel when encountering head-on traffic. Apart from the coastal road, other routes are unimproved gravel. The infamous Ruta 40, skirting the western foothills, is a rough challenge. Adding to the highway's difficulty are the toils of wind and isolation. Despite that, Route 40 conveniently connects Tierra del Fuego with the Lake District and western South America. Everyone who travels this route has stories about it. Good or bad, the difficulty of this rocky, sandy highway and its harsh beauty are unforgettable.

Throughout Argentina, at border crossings with bridges or tunnels, officials may forbid bike passage. Citing safety reasons such as traffic on the bridges and carbon monoxide in the tunnels, they insist on transporting your bike in their trucks. Authorities seem adamant on the issue.

Finally, in towns and cities traffic lights rarely work, and signs are rarely observed. Be careful at intersections and assume no one is yielding. Off the city streets and on the main highways, traffic is considerate, allowing you ample space.

MAPS. Without a doubt, buy the Automovil Club Argentino maps for travel in Argentina. Scales range from a large *Red Caminera Principal*, ideal for general planning, to excellent provincial maps, to strip maps detailing specific roads. All the maps are expensive, so if you plan only on passing quickly through a province, the general map will suffice. For detailed exploration of an area, however, the provincial map is ideal, pointing out elevations, road conditions, intersections, and distances. All the maps outshine the others available in South America. The ACA operates in every provincial capital.

Respective provinces run tourist offices, which supply free or cheap provincial maps. These maps vary in quality and usefulness; some are good, others are ridiculous. Apart from maps, tourist offices are excellent spots for obtaining provincial information and literature.

BIKE TRANSPORT. Buses in Argentina are large, fast, and comfortable. Between major destinations, companies offer both regular buses and overnight buses that cost a bit more. Make sure you arrive on time; buses leave precisely when scheduled.

On back roads and in Patagonia, bus services are limited; for example, some areas may only schedule one bus weekly, while no bus services run along Patagonia's Ruta 40. Buses along remote routes are less comfortable but more tolerant about carrying bikes. At times, companies charge for baggage by its weight, but at other times charges vary according to the number of people. The more people, the higher the bike's carrying cost.

Hitchhiking is common in Argentina, particularly in Patagonia where the lack of traffic is a problem. As a rule, the less traffic, the more likely a vehicle will stop to help.

Six different rail lines serve Argentina. Each uses different tracks and has different charges for bikes. The government nationalized most lines, but then suspended them. Buses are usually faster and more reliable.

Argentina maintains an extensive domestic flight schedule. If you need to cover a large distance quickly, planes present an excellent option. The problem with planes is the full bookings on flights. People reserve some flights weeks ahead. Argentines book flights on a whim and cancel frequently, so get on the waiting list if flying is your most attractive alternative.

BELIZE

Belize epitomizes the word *unique*. No other country in Latin America compares to it. Where else do you find a Mennonite farmer selling a hand-built chair to a Rastafarian? Where else do the people know and respect "Chocolate," a beachcomber who taxis tourists out to the cays? Where else but Belize?

TOURING INFORMATION

SCENERY. The northern area and the coast of Belize consist of low-land mangrove swamp interspersed with low grasses, azalea, and sugar-cane. Except for the intrinsic beauty of the surf and sand, the north is consistently dull.

Jungle dominates most of southern Belize. Below Belmopan the land fills with tropical plants, thousands of birds, and exotic animals (the world's only jaguar reserve is here). Another highlight, on the Western Highway toward Guatemala, is The Place, a zoo containing the country's indigenous animals. The Place feels more like a farm than a zoo, as the animals live behind chicken wire that allows you to pet and feed them.

Toward the south and west, you reach an area known as the Maya Mountains, the highest points of Belize. Here, a rough track snakes through the Mountain Pine Ridge. You can bicycle the tracks and enjoy the area's remoteness and natural beauty.

Offshore, the cays shine as Belize's jewels. Pronounced "keys," the small islands grew from mangrove swamps. A visit to the cays, with their sun, beach, and crystal-clear water, offers everyone a mini-vacation. Some cays, including Cay Caulker, are small enough that you can walk every-where. You don't need to bring your bicycle, and even if you wanted to, few launches would allow one. The cays exist for enjoyment. You can rent snorkeling gear and hire a boat to experience the unbelievable beauty of the offshore reef. Cay Caulker, with its accessibility and relaxed atmo-sphere, is the best cay to visit.

CULTURAL INTEREST. The most interesting aspect of Belize is its cultural makeup. Africans, *Mestizos*, Mayas, Orientals, Europeans, North Americans, and their combinations make up the population of 175,000. The mix of Rastafarians, British soldiers, Guatemalan refugees, German Hutterites, Oriental entrepreneurs, and bewildered tourists is in-toxicating.

The inhabitants speak and understand a variety of languages, of which German, Chinese, English, and Korean are a few. English is the official language, but most of the people speak Creole, a squashed mixture of En-glish and Spanish.

A pre-election reveler celebrates his candidate's party in Belize City.

Belize struggles to boast about its Mayan ruins. If you want isolated, overgrown ruins that look like they did when they were discovered, Belize may entice you. Xunantunich in the Upper Belize Valley and Altun Ha in the north are the two main Mayan sites. Admittedly, the extent of ancient Mayan influence in the area is still under study.

WEATHER. The coastal temperatures in Belize remain constant. Highs range from 27 to 31 degrees Celsius. Lows hover between 19 and 23 degrees. Inland, the temperatures rise higher than the coast. Maximums reach 38 degrees and lows drop to 12 degrees.

Rain can fall anytime of the year, but the driest months are from February to May. The wettest months are from September to December, while the hurricane season blows between June and October.

Winds generally blow from the northeast, blissfully cooling the coast. Inland, the wind diminishes, raising the heat and humidity.

TOUR OF BELIZE AND GUATEMALA

THE MAYAN LOWLANDS

Distance: 833 km
Start/Finish: Belize City/Belize City
Season: November–May
Terrain: Flat to slightly hilly
Scenery: **
Interest: **
Difficulty: Easy to moderate

Km	Location	Scenery	Interest	Comments
00	**Belize City**	*	*	
26	Hattieville	*		
22	The Place (Belize Zoo)	*	*	No provisions
32	Roaring Creek	*		
36	**San Ignacio** (Cayo)	*		
11	Jct. to Xunantunich			
(04)	Excursion to Xunantunich	**	**	No provisions
02	**Benque Viejo del Carmen**	**		
03	**Ciudad Melchor de Mencos**	*		
65	El Cruce	**		
(33)	**Tikal**	***	***	
30	Jct. to Dolores			
(05)	**San Benito/Flores**	**	*	
68	**Dolores**	**		
(03)	Excursion to Ixcún	**	*	No provisions
26	**Poptún**	**		
16	**San Luis**	**		
45	**Modesto Mendez**			
38	Castillo de San Felipe/ Fronterra	**	*	
34	Franceses	*		
(09)	**Morales**	*		
38	**Entre Rios**	*		
13	**Puerto Barrios**	*		
	Ferry to Punta Gorda (Tues. and Fri., 0830)			
	Punta Gorda	**		
94	Jct. to Mango Creek			
(08)	**Mango Creek**	**		
	and dugout excursion to **Placentia**			
64	Jct. to Stann Creek			
(10)	**Stann Creek** (Dangriga)	***		
67	Blue Hole	***		No provisions
21	**Belmopan**	**	*	

02	Roaring Creek	*
54	Hattieville	*
26	**Belize City**	*

GENERAL INFORMATION

GETTING TO THE COUNTRY. Getting to Belize by air is expensive. Few charter flights service Belize, so you have to board regular flights connecting through Miami. Off-season flights during the summer months offer better fares.

Flights connect Belize City to most Central American capitals except Managua, Nicaragua; for Managua you have to connect through Tegucigalpa, Honduras.

Three entrance points cross overland. From Mexico the northern Chetumal–Corozal route provides a quiet, well-paved road.

To Guatemala on the Western Highway, the road becomes hilly but paved through to San Ignacio. From there the short road hops to Benque Viejo and on to the Guatemalan border, where it becomes rough and unpaved. Beyond, in Guatemala, the Petén roads are rugged.

The last crossing into Belize and the second route into Guatemala crosses the Bahia de Amatique in the south. You take the Hummingbird Highway southeast from Belmopan to Dangriga. From Dangriga, the now unpaved road narrows to the port town of Punta Gorda. Here you board a boat to Puerto Barrios, the eastern port of Guatemala.

DOCUMENTS. Everyone needs a passport. American, Canadian, and other Commonwealth citizens do not need visas, but everyone else does. You can't obtain visas at the border; you must apply for them before crossing. Officials may ask for an onward ticket, but a show of sufficient cash will suffice. Border searches are routine and indifferent.

You must declare your bicycle by make, model, serial number, and value. Officials note this information in your passport to prevent you from selling your bike. Duties, fees, and licenses are not required in order to bring a bike into Belize.

If you plan to continue on to Mexico, try getting your tourist card at the Mexican consulate in Belize City; the card may not be available at the border. If you plan to go to Guatemala, get your visas before entering Belize; no Guatemalan consulate operates in the country. Finally, if you enter through Punta Gorda, get your exit stamps and necessary paperwork completed before leaving Belize.

There is a departure tax of BZ$1.

ACCOMMODATIONS. Belize runs expensive hotels. Comparing the quality and value of Belizean hotels to Mexico's and Guatemala's is a shock initially. Usually, Belizean hotels appear as rundown rooms and cramped guest houses where you always question the security. No youth hostels operate in Belize.

You can pay to camp in a few scattered sites around Belize, such as

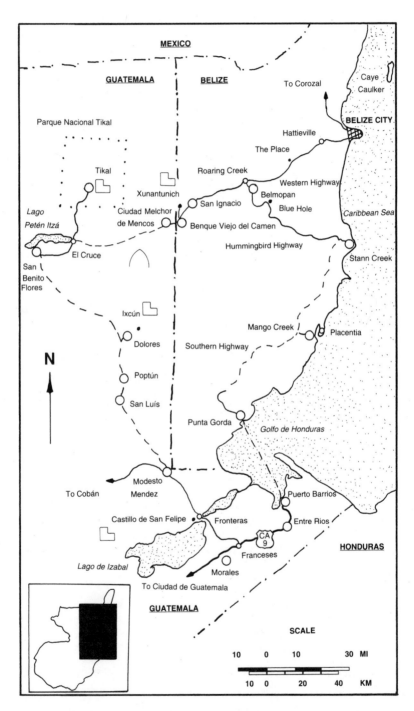

Corozal, Belize City, and cottages along the Western Highway. Security is vital when using these sites. We camped in Corozal, where the all-night, armed guard used his shotgun "to shoot only above the prowlers' heads."

Technically, wild camping in Belize is illegal. If you want to camp and avoid luring thieves, ask the landowner's permission. People outside Belize City are friendly and helpful. Camping in the Belizean jungle allows you to hear the eerie cry of the howler monkeys.

FOOD. The people of Belize import most of their food from Europe, South America, and North America. Great food that you can't find anywhere else in Central America abounds in the supermarkets. Only recently has the country started farming on a commercial basis. European and North American religious groups have immigrated and now work in an accepting environment. The government needs and promotes the food production and subsidizes staples like sugar, rice, and tortillas. In season, cheap tropical fruits and vegetables are available; otherwise, expect to pay a lot for food.

Inexpensive restaurants in Belize prepare cheaper local food, such as rice, beans, and lobster.

DRINKS. A joint Canada–Belize project overhauled the entire sewage system of Belize City, so the water in Belize City is now safe. Outside the main city, treat all water. Because of the sparse population and subsequent lack of homesteads on the Northern and Hummingbird highways, finding potable water is difficult; bottled water is expensive everywhere.

The local brands of rum and beer are cheaper than soft drinks. The country produces both alcoholic drinks, whereas they import soft drinks from Mexico.

HEALTH. Malaria prevails year-round in the rural areas except the province of Belize; however, chloroquine-resistant strains are nonexistent. Update your yellow fever and tetanus shots and stay aware of the usual tropical ailments and pests.

MONEY. The unit of currency in Belize is the Belizean dollar, written as "BZ$." The BZ$ is fixed to the American dollar at a rate of two to one.

Most exchanges happen at banks, which charge 2 percent commission for either bills or traveler's checks. You can change American dollars or traveler's checks at some import stores in Belize City for a higher rate; for example, BZ$2.05 per U.S.$1. Don't change money on the street.

If you have leftover Guatemalan quetzals or Mexican pesos, try to exchange them with other travelers at the main bus depot. You can find the best exchanges for quetzals or pesos at the borders. No matter where or how you change money, the Belizean cost of living is high.

Most shops are open from 8:00 A.M. to 12:00 P.M. and then from 1:30 P.M. to 6:00 P.M. On Sundays and holidays, small shops only open in the morning—everything else is closed.

Banks are open Monday to Thursday 8:00 A.M. to 1:00 P.M., and Friday from 3:00 P.M. to 5:00 P.M.

The market in Belize City offers color, but it's expensive to shop there because locals automatically see you as a tourist.

The holidays of Belize are: January 1, New Year's Day; March 9, Baron Bliss Day; Good Friday, Good Saturday, Easter Sunday, and Easter Monday; May 1, Labor Day; May 24, Commonwealth Day; September 10, St. George's Cay Day; September 21, Belize Independence Day; November 19, Garifuna Settlement Day; December 25, Christmas; December 26, Boxing Day.

SECURITY. Thievery has erupted. Yet most crime centers in Belize City, where a self-defensive, pioneer spirit manifests itself. Don't trust self-appointed guides for anything. They may follow you, attempting to find you a hotel room, taxi, or restaurant and afterward harassing you for money.

Outside Belize City the situation improves, but don't take any chances. Always lock your bike when leaving it unattended. The uniqueness of your bike or equipment isn't the deterrent it is in other countries.

Security Rating: B in country; D in Belize City.

CYCLING INFORMATION

BICYCLES. Belize takes cycling seriously—so seriously that every year in April, the country's brewery sponsors a very competitive cross-country bike race from Belize City to the Guatemalan border and back. Most of the racers buy their equipment and have repairs done at a shop called Santino's on 37 New Road in Belize City. If you need high-quality racing parts that are compatible with your bike, you can find Campagnolo and Shimano components. If you can't use these components, other shops stock a good variety of cheaper Taiwanese parts. Hoifues on Albert Street offers the best selection. Prices for these parts are reasonable, but the quality is questionable. You can find 700C and 26-, 27-, and 28-inch tires in the city.

ROADS. Belize keeps most of its roads well maintained except for those entering Belize City, which are badly gouged. Unpaved sections include Dangriga to Punta Gorda, a small section of the Western Highway from Benque Viejo to the Guatemalan border, and all secondary roads. Traffic is light on all roads, and compared to Mexico the bus drivers are refreshingly courteous. During the March sugarcane harvest, the roads are busy.

MAPS. Belize's road system is simple, so getting lost on the roads is impossible unless you go off into the Mountain Pine Ridge area of the Maya Mountains. If you want a good map of Belize, try the tourist office or a major bookstore in the city. Cathedral Book Shop on Regent Street stocks an adequate selection. If you plan to explore more remote areas, you can obtain 1:50,000-scale maps from the Ministry of Natural Resources in Belmopan. However, obtaining the maps is difficult and they may be outdated.

BIKE TRANSPORT. Buses take bikes for 75 percent of the normal fare. Truck transport can be arranged outside Belize City's market. In other places lining up truck travel is difficult.

BOLIVIA

In the small, darkened patio the audience has crowded in and is patiently awaiting the competition. The deep, haunting beat of a kettle drum begins throbbing through the cold night air like a boat through inky waves. Penetrating the pulse of the drumbeat, the breathless sounds of the Andean panpipes, the *zamponas*, begin interweaving a melancholy melody that was born in the austere *altiplano*. As the music builds, a procession of musicians slowly marches out from beneath the balcony steps. Swaying hypnotically, they form a circle and let their music carry them away to the time of their ancestors. The *Ayamara-Quechua, Cinco Siglos de Resistencia Fiesta* has begun.

Bolivia offers much to travelers. The Andean culture of ancient dialects, authentic apparel, and honest lifestyles magnetizes visitors, drawing those wishing to discover an age-old culture slowly regaining its beauty and identity. Bolivia offers more. Bicycling along the barren *altiplano*, llamas graze, unaffected by your passing. Snowcapped mountains sit on the horizon as if painted on a sky-blue canvas. The air seems iridescent, rarefied; everything seems bright, clear, and bursting with intensity. Bolivia is for the explorer desiring wide-open lands, deep-rooted cultures, and an austere environment where nature maintains a profound impact.

CYCLE ZONES

The Altiplano

TERRAIN. Covering the western third of the country, the *altiplano*, or high-plain area, is quixotic. Desolate and gaunt, its base is at a lofty 4,200 meters. The surrounding mountains reach higher—their goal, to touch the sky.

The widest section of the South American Andes lies in Bolivia. At their widest, the mountains spread over a 250-kilometer expanse.

Despite some of the world's highest roads along Earth's second-highest mountain range, the *altiplano* rolls ever so slightly. Traveling in the area is like traveling in a giant pie plate: The road seems flat, but the surrounding mountains at the rim always lie within sight.

The *altiplano*'s northern section is the most level area of this zone. As you progress farther south, the Andes narrow and the basin becomes more rolling.

At the western edge of Bolivia, the *altiplano* roads climb and cross the major passes of the continental divide separating Chile and Bolivia. Alternately, at the *altiplano*'s eastern edge, the roads plummet into other envi-

Fishermen on Lake Titicaca

ronments—the eastern valleys and, farther east toward Paraguay, the Chaco lowlands.

SCENERY. The *altiplano* exhibits a gaunt, forbidding presence. The landscape is reduced to basics; snowcapped mountains encircle the area, barren flatlands lie on the Argentine border, and the blinding mystery of the salt lakes wait at the country's western fringe.

Waiting for adventurers seeking a severe beauty, the area has a haunting quality that fosters an indelible feeling of isolation.

CULTURAL INTEREST. I crawled on my belly into the bowels of the hellish Potosí silver mine. I discovered the witchcraft section in the maze of La Paz's open street market. I experienced the matriarchal market in Tarabuco, where wandering men play their traditional instruments. I ascended a station of the crosses to a pinnacle overlooking Lake Titicaca. On a darkened patio, I listened to an Ayamara Indian implore to *Mama Pacha*, the Earth Mother, for a return to ancient ways. The *altiplano* offers variety and intensity.

The history of the Bolivian people, their ancient Ayamara culture, the Spanish invasion, and the natives' current struggles are all exposed for the traveler to observe. Like an open book, the *altiplano* waits to express the history of its people. The *altiplano* absorbs the traveler.

WEATHER. *Altiplano* weather pierces you. A cold, dry northeast wind gusts across the *altiplano*. A bright, intense sun turns exposed skin into leather. At sundown, as temperatures drop to −15 degrees Celsius, leftover warmth evaporates to the stars, and water bottles freeze solid.

The zone's wet season lasts from December to April, but short bursts of hail and sleet fall intermittently throughout the year. Be prepared for harsh weather conditions.

TOUR OF BOLIVIA

THE ALTIPLANO

Distance: 1,470 km
Start/Finish: La Paz/La Paz
Season: March–October
Terrain: Mountainous
Scenery: ***
Interest: **
Difficulty: Difficult

Km	Location	Scenery	Interest	Comments
00	**La Paz** (3,630 m)	**	***	Market daily
(71)	excursion to Tiawanacu	*	***	
84	Ayo Ayo (3,950 m)	*	*	
20	**Patacmaya** (3,810 m)	*		
22	**Sica Sica** (3,975 m)	*		
67	**Caracollo** (3,840 m)	*		
37	**Oruro** (3,706 m)	**	**	
61	Poopó (3,709 m)	***		
61	Challa Pata (3,706 m)	***		
93	Ventilla (4,330 m)	***		
109	**Potosí** (4,020 m)	***	***	
46	**Betanzos** (3,407 m)	**		
103	Yotala (2,905 m)	***		
17	**Sucre** (2,635 m)	***	**	Market daily
(65)	Excursion to Tarabuco (3,340 m)	**	***	Market Sat.
47	Chuqui Chuqui (1,810 m)	***		
92	**Aiquile** (2,218 m)	***	**	Market daily
75	**Totora** (2,603 m)	***		
14	**Epizana** (2,600 m)	***		
90	San Benito (2,746 m)	***		
06	Punata (2,740 m)	***	**	Market Tues.
08	Cliza (2,735 m)	***	**	Market Sun.
09	Tarata (2,730 m)	***	**	Market Thurs.
18	Return to Hwy. 4	**		
07	**Cochabamba** (2,537 m)	***	**	Market daily
15	Quillacollo (2,535 m)	***	**	Market Sun.
78	Pongo (3,910 m)	***		
80	Caihuasi (4,210 m)	***		
18	**Caracollo** (3,840 m)	*		
67	**Sica Sica** (3,975 m)	*		
22	**Patacmaya** (3,810 m)	*		
20	Ayo Ayo (3,950 m)	*		
84	**La Paz** (3,630 m)	*		

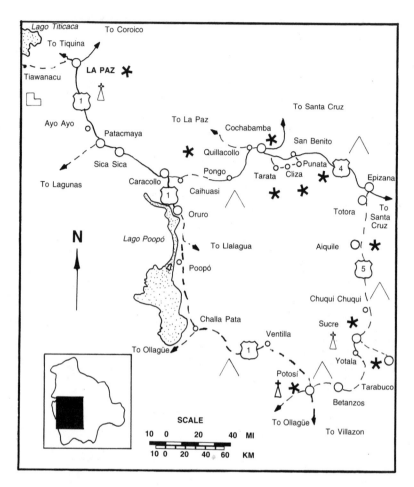

The Eastern Valleys

TERRAIN. The eastern valley zone buffers the Chaco lowlands and the *altiplano*. As the *altiplano* slopes down toward the lowlands, deep valleys and high ridges alternate through the area. Rarely does a road drop uninterruptedly; rather, the cycling through this zone ascends and descends in relentless succession. Magnified by the road conditions, bicycling in this zone is hard work.

SCENERY. The mountains in the eastern valleys provoke a feeling of envelopment. In the deeper ravines, small cracks of sky expose their blueness. At the summits, rows of mountain peaks roll onward to the distant horizon. Between the two, the changes in climate produce vegetation ranging from cactus and scrub grass to orchids and moss. The scenery is extensive, varied, and exciting.

CULTURAL INTEREST. The farther the indigenous people move from their native soil, the more they adapt their traditional lifestyles. The warmth of the valley has thawed the people's layer of stoicism and changed it into a hint of assertiveness. You can find bursts of this changing culture in Cochabamba's bustling markets and in the bistros of Sucre. However, the area's isolation and unpaved roads make reaching the interesting spots difficult.

WEATHER. Days seem springlike year-round. The valley climate is temperate enough to grow crops such as coca, bananas, and grapes.

Winds blow from the north and east, with occasional gusts tearing through the valleys.

The rainy season lasts from November to March, at times rendering the roads impassable.

The Lowlands

TERRAIN. Once into the lowlands, the terrain levels, producing rolling roads. Gone are the severe hills and knee-straining climbs of the valleys.

SCENERY. The lowlands, apart from the area around Santa Cruz, are an almost untouched area of wildlife and forest. Toward the Paraguayan frontier, the lowlands dry out and turn into scrubby grassland. Stretching north toward Brazil, the land becomes wetter, denser with vegetation, and more difficult to access.

CULTURAL INTEREST. The lowlands make up a large portion of Bolivia's land mass, yet the area contains only a small percentage of the country's people. Bolivians, afraid of the jungle's dark unknown and tropical diseases, are reluctant to relocate to the lowlands. Newly developed, the zone is of limited interest.

WEATHER. The northern lowlands have a wet, hot climate. Rain is common throughout the year, and temperatures are high across the region. The humidity of the north adds to the discomfort. In the south the humidity drops. Sporadically, cold winds from the Argentine pampas blow through the area and lower the temperature.

GENERAL INFORMATION

GETTING TO THE COUNTRY. You can enter Bolivia from Peru in three ways. The route farthest to the north, Porto Acosta, is the most difficult because of road and weather conditions and haphazard border openings. Circling Lake Titicaca, this route unveils a beautiful isolated passage that offers glimpses into the customs of the *altiplano*'s people.

The second route from Peru crosses Lake Titicaca's main island, Isla de Tiquina. On the Peruvian side, conditions are reasonable; however, the Bolivian side demands intense climbing over rough roads. A ferry connects the island to the mainland, at Tiquina. The paved road from Tiquina to La Paz makes up for the rough road over the island. Although not the

Bolivia's altiplano

busiest route to La Paz, this is the only pavement from the Peruvian border to Bolivia's main city.

The Desaguedero crossing, which is unpaved, offers the least physically demanding crossing from Peru. This route, which leads to La Paz, is flatter, rougher, and busier than the other two roads. Despite its disadvantages, the Desaquedero road offers the opportunity to visit Tiawanaku, the ancient Ayamara ruins.

The continental divide establishes the border between Bolivia and Chile. Arriving overland from Chile, anticipate formidable climbs.

Two main routes, both difficult and isolated, cross from Chile. Tambo Quemada offers rugged roads in both countries. A rougher route crosses via Ollagüe. Take care along this route, as signs are poor and you could get lost within the maze of intersecting dirt roads. Spectacular volcanoes and otherworldly salt lakes make the Ollagüe route outstanding. Whichever of these isolated routes you take, carry all the water and provisions you will need.

Three viable routes cross from Argentina, each entering one of Bolivia's three distinctive zones. The highest, most westerly passage enters at Villazón. Expect rough, high-altitude cycling in both countries. In the dry season Villazón is a long, dusty, isolated route. In the rainy season this crossing may be impassable, as few bridges span the swollen rivers.

The second route, via Bermajo and the eastern valleys, is also a dry season crossing. The chaotically bouncing topography of this route dispenses ruthless climbs to the cyclist.

The third crossing lies in the Bolivian lowlands at Yacuiba. This would be the ideal crossing for heading into the Bolivian Chaco; otherwise, it's a primitive, arduous route.

Crossing from Paraguay, you challenge the isolated, extremely difficult Chaco in both countries. The Chaco imposes expedition-level bicycling.

In Brazil the government has upgraded the road from Santa Cruz to Puerto Suarez, but in Bolivia this route continues as a long, difficult trip through lowland jungle. If you feel ambivalent about bicycling through the Chaco, take the train connecting Corumbá, Brazil, to Santa Cruz, Bolivia. To bicycle the Chaco, you must have a determined attitude and a craving for challenges. The distance between provisioning stops averages 100 to 250 kilometers, and only a minimum of traffic travels this road. You cannot rely on external assistance in case of breakdown or illness.

Three international train services operate to Bolivia. The first, at Ollagüe, crosses at the Chilean border. This route subjects you to intense and meticulous border searches. The second train service runs from Argentina via Villazón. This route suffers from intermittent service because of Argentine government cutbacks. The complementary Bolivian train from the border into the interior is financially sound and reliable. The third train crossing is the aforementioned Brazilian service to Corumbá. This is by far the best method for crossing the Bolivian Chaco.

DOCUMENTS. Everyone requires a passport and most nationalities need visas, which are obtainable at border crossings. A visa is valid for thirty days, renewable for another thirty days at immigration offices of large cities. Renewing a visa costs up to U.S.$25, depending on your nationality. If you travel near a border, it may be easier and less expensive to cross the border and redo the paperwork than to renew the visa in Bolivia. Peruvian and Argentine border crossings are straightforward, but the Brazilian and Chilean crossings are not. Those two countries are drug-conscious, and officials search travelers' possessions thoroughly. Always carry your passport with you; authorities do not accept photocopies as identification.

ACCOMMODATIONS. Bolivian hotel standards are higher than Peruvian standards, but lower than those of Chile or Argentina. Locals call their hotels *residenciales*, *alojamientos*, or simply *hoteles*. A *pension* is only a restaurant. Also, be aware that in smaller villages the term *hotel* may only mean a restaurant.

The Bolivian hotel network is limited. Most towns and villages do not have hotel facilities. Distances between large cities containing hotel facilities usually lie beyond a day's cycling, so you must have camping capability.

Luckily, you can camp wild easily and safely. In the *altiplano* you can usually find a wall or small gully to use as a windbreak.

Use cold-weather gear for camping in the *altiplano*. Temperatures at night fall quickly and drastically; normal night temperatures can drop to –20 degrees Celsius. It helps to have a high-altitude stove if you want cooked food.

You can easily camp in the eastern valley area as well. The best camping sites to look for are dry riverbanks. Rarely do the mountainsides offer a flat clearing uncluttered by cacti or rocks.

The locals maintain an easygoing attitude in giving cyclists permission to camp. For the *campesinos'* benefit, watch where you pitch your tent, as their *canchas* barely provide sustainable yields in normal conditions. The locals will find your presence more tolerable if you have small gifts handy. Coca leaves and cigarettes help to ease the locals' discomfort.

Camping gas and GAZ cartridges are impossible to find. You can obtain gasoline from either drums (*sueltas*) or pumps (*engritos*). Most villages do not have gasoline pumps.

Finding camping equipment is like a quest for El Dorado. One source for gear is at the Club Andino, on 1638 Calle Mexico, La Paz. In Cochabamba a sports store, Caminate, at 391 Norte on 25 de Mayo, offers a limited selection of gear.

FOOD. Bolivians generally call restaurants *pensiones* or *comedors popular*, and in smaller villages they're known as *hoteles*. Although accommodations in these smaller villages are difficult to find, truck stops pepper the roadsides, offering decent, though monotonous *almuerzos*. Restaurants offer little variety in their meals.

Apart from the truck stops, buying food in certain areas poses problems. In remote villages locals have developed a system of self-sufficiency, so stores stock a small selection. Most *campesinos* grow and dehydrate their food for year-round use. The easiest foodstuffs for the traveler to find consistently are bread, eggs, and pasta. Rice, fruit, and vegetables are difficult to buy on the *altiplano*. Before departing on remote stretches of roads, buy as many necessities as possible.

The amount of imported food available in La Paz makes the city a smorgasbord. Locals haul food from Chile, Brazil, and Argentina to sell in La Paz's street markets. Most local food sold in the country is limited to fruit and vegetables. Bolivia imports most of its processed food.

Any food's availability and cost depend on the distance the food has traveled. For example, you can buy twenty-five oranges for a boliviano in Sucre, but in Potosí, 170 kilometers away and 1,700 meters higher, the price for twenty-five oranges increases to 4 bolivianos.

Bolivians tend to eat a light breakfast of bread and coffee. In La Paz the people breakfast on *salteñas*, a traditional, small pastry filled with chicken or meat stew.

The cheap milk products offer an excellent value. You can purchase safe yogurt and milk products from a city's government-run PIL outlet.

Markets characterize Bolivia. With the economic collapse of the eighties, the people had to develop an entrepreneurial spirit to survive. Now everyone seems involved in the market activity. Every city maintains at least one market, with some cities boasting two or more. La Paz seems to exist as one huge market, reserving entire city sections for the dense array of stalls.

DRINKS. Bottled water is difficult to find. Adding to the difficulty, all other water must be treated.

Bolivians call soft drinks *sodas* or *refrescos*. Stores sell noncarbonated soft drinks with fruity flavors, including pomegranate, papaya, and quinoa. An interesting hot breakfast drink is *api,* which is made from maize and sold in most markets.

Bolivians maintain the Andean coffee tradition of sludge served at your table. The coffee tastes as bad as it sounds.

Local beer is good but expensive. You can find the local grape brandy, called *singani*, and the locally fermented corn beer, *chicha*, in most markets.

HEALTH. Paying strict attention to hygiene is important when traveling in Bolivia. Amoebic dysentery, worms, and hepatitis flourish. Cholera has spread into many poorer villages that are unable to afford plumbing.

There is a malaria risk at altitudes below 2,500 meters. *Falciparum* malaria exists in Bolivia's northeastern section, which borders Brazil. Chagas' disease also threatens in the lowlands. The disease is transmitted by the bite of a beetle that lives in thatched ceilings of huts and bites its victims at night.

If you arrive too quickly in the *altiplano,* you could suffer from altitude sickness.

MONEY. Bolivians use bolivianos for money. Occasionally, Bolivians may refer to pesos, the currency's previous name.

The easiest city to exchange currency in is La Paz. Because street changers in the city bid the same or a worse rate than the exchange houses, they are not worth the trouble unless you find yourself short of money on the weekend or a holiday.

Many *casas de cambio*, located throughout La Paz, offer the best rates of exchange. At the houses you can exchange dollar traveler's checks not only for bolivianos but also into American bills. If you plan on continuing to either Brazil, Peru, or Argentina, La Paz offers an excellent opportunity to stock up on hard currency.

The exchange rates outside La Paz are lower than anywhere else in the country, so try to stock up with what you need before leaving. If you need to change money outside the city, search for stores with a *Compro Dolares* sign. These stores are usually import shops that require hard currency to purchase inventory.

Borders are a risky place to exchange money because many counterfeit notes circulate there. Before changing money at the borders, be able to recognize the bills you need.

For the traveler the cost of living is low. The inflation rate has dropped significantly from its staggering 1,000 percent levels of the early eighties. With severe cutbacks that took a heavy social cost, Bolivia has beaten inflation down to a tolerable level.

Opening times vary in Bolivia. In well-populated areas most shops and services close from 12:00 P.M. to 2:00 P.M. for lunch and open again until 7:00 or 8:00 P.M. On weekends shops close at noon Saturday and do not re-open until 9:00 A.M. Monday morning.

In smaller *pueblos,* shops open early and close at nightfall, rarely closing for siesta or the weekend.

Bolivia celebrates the following national holidays: January 1, New Year's Day; Carnival Monday, Shrove Tuesday, and Ash Wednesday; the Thursday, Friday, and Saturday of Holy Week; May 1, May Day; August 5, Corpus Christi; August 7, Independence Day; October 12, Columbus Day; November 2, Day of the Dead; December 25, Christmas.

Post office service is moderately expensive. According to the postal authorities, Bolivia has no surface mail so you must ship everything air mail. International parcels must be cleared at customs, which is located in the same building as the post office. Bring your own glue, string, and paper, as no packing materials are provided at the post office. Finally, the post office and telephone system are open from 8:00 A.M. to 8:00 P.M.

SECURITY. If you take normal precautions against pickpockets, men posing as police, and condiment sprayers, Bolivia is a safe country to visit. Compared to its northern neighbors, Peru and Brazil, Bolivia is safe. However, you should take care in the northern Yungas area and the lowlands surrounding Santa Cruz. Coca production occurs in these areas and locals are suspicious of strangers.

Bolivia, despite holding the Latin American record for military coups, has become a stable democracy. Two minor guerrilla groups operate, but they pose no major threat to tourists.

Security Rating: B.

CYCLING INFORMATION

BICYCLES. In the *altiplano*, bicycles are limited to one-speed roadsters. However, the *altiplano* is not the bicycle capital of Bolivia. In Cochabamba and the lowland areas, there are more mountain bikes. These mediocre bikes are admittedly insufficient for touring, although you could glean parts from them.

Few bike shops operate in Bolivia. Parts for anything but the roadster are almost impossible to find. In the markets there are *caritas*, market carts laden down with a potpourri of pedals, chains, pumps, and tires. These carts stock everything available in a Bolivian hardware store. Forget 700C tires, but 27- and 28-inch tires are fairly easy to find. Twenty-six-inch tires require more searching. The best shop in the country is in La Paz, at 606 Buenas Aires. Although a poorly maintained shop, it does stock obscure parts.

Bike shops are limited in their ability to handle sophisticated repairs. For example, it seems no bottom-bracket or headset tools exist in the entire country. If convenient, use repair facilities in Argentina or Chile. Bolivian bicycle touring requires bicycle independence. Bring all your expected spares; you cannot expect to find parts or repairs if you run into problems.

ROADS. At 3 percent, Bolivia has the lowest percentage of paved roads in Latin America. Bolivia's main road connects Tiquina on Lake Titicaca, enters La Paz, and continues to Cochabamba in the eastern valley area. Yet even along this main route, there are unpaved stretches.

Farther westward, two routes run between Cochabamba and Santa Cruz. Picking a route depends on how long you want to stay in the mountains. The northern route has more pavement than the southern route; the southern route, however, unveils more mountain scenery. The main highway between La Paz and Cochabamba connects with the short paved route to Oruro. Every other road in Bolivia is unpaved.

Road conditions vary, depending on when the road was last graded.

Conditions range from reasonable to atrocious. Mountain roads are usually the worst for dust, rocks, and ruts. Additionally, these roads are so narrow that when two trucks meet, one has to backtrack to the last passing area. These narrow roads are a concern for cyclists because the potholes and loose sand make traction a problem. When a truck passes you on the road, its wheels get dangerously close. Stop and let trucks pass.

You don't need to stop for traffic very often. Outside the major population centers, few private vehicles travel on the roads. Transport trucks delivering goods and people throughout the country make up most of the traffic. Usually, only three or four vehicles per morning pass, because most truck drivers prefer traveling at night.

Road grades over the mountains vary greatly. Climbs range from gradually rising up a tributary valley to tortuously scaling 600 meters in 8 kilometers. Before bicycling in Bolivia, get the smallest gears possible; the grades and road conditions can be Herculean.

Finally, few road signs exist to direct you. You can ask directions from the first *campesino* you meet, hoping he knows how to get to where you want to go, or you can buy a good map and orient yourself.

MAPS. Few good maps of Bolivia are available. The best map of the country is the Servicio Nacional de Caminos (SNC) *Red Vial* map. This map, a Landsat photograph of the country, has roads and towns superimposed on the photo. Although it does have accurate distances and towns marked on it, the topographical lines are the gross contours seen from the satellite, and the map lacks railway and river markings. Despite these problems, it is the best Bolivian map available. You can buy it at the SNC in La Paz, on 20 de Octubre near Avenida Otero, or in bookshops.

The Instituto Geográfico country map is poor and difficult to read, but the departmental map for the Yungas and La Paz area is excellent for planning even though it has no distance markings.

BIKE TRANSPORT. Bolivia is the easiest Latin American country for bike transport, and the easiest method is by the ubiquitous truck. Covering every route and connecting every village accessible by road, trucks carry every type of cargo, animal, vegetable, and mineral. Transporting your bike is never a problem. Negotiate the fare for yourself and the bike together. Once on, make sure you have easy access to food, water, and cold-weather gear. Traveling in the back of a truck in the middle of an *altiplano* night exposes you to extremely harsh conditions.

The second-easiest method of transporting your bike is by bus. Although routes and times are limited, buses are definitely more comfortable than trucks. Another advantage is buses cover their cargo with a tarp, keeping the road dust off your gear.

Trains pose more of a problem. Few and far between, they require extra care concerning baggage and security.

Bolivia operates two airlines, Lloyd Air Boliviano (LAB), the commercial airline, and Transportes Aereas Militares (TAM). Fares are cheap, and if you want the convenience of getting to a destination quickly, arrange a flight. After taking one too many eighteen-hour truck rides, this option begins to look more appealing. Arrive early to clear baggage requirements.

BRAZIL

Brazil is South America's most diverse country. Argentina may have sophistication, Ecuador may have native culture, and Colombia may have outstanding scenery, but Brazil boasts all that and more. This immense country includes 3,000-meter-high mountains and the world's largest river basin. Unadulterated Indian tribes live in the Amazon, while the sophisticated megalopolis of São Paulo holds a population of 13 million. West of São Paulo, in a far-off corner, lies the Pantanal, a habitat for the continent's greatest concentration of wildlife, while Rio de Janeiro's beaches exhibit the world's wild life. Brazil thrives on extremes.

CYCLE ZONES

Amazonas

TERRAIN. The Amazon basin covers a third of the country. Stretching 5,000 kilometers, it connects Brazil's farthest eastern and western points. At its widest, near the Peruvian border, its width extends to 1,400 kilometers, but it narrows to less than 100 kilometers between the Guinea highlands and the Planalto.

The basin is less than 250 meters in altitude, but the road rises and drops as it makes its way through the jungle. Don't expect totally flat cycling, as the engineers rammed through the jungle and left difficult grades on the roads.

SCENERY. The beauty of the rainforest depends on how far the area's settlers have slashed into the jungle. Along the Trans-Amazon Highway and its access roads, you find 100-kilometer stretches of charred forest quickly turning into hard-packed desert. Thousands of settlers continue flocking to the area, vainly hoping the Amazon basin can be turned into the country's breadbasket. The basin's fertility is deceiving. The rainforest's foliage is self-reliant, with plants living off the constant cycle of decay and growth. Beneath this fragile humus is infertile clay. Still, farmers plunge into the forest, slash and burn, grow their crops until the soil is exhausted, and then turn it into pastureland, eroding the area completely. These assaulted areas sadly remind you of man's desperate and arrogant hopes.

When you stumble on regions of untouched forest, seeing wildlife is difficult. Nestled in the high and middle forest canopies, some birds and animals live their lives without ever touching the ground. The best tracts to view wildlife are at the forest edges, where bare land lies next to the forest.

Do not venture too deeply into the jungle. Although it is not the mass of impenetrable vines that Hollywood likes to depict, getting lost is easy. The

*Everything grows larger in the Amazon: aquatic lilies (*Victoria regia*), native to the region.*

best way to intensely tour the interior jungle is with a guide.

CULTURAL INTEREST. Ancient cultures left few vestiges of their existence. Instead of stone gods, cultures worshiped their jungle. The rainforest was their pantheon of gods, and every god lived in the rainforest. Everything was connected to nature. There were no elaborate rituals or priestly castes.

Remote tribes still carry out an ancient jungle culture passed down from their ancestors. Most of the discovered tribes now live in reserves, and because of the threat from poachers and gold-diggers, travelers wanting to visit reserves require advance permission from Brazilian authorities.

Today the Amazon has a frontier mentality; its people either welcome you openly, wanting to share the glory of their hardships, or are frighteningly paranoid, their survival bleak and their lives cheap. The towns, pioneer settlements, fill with cowboys, prospectors, and ranchers.

WEATHER. Temperatures and humidity levels remain high year-round. Highs in Manaus range from 30 degrees in January's dry season to 37 degrees Celsius in December. From January to June, expect one strong rainstorm daily. Rainfall is relentless. Belém, at the Amazon's mouth, receives almost 3 meters of precipitation yearly. Rain causes the biggest impediment to cycling; the best time to visit is during the dry season, from June to December. Outside of these months, temperatures, coupled with road conditions, make cycling oppressive.

Paranagua Basin

TERRAIN. The Paranagua basin, delineated by the Amazon basin, the Paraná River, and the borders of Bolivia and Paraguay, sits like a giant bowl in Brazil's central west. Around its southern and eastern rim, the basin's edge rises sharply into the Planalto. North, toward the Amazon, the basin's edge is shallower, cut by river valleys flowing either southward into the Pantanal or becoming part of the Amazon River system to the north.

SCENERY. The area's biggest attraction is the huge inland marsh, the Pantanal. Luckily, it's also the continent's best secret. The Pantanal contains the largest concentration of birds and wildlife in the Western Hemisphere. Unlike the Amazon, the Pantanal presents open forest and scrubland that allows you easy access and open views of the wildlife. You can easily see monkeys, alligators (*jacaré*), giant amphibious guinea pigs (*capybara*), tapirs, anacondas, and hundreds of bird species, from toucans to pink flamingos.

Only a small portion of the Pantanal is protected as a national park. Cattlemen and their livestock share the rest of the marsh and woodland. Despite cattle overrunning some areas, poachers killing relentlessly, and tourists increasing the demand for resources, the area remains rich in species and natural beauty.

You can visit the Pantanal in two ways. The first is by organized excursion, ranging from formal U.S.$100-per-day groups to inexpensive, unpredictable three-day visits for U.S.$50. Most tours consist of a trip to a hut deep in the Pantanal where you participate in walks, fish for piranha, and search out animals to photograph.

The second method of traveling through the Pantanal is independent of excursions—bicycling. Two main roads cross into the Pantanal. From Cuibá the Transpantanaria slips 140 kilometers deep into the Pantanal, ending at a small ranching center, Porto Jofre. Finding provisions along the road is impossible, so prepare for any emergency. During the dry season, seeing animals on the sides of the road is common. During the rainy season, the road is submerged and animals use any raised surfaces for refuges.

The second road through the Pantanal, which connects the city of Corumbá to the rest of Brazil, bisects a small portion of the Pantanal. Two roads follow this route: the major, paved route and the less used, much rougher road farther north. The major route is uninteresting, while the secondary route affords exciting exposure to the area's flora and fauna.

CULTURAL INTEREST. Although the Paranagua basin is Brazil's fastest-growing region, there is very little of interest to the traveler.

Ranchers, farmers, and the coastal poor, all searching for a better existence, have blighted the area's wilderness.

WEATHER. When planning an excursion into the Paranagua basin, you must consider the rainy season. From November to March, when most of the rain falls, the roads become impassable, particularly in lowlands and marshes. The further into the dry season you visit, the more comfortable and enjoyable your trip. Winds are rarely a problem.

The Planalto

TERRAIN. The Planalto is an enormous escarpment, stretching from the Uruguayan border to the Amazon basin. The Planalto rises abruptly from the southern coast. From the central coast, the escarpment rises in stages. Farther north, it fades to the Amazon.

The Planalto's altitude averages only 300 meters. Yet the area's highest peaks rise to 2,000 meters in the Minas Gerais region, north of Rio de Janeiro. This region is Brazil's most mountainous, and the roads fall and drop between the valley floors. Few flat sections exist; most of the terrain either rolls along or challenges with knee-cracking climbs.

SCENERY. Scenery consists of hills, either forested with pine or planted with coffee plants. Lakes and rivers add their charm. Unfortunately, mining corporations, intent on denuding and raping the land, have assailed expanses of Minas Gerais. Yet thousands of kilometers of back roads and forgotten mining routes still offer satisfying scenery.

In the northeast the escarpment dwindles toward the Atlantic Ocean. The area, known as the Seratão, exists as a scrubby, drought-ridden area, inhabited by thorny cacti and low shrubs.

CULTURAL INTEREST. The interest rating in the Planalto is high. In the southern area of Rio Grande do Sul, European immigrants have settled successfully, and the ranchers who dominate the area follow the Argentine *gaucho* tradition.

The Minas Gerais region is perhaps the most interesting. Through the eighteenth century, Europeans colonized and exploited the area's mineral wealth. During this gold-rush era, beautiful cities such as Diamantina, São João del Rei, and the gem of the mining area, Ouro Prêto, were built, becoming cultural landmarks over time. Today the cities and towns retain their churches and sculptures, preserving the area's colonial identity.

Farther north is Brazil's capital, Brasília. Placed in the middle of nowhere, Brasília has typified everything that is wrong with Brazil. The concept started as a plan to decentralize the government, reduce the population density along the littoral, and boost Brazil into the twenty-first century. Instead, Brasília became an ostentatious undertaking beyond the capability of its people. No one wanted to live in this wasteland devoid of culture, recreation, or natural beauty. The city has never been accepted. On weekends the inhabitants shuttle to Rio de Janeiro and leave the city to the poor *favela* inhabitants.

Farther north, the Seratão's inhabitants include dusty cattle, emaciated horses, desperate farmers, and pitiful cowboys. The region is a forlorn area, isolated and forgotten by the rest of Brazil.

WEATHER. The weather varies within the region. In the southern hills, winter frosts occur, while in the northern Seratão, yearly droughts are common.

In the southern Planalto, most rainfall occurs from June to September. During these winter months, daytime temperatures, which average 12 degrees Celsius, drop dramatically to produce overnight frosts. Summer temperatures are ideal for bicycling.

Farther north in the Minas Gerais region, temperatures are more moderate than the cold winter temperatures of the south or Rio de Janeiro's tropical heat. Minas Gerais' rainy period stretches from November to March, with a definite dry period from May to September. Days are mild and nights are refreshingly cool, ideal for comfortable sleeping.

In the Seratão, precipitation becomes more scarce, with a spotty rainy season from March to June. The area temperatures become oppressive as the plateau slides toward the equator.

Winds generally blow from the northeast.

A stone saint watches over the colonial town of Ouro Prêto.

TOUR OF BRAZIL

MINAS GERAIS

Distance: 631 km
Start / Finish: Belo Horizonte/Belo Horizonte
Season: April–October
Terrain: Hilly
Scenery: ***
Interest: ***
Difficulty: Moderate

Km	Location	Scenery	Interest	Comments
00	**Belo Horizonte**	**	**	
19	**Sabará**	*	***	
21	**Caeté**	**	**	
25	**Barão de Cocais**	**	*	
12	**Santa Bárbara**	**	**	
17	Catas Altas	***	**	
27	Antonio Pereira	***	*	
11	**Mariana**	***	**	
12	Ouro Prêto	***	***	
18	Jct. at left	***		
15	Jct. at left	***		
32	Jct. BR-040	***		
09	**Congonhas**	**	**	
09	Return to BR-265			
35	**Entre Rios de Minas**	***		
33	Lagoa Dourada	***		
23	Jct. to Prados	**		
12	Prados	**	**	
12	Dores de Campos	**		
12	Barroso	**		
25	Jct. to Tiradentes	**		
04	**Tiradentes**	***	***	
04	Return to BR-265	**		
10	**São João del Rei**	***	***	
49	São Tiago	***		
26	Morro do Ferro	***		
21	Passa Tempo	***		
07	Jct. at left	***		
17	Piracema	***		
30	Crucilândia	***		
46	Brumadinho	***		
38	**Belo Horizonte**	**		

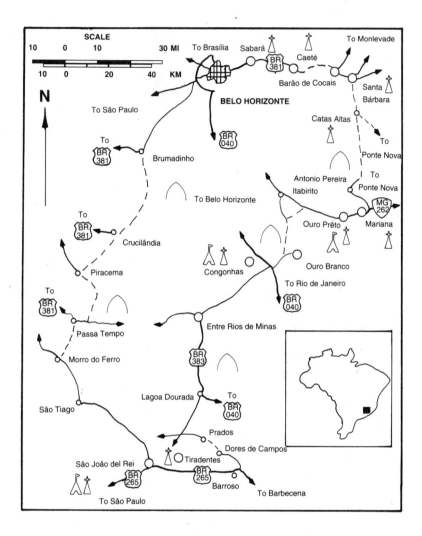

The Littoral

TERRAIN. The littoral, the coastal strip, stretches 4,200 kilometers from the busy Uruguayan border to Fortaleza's deserted beaches. The coast's southern half holds a series of small bays, rocky islands, and granite peaks. You find a microcosm of the littoral's terrain in Rio de Janeiro. Beside the famous beaches of Copacabana and Ipanema stand the celebrated peaks of Sugarloaf Mountain and Corcovado, both world-famous Brazilian landmarks. Rio's main roads connecting different sections of the city burrow through solid granite walls.

Farther north, past the irregular bays and stupendous mountains, lie flatter, wider lands. The beachfront expands, the climbs to the Planalto lessen, and the terrain becomes easier.

SCENERY. If enticing seascapes, luscious beaches, and luxuriant wooded hills can lure you, then you'll love the littoral. On certain sections of highway, your cycling progress will slow to a snail's pace as you stop and savor the differing qualities of each beach. Every beachfront strip has its own identity—lively or lonely, calm or rough, sandy or rocky, white sand or black pebbles. Each coastal bay is unique.

CULTURAL INTEREST. The littoral doesn't only consist of hedonistic beaches. Seventy-five percent of the country's population lives along the coast. Each of these people, from the German industrialists to the Afro-Brazilians, add their color to the coastal scene. ·

On the southern coast, the majority of European immigrants celebrate their culture at Blumenau's yearly Oktoberfest. These recent arrivals have brought their skills and capitalist values to their new land.

São Paulo is the country's mighty industrial heart—a heart that is having palpitations. With a heterogeneous population of 13 million people, it's the world's fastest-growing city. Every day another thousand rural Brazilians, looking for work and a spark of hope, migrate to São Paulo. Often what they find is slums and desperation.

On Rio de Janeiro's surface, the city prospers. The wealthy cavort on the beaches, world-class boutiques sell designer bikinis, and the nightlife matches the world's liveliest. Rio's displays of hedonism climax in the orgiastic frenzy of Carnival. However, deeper in Rio's bowels lurk disfranchised youth, hopeless men, and desperate families. Rio is the city where Brazil's division of wealth is the most profound.

Twelve hundred kilometers farther north, Salvador's people center themselves on religions based on ancient African traditions. Africans, resistant to European diseases, were brought over as slaves to cut sugarcane. They also brought their religions and traditions. Many gods, each with its weekly day of celebration, manifest *Candomblé*, the Afro-Brazilian religion. Ogun, the *orixá*, or god of war, is identified with the Roman Catholic Saint George. Check at the Salvador tourist office for religious ceremonies open to the public. The locals also believe in and practice *Umbanda*, a form of spiritualism. Salvador represents mystery and magic.

In Brazil's forgotten northeast corner, the Seratão supports Brazil's poorest people. Farmers and cowboys try scratching a living from the alternating periods of rain and drought. Here the people's attachment to the land is deeply rooted. Family bonds and daily hardships characterize this strong, proud culture.

The entire coast is magnificent in its scenery and attractions. To encapsulate the coastal experience, bicycle between Santos, São Paulo's port, and Rio de Janeiro. You'll find hundreds of beaches, wooded hills, and charming villages.

Apart from the spectrum of people, this gorgeous ride also has the fascinating colonial ports between São Paulo and Rio de Janeiro. This area

Everyone, regardless of age, celebrates Brazil's Carnival.

is sprinkled with small, picturesque towns such as Caraguatatuba, Parati, and Angra dos Reis.

WEATHER. Weather cycles are similar to the Planalto. But on the littoral, the precipitation and temperatures intensify. Temperatures range from 32 to 42 degrees from December to March, the summer season, while the winter months, June to August, range from 22 to 32 degrees Celsius. During the rainy season, from December to April, vicious thunderstorms arrive daily. Preceding rainy weather are the southeast winds, while winds heralding good weather blow from the northeast.

TOUR OF BRAZIL

THE LITTORAL

Distance: 630 km
Start/Finish: São Paulo/Rio de Janeiro
Season: March–September
Terrain: Hilly
Scenery: ***
Interest: **
Difficulty: Moderate

Km	Location	Scenery	Interest	Comments
00	**São Paulo**		**	
60	**São Vicente**	**	*	
03	**Santos**	**	**	
08	Ferry to Guarujá			
04	**Guarujá**	**	*	
33	**Bertioga**	***	*	
67	Maresias	***		
27	**São Sebastião**	***	*	
	Ferry excursion to **Ilha São Sebastião Ilhabela** (every 2 hours)	***		
28	**Caraguatatuba**	***		
51	**Ubatuba**	***	*	
71	**Parati**	***	**	
46	Mambucaba	***		
46	Jct. Angra dos Reis	**		
04	**Angra dos Reis**	**	**	
	Ferry excursion to **Ilha Grande** (Mon., Wed., and Fri., 1500)	***		
04	Return to BR-101	**		
68	**Itacuruçá**	***	*	
18	**Itaguaí**	**		
10	**Santa Cruz**	**		
46	Jct. left through Parque Nacional da Tijuca	***		
36	**Rio de Janeiro**	***	***	

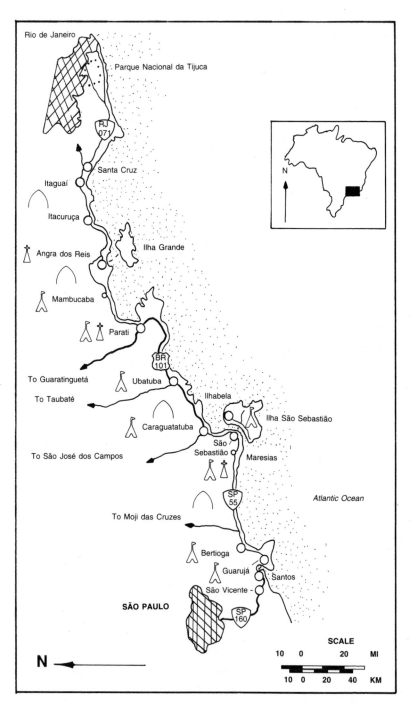

GENERAL INFORMATION

GETTING TO THE COUNTRY. Brazil borders every South American country except Chile and Ecuador. Some countries have road crossings into Brazil every hundred kilometers, while others have only one riverboat crossing.

Only one road crosses from Venezuela, at Santa Elena. In both countries the route passes through isolated terrain. Through Venezuela's beautiful Gran Sabana, provisions are poor, but the newly paved road is excellent. In Brazil, from the border to Boa Vista and southward, the road is isolated and difficult. You must contend with long stretches of jungle, Indian reserves, health hazards, and scarce provisions.

From Colombia the most common way of entering Brazil is to fly to Leticia and then canoe across the river to Tabatinga, Brazil. Once you complete immigration formalities, float by boat down the Amazon for 1,200 kilometers to the first road at Manaus.

Peru's northern crossings follow the same method as Colombia's. Reaching Iquitos from the road's end at Yurimaguas or Pucallpa, take a riverboat destined for Iquitos. From there regularly scheduled boats ply the water from Iquitos to Tabatinga.

The only road crossing from Peru to Brazil is for the adventurous. From the southern mining town of Puerto Maldonado in Peru, cross a rough, isolated track. Struggle through mud and ford rivers until you reach the first major town along the Trans-Amazon Highway, Rio Branco. Provision carefully and plan for every type of emergency. Good luck!

From Bolivia the main route passes through Corumbá, near the Pantanal's center. Rail travel is the most popular method of reaching the Bolivian border at Puerto Suarez because the road route is difficult, isolated, and subject to washouts. On the Brazilian side, the main route out of Corumbá and onward to Campo Grande is paved and in reasonable shape.

Out of Paraguay, three routes cross the border. The main route connects Asunción to Foz do Iguaçu and continues to Curitiba, near the Atlantic coast. On the Brazilian side, the area is busy, but many side routes twist through the hills. The second route connects Paraguay's second city, Concepción, to the border at Pedro Juan Caballero. The main street acts as the border for both Caballero and the town of Punta Pora in Brazil. This secondary route connects Paraguay with the Paranagua basin, as opposed to first crossing into the Planalto farther south. A third method of entering Brazil is by the twice-monthly riverboat that travels upriver from Asunción. This relaxing three-day voyage ends in the Pantanal's main city, Corumbá.

From Argentina the obvious crossing lies at Iguazú, one of South America's most spectacular sights. Crossing at Iguazú allows you to enjoy the benefits of seeing the falls from two perspectives, Argentina's close-up views and Brazil's encompassing distant views. If you visit the area, both borders allow for one-day visits to see both sides, eliminating the need for visas.

If for some reason you want to miss the falls or avoid Uruguay, a crossing exists in the heart of the pampas at Uruguaiana, Brazil, and its Argentine counterpart, Paso de los Libres.

From Uruguay three routes cross the border. On the Brazilian side, all routes are paved, but most of the pavement on the Uruguayan side, except for the Chuy crossing, is spotty.

This coastal route, the Barra de Chuí, is the main international route, carrying the bulk of traffic between Brazil and Uruguay. Both sides' roads are well maintained but busy.

The next major crossing passes through the Rivera crossing at Santa do Livramento. This crossing, which lacks pavement on the Uruguayan side, slogs through Uruguay's interior and the isolated section of Brazil's Rio Grande area.

Uruguaiana, Brazil, acts as a double border city for Argentina and Uruguay. Snuggled into this far corner of Brazil, this ranching city sits quietly on the Rio Uruguay, which runs past Uruguay's Bella Union.

DOCUMENTS. You need a passport to enter Brazil and some nationalities also need a visa, which varies in cost according to nationality. If you require a visa, you need to provide a photograph and either proof of funds or an onward ticket. If you arrive by air, the onward ticket is necessary, but if you travel overland the ticket requirement is usually waived.

Everyone arriving at the border must fill out a tourist card that is valid for ninety days. Officials might document your bicycle on the card.

Renewing a visa or tourist card is a time-consuming, tedious procedure. First you must show proof of funds (a credit card is the best for impressing officials). Then show your passport. Then go to a Caixa Economicá Bank and have a DARF form filled out, return it to immigration, and finally pay the officials for the extension. The entire process is a headache.

You must always carry your passport with you. In larger cities you may get away with carrying an embassy-authorized copy of your identification, but in remote areas you should always carry your originals.

LANGUAGE. Just about everyone traveling to Brazil believes that knowing Spanish is sufficient. Once you get there, you'll discover that most of the people understand what you're trying to say, but you won't understand what they're saying. Brazil's official language is Portuguese, and you should try to understand at least its basic pronunciation.

ACCOMMODATIONS. Brazilian hotels run the gamut from internationally renowned five-star hotels to flea-bitten whorehouses furnished with squalid round beds. Cheaper accommodations begin with *dormitórios*, a room with three or four beds. If there's no demand for the room, you can usually rent it for the price of a normal double room. Hotels offering dormitory rooms and other styles of rooms are called *hospedárias* and *pensãos*. *Quartos* are private rooms without a bath, and rooms with private baths are *apartamentos*. You can find most of these cheaper accommodations around the bus and train stations, but you can also find quieter rooms with more character in the town center.

Avoid rooms facing a main street, as they are always noisy. Some hotels have poor security, so always lock your belongings, including your bike, in your room. Finally, all shower facilities are heated by the infamous electric showerheads—be careful.

An accepted Brazilian institution is the motel. Provocatively advertised, motels offer a short-term hideaway for couples wanting discretion and privacy. The higher-quality motels offer whirlpools, high-security fences, and piped-in music. During a quick stopover, you could splurge, renting these motels for a half-day period. The lower-quality motels are usually in rougher sections of town that are populated by prostitutes. Furnished with gaudy, round beds, the motels usually offer a private shower. Nothing is wrong with them; just be careful of security.

Brazil runs an extensive campground network operated by either the municipality or the Camping Club do Brasil. Most cities operate campsites 5 to 20 kilometers from town. Municipal camping is inexpensive but lacks facilities. However, the Camping Club is expensive and contains every camping luxury, from showers to laundry basins to swimming pools.

All campgrounds are busy during the hectic December-to-March tourist season. Because of this intense demand, it may be impossible to rent a spot at a club site without being a member and making a reservation.

Don't try wild camping anywhere near a city. Since most cities have surrounding rings of slums, called *favelas*, a tourist's presence and wealth could attract trouble.

In the Planalto or on deserted beaches, finding wild camping is easy. In the Planalto most land is fenced for pasture, but since so few people live in this area, helping yourself to an isolated spot is easy. Along the littoral set up your tent after dark and do not camp directly on the beach. Robbers and joyriding drunks present two potential hazards. Also, beaches may be private, and the wealthy class is paranoid about squatters moving onto their land and setting up homes. If the authorities confront you, they usually allow you to stay the night once you explain your situation. In the Amazon, camping is a necessity, not a choice. Distances between shelters are too great. Camp as well off the road as is comfortable, but in the jungle maintain your bearings. Waterproof your gear, disregarding the saunalike condition you'll create in your tent. Finally, be wary of robbers, vermin, pests, and dangerous animals, such as snakes and wild dogs.

Fuel for every type of camping stove is easy to find. Low-octane gasoline is expensive and poorly filtered. You can also find alcohol, produced from sugarcane, at gas stations. The country's current economic situation causes shortages for drivers needing large quantities. GAZ cartridges are available at most supermarkets and camping stores.

Brazil manufactures mediocre camping equipment, including tents, sleeping bags, and GAZ stoves. Most equipment is designed for occasional weekend use and not for long-term expeditions.

FOOD. Food varies by region and season. For example, the southern ranching area of Rio Grande do Sul specializes in beef, whereas the Amazon produces an abundance of exotic fruit, vegetables, and fish. Despite these differences, Brazil produces such an enormous amount of food that finding staples is not a problem except in isolated sections such as Mato Grosso and the Amazon basin.

In every city there are supermarkets that stock vast arrays of food; many groceries even include a hot and cold delicatessen and health food sections with whole-wheat breads and brown rice. If you've spent any time in the Andean countries, the variety and quantity of food will astound you.

The cheapest restaurant deals are the side carts and mobile trailers selling *lanches*, fast foods such as X-burgers (hamburgers). In restaurants the day's set meal is the *prato del dia*. The *prato* usually consists of two starches, a bit of salad, and a slice of grilled meat. If the *prato* is not enough for a full cycling meal, the *surtido* is larger and not much more expensive. Even better is the *comercial*, separate dishes filled with generous helpings, the price calculated per person.

DRINKS. Brazil has cornered the market on methods of selling bottled water. Four-liter and one-liter plastic containers, small glass bottles, plastic sachets and one-quarter-liter plastic cups are sold in most supermarkets. All tap water should be treated; however, some hotels and restaurants have installed filters that purify the drinking water.

Brazil's large variety of fruit makes for delicious combinations of juices. Types of fruit juices, *sucos*, vary by season and area. Traditionally, *sucos* have sugar and ice added. If you don't want a repulsively sweet drink, order it *sem gelo e açúcar*. Brazilians add endless supplementary ingredients, among them protein powder, eggs, and milk. If you want a simple *suco*, order it *natural*.

You can find soft drinks, *refrigerantes*, everywhere. They're also cheaper than water, beer, or juices.

Soft drinks are not the nation's most popular beverages; everybody drinks beer. Sold in stores, by street vendors, and in bars, you're never far from beer. Wine and alcoholic drinks are less in demand except around Carnival, when homemade liquor is added to powdered-fruit punches.

Drinking a cup of coffee, a *cafezinho* in Brazil, is a national pastime. Drank everywhere and anytime, the small cup of black coffee is a societal mainstay. Children develop a taste for coffee early, and it continues as a part of every Brazilian's life.

HEALTH. Health concerns vary depending on a region's urbanization. For example, health concerns in Rio de Janeiro, the healthiest area in the country, are small. You can swim in the oceans, eat most foods, and drink filtered water. However, in remote areas bizarre diseases appear.

The more common ailments throughout Brazil include hepatitis from fruits and vegetables, intestinal parasites from just about everything you touch, and dysentery and typhoid from impure water. Inoculations you should get before traveling in Brazil include polio, typhoid, a TB skin-test, gamma globulin, hepatitis, and yellow fever.

Intestinal parasites are easy to catch, and it seems inevitable, if you travel extensively in Brazil, that you will contract at least one type of parasite. Colestase, a drug for parasites, is a reliable local brand that can be purchased at any pharmacy.

Malaria is increasing in Brazil. In the Amazon basin new strains appear constantly. Below 900 meters in rural areas, the following states have a year-round malaria risk: Acre, Rondônia, Amapá, Roraima, Amazonas, Pará, Goiás, Maranhâo, and Mato Grosso. No risk exists in urban areas except in the Amazon river region. Throughout the interior Amazon region, you can encounter chloroquine- and Fansidar-resistant strains of malaria. Avoidance is becoming the best precaution. Keep exposed skin covered, particularly at dawn and dusk; sleep under a mosquito net or fan; and use insect repellent. The Brazilian brand of repellent works well.

The Amazon holds the world's most exotic diseases. Guarding and protecting yourself against every new strain of a malady that comes along seems impossible. So, as with anti-mosquito precautions, the best precautions lie in reducing your risks instead of relying on pharmaceuticals. Treat all your water, pay strict attention to your hygiene and eating habits, and, since many parasites enter through the soles of the feet, don't walk barefoot.

When you enter the Amazon region, officials stationed at highway roadblocks check everyone's yellow fever status. You must show your inoculation card verifying that you have had a yellow fever shot. If you can't, they inoculate you before allowing you to continue.

Beaches hold their inherent dangers. First, the sun is fierce at these latitudes, and the glare of bright sand and sea intensifies the sun's burning power. Brazil sells excellent, though expensive, sunblocks ranging in protective factors from two to thirty.

The heat and sun's rays also make you susceptible to heat exhaustion and sunstroke. Drink lots of liquids and keep your skin loosely covered to prevent dehydration.

All this talk of sun, sand, and hedonism brings us to the topic of sex and sexually transmitted diseases. Brazil has a high number of AIDS cases. Propagated by the wildness of Carnival and the more liberal morals than other South American countries, sexually transmitted diseases make Brazil a country where practicing safe sex is essential.

Lastly, a discussion about the natural vermin of the beach, the dreaded *borrachuda*. You are lying lazily on the beach, or you find an excellent camping spot in some secluded woods. The sun sinks, supper is about ready, and then your ankles become itchy and swollen. Small dots of blood appear on the more susceptible areas of your body, and you notice the small black specks hopping about on your skin. The sand fleas, seemingly all jaw, inhabit every rural or undeveloped beach. After they chomp, the bites become itchy, red, and swollen. To combat these little devils, keep your body's softer areas covered, especially at dusk and on wild beaches. Repellent also deters the fleas for a short period, but ultimately the *borrachuda* is relentless and the subsequent itching is maddening.

PHOTOGRAPHY. Brazil is an expensive country for restocking photography supplies. Film, slide and print, is expensive, and prices for accessories are astronomical. The convenience of twenty-four-hour developing will also cost you.

MONEY. Three rates exist for converting foreign currencies into the Brazilian cruzeiro ouro. The official bank rate is the lowest possible, so banks are poor places for exchanging money or having money sent to you.

The second exchange rate is the tourist rate. The government's economic policies periodically ban this market. An economic crackdown will result in Brazil's becoming an expensive country. If the government is tolerating the market and loosening economic policies, changing money is simple and the cost of living lower. You can usually get a feel for the black market's legality by how open the money changers are. If they act worried and conduct business in doorways, be more wary. The major newspapers list the daily exchange rate on the front page. *Casas de trocar* sell at close to the tourist rate, and you get slightly less for traveler's checks. Exchange facilities differ between regions. In some places banks may change at the tourist rate; in other spots *casas de trocar* are nonexistent, so you might have to ask where you can change money and then compare rates. Hotels and travel agencies usually have reasonable rates of exchange.

Some travel agencies may change money at more than the tourist rate. This parallel rate is the final tier of a confusing system. Found on the streets, in some hotels, and at travel agencies, it is the most favorable but riskiest market. Robbery, sleight-of-hand, or simple ignorance could result in losing money.

Brazilian economics is insane. Plagued by bad debts, a large deficit, high unemployment, extensive corruption, and notable class discrepancies, the economy has been subjected to a variety of extreme measures. Inflation and the cost of living fluctuate at the whim of government and business. As an example, the first time I entered Brazil, living was extremely inexpensive. I received 87 cruzados (then the currency) per U.S. dollar. At month-end, just before people were paid, every business, supermarket, and gasoline station increased their prices by 25 percent. The reason for the inflation was the sudden increase of circulating money. Disappointed, I left for Paraguay. On its first day in office, the newly elected Brazilian government froze everybody's bank accounts over U.S.$700. This stroke of economic genius took billions of dollars out of circulation, and inflation was obliterated. But this lack of funds eliminated the speculation on the normally safe investment of American dollars. The exchange rate dropped to 30 cruzados, a third of what the dollar was worth a month earlier. Brazil became an exorbitant country to visit. Slowly, the currency stranglehold loosened, and inflation and the U.S. dollar again began to creep upward. The Brazilian economy is too volatile to predict its cycles of inflation and austerity.

The closed-market system inhibits the traveler from buying American currency for travel to other countries.

Most shops are open from 8:00 A.M. to 6:00 P.M., closing an hour or two for siesta; yet these times are less formalized in rural areas. Most shops except supermarkets, general stores (*mercerías*), and bakeries (*panaderías*) close Saturday at midday and do not open until Monday morning.

Brazil observes the following holidays: January 1, New Year's Day; the three days preceding and including Ash Wednesday of Carnival; April 21, Tiradentes; May 1, Labor Day; June, Corpus Christi; September 7, Independence Day; October 12, Nossa Senhora Aparecida; November 2, All Souls' Day; November 15, Republic Day; December 25, Christmas.

SECURITY. After Peru and Colombia, Brazil is South America's most dangerous country. It's not rife with drug-related violence or revolutionaries threatening to bomb every government facility. Outside the major cities, crime is not a serious problem. Most of Brazil's criminal elements thrive around major cities, particularly Rio de Janeiro, São Paulo, and Salvador de Bahia. In them, criminals mark tourists as easy targets. Foreigners don't know the language, are often disoriented, and always have valuables—tourists are easy game.

Brazil's jails maintain a stock of travelers who attempted to smuggle drugs in or out of the country. Brazilian jail terms average fifteen years, whatever your nationality. If you are convicted on a drug charge, do not expect leniency or help from your embassy. Baggage searches are intense at border crossings with Bolivia, Peru, and Colombia. Try not to look like a "hippie" and do not attempt to smuggle drugs.

Security Rating: C.

CYCLING INFORMATION

BICYCLES. Brazilians with money and an interest in bicycling import their gear from the United States. Although Brazil manufactures its own line of Caloi bicycles, including mountain bikes, cruisers, and semi-racers, their parts are not interchangeable with those made elsewhere. Specialized parts made outside Brazil are difficult to find. Basic parts, bearings, tires, and races are available. The only tires fitting 26-inch rims are the Industria de Brasileria 26 x 2.175. Other sizes do not fit standard 26-inch rims.

Bicycles are uncommon in the larger cities, but where the natural terrain is flat and traffic levels low, bicycles are more popular. You can locate bike shops and mechanics more easily in smaller towns. In larger cities bike shops hide in small alleys and streets.

You can find basic shops at the following locations: in Florianopolis on Avenida Mauro Ramos between Rua Clement and Rua Osvaldo; in Foz do Iguaçu on Avenida Barabosa between Barbosa and Batholomeu de Gusamo; and in Curitiba at 1803 Negrâo. Rio de Janeiro has an excellent source of bicycling information at the Federaçao de Ciclismo on Avenida Rio Branco 277, gr. 501.

ROADS. The Brazilian road network encompasses 1 million kilometers. Of that, 90,000 kilometers are paved. The extent of the road network is a result of the enormous distances between destinations. The Trans-Amazon Highway's length is over 4,000 kilometers. From Brasília, in the center of the country, to Belém, at the mouth of the Amazon, is 2,100 kilometers, and from Salvador to the Uruguayan border, a mere 4,500 kilometers. With an average cycling day of 100 kilometers, it would take almost seven weeks to cover this distance and six weeks to cover the Trans-Amazon's length.

The Trans-Amazon's length is only part of its difficulty. Unpaved roads can feature slick, impassable mud or billowing red dust that engulfs your gear and fills your lungs. Some rivers can only be crossed by ferry, and delays are inevitable. Finally, provisioning is difficult along most stretches of the road.

Along the southern littoral, traffic intensifies. International traffic between Uruguay, Argentina, and Brazil follows the littoral's road, the BR-101, also known as the *Pista do Morte*. Try using whatever secondary routes exist—for example, the excellent coastal road from Santos, São Paulo's port, to Rio de Janeiro. Because of the new expressway farther north, this is a first-rate cycling route in Brazil. Farther north along the littoral, the road deteriorates, culminating in the poor northeastern region, where roads alternate between dirt and pockmarked pavement. Luckily, coastal traffic here decreases because inland roads are shorter.

In the Planalto excellent alternate roads that are almost deserted run between most cities. These secondary roads are more demanding because of the extreme grades and the varying road surfaces. Some roads may be mining tracks, while others are ideal routes, forgotten about when a new expressway was constructed. Either way, secondary roads are usually longer and less direct, so time and motivation are considerations when choosing these routes. Despite the conditions, exploring these secondary roads, especially in Minas Gerais, generates excellent bicycle touring. Since you can get lost at some intersections, not only in Minas Gerais but throughout Brazil, use a recent map detailing the secondary roads.

MAPS. The best guide and map to obtain is the *Guia Quatro Rodas*. Published yearly, this compact guide illustrates and describes every major Brazilian road. The guide also details the national parks and tourist areas. There is an alphabetical listing of every relevant Brazilian town, describing accommodations, camping, attractions, and services. If you plan on bicycling anywhere in the country, the book is invaluable. The only drawback is that it is only published in Portuguese. Luckily, the guide uses extensive symbols, so even if your Portuguese is poor, the book is worthwhile. You can buy the guide at every bookstore and kiosk in the country.

A large country map is included with the *Guia* guide. The map is excellent for planning and complements the guide's strip maps. If you want more detailed maps, bookstores sell state maps of varying usefulness. Each map is published independently. Petrobras, the country's oil company, distributes state maps, but availability and prices vary from place to place.

None of the above maps contain elevation markings. The best large-scale maps of the country detailing elevations are available through the Ministerio do Planejamento e Coordenaçáo, General Departamento de Cartógrafia. The ministry departments are in Rio and Brasília. If you want a greater selection of Brazilian maps or other maps of South America, an excellent bookstore in Rio de Janeiro is Paulini, on Rua Lelio Gama 75.

BIKE TRANSPORT. The Brazilian bus network is excellent. Every city has its terminal, the *rodoviária*, where buses connect and depart for short- and long-distance destinations. Regular buses are large and luxurious. Overnight services, called *leitos*, provide extra comfort but are reluctant to take bikes. Most regular buses hold bikes, and prices vary from free to half the passenger fare. Before buying a ticket, ask the attendant about carrying your bike. At times you have to clear it with the baggage department, the *economienda*. If after all your forethought the conductor is still reluctant to take your bike, be assertive. Twist your handlebars, take off a wheel or two, put it on the bus, and prove to the conductor how small a space the bike occupies. Once the bike is loaded, the conductor is unlikely to remove it.

Hitching rides is difficult. Trucks expect payment for transportation in remote areas. In intense traffic areas, trucks do not stop—period. Recently, an advertising campaign has dissuaded drivers from picking up hitchers after both parties were getting robbed and murdered.

If your time is limited and there are specific areas you would like to tour, take a plane. As with buses, check baggage requirements and prepare to dismantle your bike.

Few passenger trains still operate. The most significant are from Corumbá to São Paulo, and São Paulo to Brasília. Baggage handling is straightforward and safe but expensive (a bike costs the same as a passenger). If the current cost of living is high, trains are expensive and constraining.

The most likely places to travel by boat are along the Amazon and its tributaries. Riverboats, running on set schedules, ply up and down their routes. Buy first-class tickets. The difference in price is not worth the amount of noise and fumes on the second-class lower deck. Secondly, although a certain degree of trust is shared among the passengers, watch and lock your belongings while on board. The fares include meals, but on a long trip the chicken and rice gets monotonous quickly. Bring along snacks and fruit. Lastly, boats do not charge for bikes.

CHILE

Chile's 4,300-kilometer length encompasses an astounding array of scenery. In the north the barren Atacama Desert hasn't felt rain in a hundred years. In the south, in a forgotten corner of the world, Tierra del Fuego's mountaintops, divided by advancing glaciers, are permanently blanketed in snow. Between these extremes lie fruitful valleys, a magnificent lake region, and an area cut by fjords, wrapped in forests, and peppered by volcanoes.

Chile's people can be hesitant with strangers. During periods of harsh dictatorship and censorship, people were careful of their speech and actions. Today an era of democracy has arrived, and Chileans feel more relaxed and secure. Longstanding introversion now mixes with hospitality, producing an attitude that's friendly without being overwhelming.

CYCLE ZONES

Northern Chile

TERRAIN. The northern zone of Chile extends from the Peruvian border to La Serena, 500 kilometers north of Santiago. In a longitudinal direction, the area's topography varies from flat to very hilly. As you travel farther south, routes become more hilly as the Andes send transverse spurs toward the ocean. Following the Andes' crest, Chile's border with Argentina has passes over 4,700 meters high.

SCENERY. The northern zone provides a tremendous amount of monotonous scenery. For hundreds of kilometers, you're subjected to barren hills, dried salt lakes, and an endless supply of sunbaked rocks.

This part of Chile is one of the world's driest areas. The Atacama Desert is sterile; no plant life grows. Cities pump their water supply through irrigation pipes hundreds of kilometers long.

In the northern zone, the Andes remain close. At the extreme northern end, traveling away from the desert and into the mountains, there is an exquisite jewel, Lacuna National Park. The park holds some of South America's most stunning scenery and most visible wildlife.

CULTURAL INTEREST. If you want either natural beauty or human interest, you must ride off the area's main route, the Longitudinal Highway. For example, outside Calama, 90 kilometers off the highway, you can visit the world's largest copper mines. If this doesn't sound too exciting, a day's ride from Calama sits the town of San Pedro de Atacama, once the center of Paleolithic civilizations. One side-road possibility is a circular tour of the area's ancient rock sites.

Farther north, near Arica, archaeologists have found a zone complete with mummies from 5000 B.C. Visitors can examine the relocated mummies at Arica's University of Taracapa.

WEATHER. Weather conditions are harsh. Wind, sand, aridity, and an unrelenting sun produce difficult bicycling conditions. Temperatures are fairly constant throughout the year, with slight variations between summer and winter. Daytime temperatures are mild, while night lows plunge.

You don't have to worry about a rainy season because precipitation is rare. However, El Niño affects the area about every seven years, producing weird, unpredictable weather conditions.

Winds generally blow from the west, occasionally producing severe sandstorms.

Central Chile

TERRAIN. Central Chile covers the zone from La Serena to Temuco, 677 kilometers south of Santiago. The northern area between La Serena and Santiago becomes more mountainous as you approach the capital. Ranges become more frequent and climbs longer. South of Santiago the Pan-Am follows a central valley lying between the low, coastal mountains and the Andes. With fewer climbs, bicycling in this valley is easier.

Toward the Andes, passes range from 2,000 to 4,000 meters. Pass altitudes decrease as you travel south.

SCENERY. Traveling along the central valley, you will be tantalizingly close to the mountains. To experience them, detour off the main highway and rejoin it farther south. Worthwhile side trips into the mountains include visiting the towns of Conquimay and Curacautin.

The central valley's 1,150-kilometer length varies in its landscape. In the north, vineyards predominate. Farther south, beyond Santiago, fruit orchards and vegetable farms provide the country's produce, and as the weather becomes cooler and the soil less fertile, cattle ranches produce world-class beef. This grazing land gives way to forested hills.

CULTURAL INTEREST. Most of Chile's population lives in this central valley, where the country's commerce, industry, agriculture, and capital are congregated. Aside from the artisan centers of Quinchamil and Chilan, there is little of cultural interest here.

WEATHER. Central Chile has a Mediterranean climate, with warm, dry summers and cool, rainy winters. Winds predominate from the southwest, increasing in velocity through the day. Low-pressure systems carrying rain usually arrive from the northwest; rain increases farther south.

Archipelago Chile

TERRAIN. Chile's archipelago is the area south from Temuco, including the Lake Region, to Cape Horn, South America's southern tip. Most of this area is mountainous, which means the riding is a continual series of climbs and drops. Hilly and flat sections alternate between Puerto Montt

Weaving through the mountains of the Camino Austral

and Tierra del Fuego. Passes over the Andes drop from 1,100 meters in the Lake District, to 122 meters in the Austral region, to sea level on Tierra del Fuego.

SCENERY. The archipelago's scenery is Latin America's most magnificent. In the famous Lake District, east of Puerto Montt and straddling the border of Argentina and Chile, there is a breathtaking panorama of lakes and snowcapped volcanoes.

Farther south, the Austral highway is a nearly uninhabited ribbon of road that runs across wooded hills, beside glaciers close enough to touch, and into fjords covered in wild flowers and waterfalls—an outstanding road. In Patagonia, South America's densest array of striking peaks, Torres del Paine, rises majestically. Travel in the area; enjoy its splendor and isolation.

CULTURAL INTEREST. The area's two main points of interest are the Mapuche Indians who hold an extensive market in the town of Temuco and the *estancias*, the enormous sheep farms found in Patagonia. The 3 percent of Chile's population that lives south of Puerto Montt is extremely friendly and has a frontier spirit. The lack of people is the charm of Chile's archipelago, yet with extensive traveling through the area, the sporadic signs of people are welcome.

WEATHER. The archipelago is one of the few areas in South America where it is impossible to bicycle year-round. While summers are warm and sunny, winters are cold and snowy. The best time to travel in the area is from November to March, but as you travel farther south the ideal period shortens. In the Lake District, snowfalls make roads impassable. On Tierra del Fuego, snow is frequent, covering the ground for the winter.

In the Lake District and the Austral region, winds generally blow from the northwest, but in Patagonia winds veer directly from the west. Winds in Patagonia can be brutal. In the spring, wind speeds commonly reach 70 kph, slowly diminishing through the summer and fall and becoming nonexistent in the winter.

TOUR OF ARGENTINA AND CHILE

THE LAKE DISTRICT

Distance: 732 km
Start/Finish: San Carlos de Bariloche/San Carlos de Bariloche
Season: November–April
Terrain: Hilly
Scenery: ***
Interest: *
Difficulty: Moderate

Km	Location	Scenery	Interest	Comments
00	**San Carlos de Bariloche**	***	**	
19	Jct. with Hwy. 231	***		No provisions
63	Jct. to Angostura	***		No provisions
03	**Angostura**	***		
03	Return to Hwy. 231	***		No provisions
11	Jct. with Hwy. 234	***		No provisions
63	**Lago Hermoso**	***		
11	Jct. with Hwy. 19	***		No provisions
26	**San Martín de los Andes**	***		
47	Paso de Hua Hum (659 m) Border with Chile	***		
12	Ferry dock on Lago Pirihueico Ferry to Puerto Fuy (1 daily, time variable) Puerto Fuy	***		No provisions
21	Choshuenco	***		
47	**Panguipulli**	***		
60	**Los Lagos**		**	
29	**Paillaco**		**	
26	Jct. to Rio Bueno	**		No provisions
04	**Rio Bueno**	**		
49	Jct. Hwy. 215 to Entre Lagos	**		No provisions
12	**Entre Lagos**	***		
36	Jct. U-99	**		No provisions
06	Jct. U-55 to Puerto Octay	**		No provisions
09	**Puerto Octay**	***		
25	Frutillar Alto	***		
(04)	**Frutillar**		***	
17	Llanquihue	**		
06	**Puerto Varas**	**		

(17)	Excursion to	**	
	Puerto Montt		
48	**Ensenada**	***	
18	**Petrohué**	***	
	Ferry to Peulla	***	No provisions
	(daily, 1100)		
	Peulla	***	Accommodations
26	Paso de Perez	***	No provisions
	(1,022 m)		
	Border with Arg.		No provisions
03	Puerto Frías	***	No provisions
	Ferry to Puerto	***	
	Alegre (1 daily)		
	Puerto Alegre		
03	Puerto Blest	***	No provisions
	Ferry to Puerto	***	
	Llao-Llao (1 daily)		
	Puerto Llao-Llao	***	
27	**San Carlos de**	***	
	Bariloche		

Stopping beside a "monkey" tree at the foot of Volcan Osorno in the Lake District

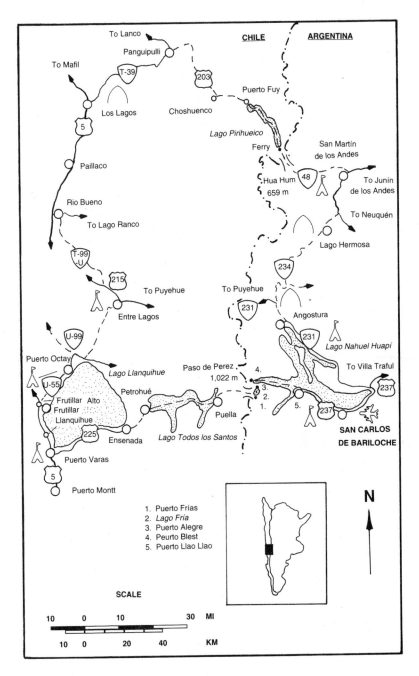

CHILE   ARGENTINA

To Lanco

Panguipulli

To Mafil

T-39

Los Lagos

5

Paillaco

Rio Bueno

To Lago Ranco

T-99 -U

215

To Puyehue

Entre Lagos

U-99

Puerto Octay

U-55

Lago Llanquihue

Frutillar Alto
Frutillar
Llanquihue

225

Ensenada

Puerto Varas

5

Puerto Montt

Choshuenco

Lago Pirihueico

Ferry

Puerto Fuy

203

San Martín
de los Andes

Hua Hum
659 m

48

To Junín
de los Andes

To Neuquén

Lago Hermosa

234

To Puyehue

231

Angostura

231

Lago Nahuel Huapí

To Villa Traful

Paso de Perez
1,022 m

4.

3.
2.
1.

5.

237

237

SAN CARLOS
DE BARILOCHE

Petrohué

Puella

Lago Todos los Santos

1. Puerto Frías
2. *Lago Fría*
3. Puerto Alegre
4. Peurto Blest
5. Puerto Llao Llao

N

SCALE

10   0   10   30   MI

10   0   20   40   KM

TOUR OF CHILE

THE CAMINO AUSTRAL

Distance: 863 km
Start/Finish: Puerto Montt/Puerto Montt
Season: September–March
Terrain: Hilly to mountainous
Scenery: ***
Interest: *
Difficulty: Moderate to difficult

The continuation of Route 7 east of Puerto Montt to Chaitén is open only in January and February. These are the only months when the necessary ferries run. If you take this route at other times, bring lots of extra food and wait for fishermen who can ferry you across the straits.

Km	Location	Scenery	Interest	Comments
00	**Puerto Montt**	***	*	
56	Pargua	*		
	Ferry to Chacao			
	(12 per day)			
	Chacao			
27	**Ancud**	**	*	
81	**Castro**	**		
23	**Chonchi**	**		
	Ferry to Chaitén			
	(Tues., Thurs., and			
	Sat., 0800)			
	Chaitén			
44	**Puerto Cárdenas**	***		
104	**La Junta**	***		
44	**Puerto Puyuguapi**	***		
60	Turnoff for Puerto	***		
	Cisnes			
(33)	**Puerto Cisnes**	***		
89	**Villa Mañiguales**	***		
10	Turnoff for Puerto	***		
	Aisén (Hwy. X-50)			
(66)	**Coihaique**	***		
(10)	Return to turnoff for	**		
	Puerto Aisén			
(52)	Puerto Aisén (Hwy. 240)	***		
58	**Puerto Aisén**	***		
14	Puerto Chacabuco	**		
	Ferry to Quellón (Mon.,	***		
	Wed., and Sun.)			
	Quellón			

Negotiating a typical traffic jam in Patagonia

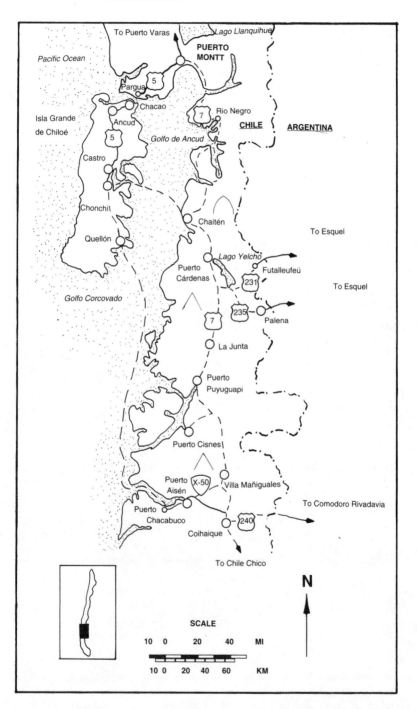

GENERAL INFORMATION

GETTING TO THE COUNTRY. Only one access crosses from Peru into Chile, at Arica. This crossing is dangerous on the Peruvian side because of the smuggling, corruption, and crime. If you can make it through the Peruvian desert and its minefield of crime, Chile will be a relief, despite its desert.

Two routes cross from Bolivia into Chile. The first is via the 4,700-meter Chana pass, a beautiful route passing through the impressive scenery of Lacuna National Park. Because of poor road conditions and lack of provisions, the route is difficult.

The second Bolivia–Chile route is through Ollagüe. Bicycling this route is more difficult in terms of road conditions and provisioning opportunities. The scenery through this area, although not as spectacular as Chana pass, is in a more southwesterly direction that avoids the harshness of the Atacama Desert and passes through the interesting Calama area.

At least twenty different routes pass between Chile and Argentina. The farthest northern route, tough on both sides of the border, skirts around Bolivia, heads in a northwest direction, and confronts harsh, isolated surroundings. The pass culminates at 4,275 meters.

The main crossing into central Chile is via Mendoza, Argentina, and Los Andes, 88 kilometers from Santiago. This excellent route is fully paved, rising gradually on the Argentine side. At 4,200 meters the pass culminates at a tunnel prohibited to cyclists. You are left with the options of either continuing over a rough dirt track or allowing the officials to throw your bike into their truck and shuttle you through.

If you travel westward toward Chile, the wind rushes violently from the slopes straight into your face. Bicycling is agonizingly slow—at times, walking feels easier. Luckily, provisions are easy to find, and the descent from the tunnel into the *caracoles*, named for a snail shell, is exhilarating.

Through the Lake District, five routes cross the border—all of them unpaved, hilly, and beautiful. In the district's northern section, the Paso de Maul Malal (1,207 m) reveals some steep sections, a lengthy climb, and fair provisioning. This route is the least scenic of the five. The second pass crosses at Paso de Carririne (1,723 m). A rougher ride than farther north, it is also a steeper route. The third pass, Huahum (659 m), requires a boat hop over Lago Pirihueico. Huahum is a beautiful route, but is logistically tricky. Portezuelo de Puyehue, at 1,308 meters, is the main road through the area. This all-weather road shifts to pavement shortly after the 43-kilometer descent from the pass. After the pavement, the road carries on briskly to Osorno and the Pan-Am. This is another gorgeous route, with heavy traffic only during the summer season. The final route into Chile's Lake District may be the most beautiful, but is undoubtedly the most expensive. Paso de Perez Rosales (1,022 m) requires three boat jaunts. You cross the first lake, Lago Nahuel Huapi Fria, at Llao-Llao, Argentina. A short, steep road section follows, then you cross Lago Fria. After yet another short, steep hill, you cross the border and hop onto the next boat to cross Lago Todos los Santos. Since these boats are operated for tourists, fares are high and a bike fare is the same price as a passenger ticket.

In Austral Chile numerous secondary routes cross the border, but not all have border facilities. Paso Coihaique Alto (795 m) is probably the best crossing from Argentina. From the border it is a short 52-kilometer ride to the largest town in the area, Coihaique. This route is rapidly becoming deforested because of local exploitation. In Argentina there is a substantial section of rough, semi-isolated road.

Farther south the last main route in the Austral region crosses at Chile Chico. The Paso Rio Jeinemeni sits at a low 231 meters. Your map will show the pass as a river because that is exactly what you will confront. No bridges span the 3 kilometers of streams and rivers. You have to ford each one. The strength and depth of the currents vary depending on the season, but the rivers always pose a challenge. Four-wheel-drive trucks transport people over the rivers and across the border, so wait for a lift if you don't want to take the risk of losing your bike in the river. Finally, to continue north from Chile Chico, you can wait for the boat making its twice-weekly crossing between Chile Chico and Puerto Ibañez. Otherwise, you face a rough, 230-kilometer circumnavigation around Lago Carrera. Chile Chico is the last reliable border crossing along the Camino Austral.

Tierra del Fuego stands out as its own entity. To reach Chile's subantarctic area, you have to crisscross between Argentine and Chilean frontiers. In the Porto Natales area, two routes exist, both convenient for visiting Torres del Paine Park.

The next crossing, much farther south, is at a small hostel named Morro Chico. This route is occasionally unmanned and is kilometers from anywhere.

The major crossing in the area is 60 kilometers south of Rio Gallegos at an isolated, windy spot called Puerto de Integrácion Austral. Rougher than the Chilean side, the Argentine side continues onward to Tierra del Fuego. A ferry crosses the Straits of Magellan.

The last southern crossing, at San Sebastian, sits in the northern part of the island. The crossing, over reasonable dirt roads, is straightforward. This final frontier invokes an austere feeling of being on the world's edge.

Crossing between Argentina and Chile at Tierra del Fuego, where each country's sovereignty is still in question, can be politically tense.

DOCUMENTS. All non–South Americans require passports, but few nationalities need visas. Upon arrival all travelers receive a free tourist card that the officials have filled out with your particulars.

Each border post has a different method of dealing with your bike. Some officials don't pay any attention to it, others type it on the tourist card, and yet others fill out an entire "Declaration of Ownership" document, used for cars, and demand to see bike papers. To avoid problems when leaving, upon entering you should have an official fill in your bicycle details on the "Observations" section of the tourist card.

For whatever reason, customs and immigration offices are occasionally at different spots. Immigration will be near the border, while the customs office is 10 or 20 kilometers farther down the road. To avoid backtracking, question the officials to determine proper procedures.

In certain regions of the country, particularly on remote routes, immigration formalities may not occur at the border itself. You may have to travel 50 to 60 kilometers into the country before you find the immigration and customs offices. Before traveling these routes, ensure your documents are in order—you don't want to be turned back and forced to return through these isolated areas.

It's forbidden to import any fresh food—no meat, vegetables, or fruit. This requires careful planning for crossings, as distances between provisions in northern, Austral, and Patagonia Chile are large.

When leaving the country, particularly in the Austral area, check exit requirements before leaving the last town, as every border seems to react differently to exits. At one point we had to have a *carabinero* in the remote Austral region telex Santiago. When he was satisfied all the requirements were met, he issued a *Salvo de Conducto* pass that was never asked for when we crossed the border. The pass did make an interesting souvenir, but the lesson was not to take remote crossing for granted—check beforehand.

ACCOMMODATIONS. Accommodations are of four types: hotels, *residenciales* or hostels, *alojamientos*, and *albergues de juveniles*.

The government grades all Chilean hotels on a five-star rating, based on the quality of amenities they provide. Most cities have these higher-priced, comfortable accommodations.

Residenciales are also supposedly ranked by the government on a three-star system. These smaller hostels proudly display any stars they can get on the front of their building. (Some unscrupulous owners put up unofficial stars. Check the room before accepting it.)

The third type of accommodations and the best value is the *alojamiento*. Unregulated by the government, these small, family-run houses offer travelers a small room with a bed or two. You can always secure your bike, as the family usually has safe storage. Every town has these small hotels, it's just a matter of asking at a tourist office in a large city, or in smaller centers inquiring of anyone on the street, or simply by looking for *Alojamiento* signs.

The last option in accommodations is youth hostels, known as *albergues de juveniles*. To use youth hostel facilities, you must buy a Chilean hostel membership. Apparently, for an extra 4 dollars you can extend its use through Argentina, Uruguay, and Brazil. How much use you will get out of one is debatable. During the months the hostels are open, you usually need a reservation, as they are overrun with school groups. Youth hostels are a poor value when compared to the relative serenity of a family-run *alojamiento*.

Paid camping is available but generally expensive. Private campgrounds, centered in tourist areas, charge by the site, not by the number of people or tents. For the price of a site used by two people, you're better off renting a private room. However, municipal campgrounds found outside some cities are often a reasonable value, with facilities that range from swimming pools and toilets to nothing more than a spot for your tent.

Camping wild depends upon the area of the country. For example, in the desert north, camping is easy: you pick a time to stop, move well off the road, and set up camp. However, central Chile, with its dense population pockets and extensive agriculture, is more difficult. An excellent spot to try is municipal stadiums. I've found many free spots on soccer fields, complete with hot showers and toilet facilities. Simply ask the caretaker for permission. The backs of gas stations are also convenient, and they sometimes have shower and bathroom facilities. Most gas stations along the Longitudinal Highway have shower facilities, and for a nominal fee they offer all the hot water you can stand.

Bicycling through the Austral region and Tierra del Fuego, you must have camping capability. You may find ranches and *estancias* willing to put you up for a night, but too many intangibles—rain, wind, and road conditions—make it far from a sure thing. Carry a good, low-profile tent for wind protection.

Stove fuel, *gasolina* and *benzina*, is available at every gas pump. *Especial* contains 93 octane, while regular *(corriente)*, at 85 octane, burns less hot and clean. Finding white gas is difficult. Kerosene can be bought at local town pumps, but few stations along the Longitudinal Highway sell kerosene. You can find GAZ cartridges and stoves more easily than in most South American countries; try sports stores. You can buy camping equipment of dubious quality.

FOOD. The types and prices of food offered in Chile depend on the area you visit. As a rule, the farther you travel from Santiago, the less variety and the higher the prices. In the northern region, fish and seafood are main staples of the people's diets. Food is expensive and you must routinely pack supplies to cover 300-kilometer distances.

In the central region, every type of food is available: fish, produce, grains, and dairy products. An abundance of inexpensive food is available in central Chile, and provisioning is easy. In fact, the roadside stands along the Pan-Am sell the current crop—and you won't even need to dismount from your bike.

South of Puerto Montt, food again becomes scarce and expensive. Beef and seafood are the main staples of the region. Fresh produce is expensive and difficult to find. Most locals buy canned and boxed food shipped in from the central regions. Food is available only in substantial towns. No stands or truck stops sell food along the Camino Austral, so planning is important.

Predictably, in Patagonia lamb and root crops make up the locals' diets. Processed food is expensive and your options in this area are limited. Packing and cooking a leg of lamb is not the easiest thing to do while bicycle touring.

The few active markets in Chile tend to be more expensive than the supermarkets. Individual entrepreneurship causes higher markups.

Supermarkets, particularly in central Chile, offer an impressive variety of food, including health food. In smaller towns supermarkets are rare, and to find the type of food you want, you have to search around in specialized shops such as *panaderías* and *fruterías*.

Restaurants range from the extravagant to the simple. Chileans have a more Westernized concept of dining for pleasure, so cheaper restaurants catering to basic feeding, such as those found in Bolivia and Peru, are rare. Look for restaurants popular with locals and order what they do. The typical places offering the day's cheap meal, *almuerzo*, are called *hosterias*. Finally, don't be fooled by *completas*—they're only hot dogs sold by street vendors.

DRINKS. Unlike much of Latin America, water is safe to drink in Chile's larger cities. This is convenient, as mineral and bottled water is expensive. Outside the larger cities, you should treat the water. The most difficult aspect of water is its scarcity in the northern desert. Typically, water supplies are 200 to 300 kilometers apart. If you can't or don't want to carry two to three days supply of water, you might flag down a vehicle and ask if they have water to spare. I don't recommend this unpredictable method, so ration your water supply.

Beer is cheap, but you should revel in the world-class wines that Chile offers. For the price of a couple of soft drinks, you can buy an excellent wine to complement an evening meal.

HEALTH. The most common health risks are hepatitis, typhoid, parasitic infections, and food poisoning. The best method of minimizing these risks is by treating dubious water, cooking vegetables, peeling fruits, and disinfecting ground-hugging fruits, such as strawberries. Supermarkets and pharmacies sell food disinfectants.

If you become ill, Santiago has an excellent supply of reasonably priced clinics and hospitals staffed with English-speaking specialists. Pharmacies sell every type of generic and brand-name pharmaceutical.

Prepare yourself for a harsh climate. In the northern desert and southern Patagonia, use a face mask for dust and sand and keep layers of additional clothing handy. Sunscreens are necessary against the increasing depletion of the ozone layer that is rapidly occurring in Chile. Finally, from May to August smog levels in Santiago are dangerous, so it's wise to use a smog filter.

PHOTOGRAPHY. Film is reasonably priced in Santiago, and it's always possible to get a discount if you buy it in bulk. However, check whether they've included the developing price in the total. (For certain brands, that developing can only be done in Chile.) All processing is mediocre.

Imported camera equipment is generally expensive, but it's possible to buy the latest technology. Equipment is better and cheaper than anywhere else in South America.

MONEY. There are two rates for peso trading. The first is the official rate found in banks and official *casas de cambio*. Official exchange houses vary in their commissions. They charge from nil to 5 percent, so shop around for the best rate. Through these facilities, you can buy American notes at a 1 percent commission. Traveler's checks are not as popular as hard currency and can only be changed in large cities and heavily traveled border posts at a rate 0.5 to 1 percent lower than for cash.

The parallel market offers the second rate of exchange. By strolling the main streets or prowling in tourist offices, you can find a "runner" who takes you to a central, unofficial *casa de cambio*. Rates are usually from 5 to 10 percent better than the official rate for hard currency and traveler's checks. The parallel market is tolerated, and using it is risk-free.

Chile's current economy is stable, and inflation is not a concern.

Most shops open at 9:00 A.M. and close between 6:00 and 8:00 P.M. Most shops, excluding supermarkets, close from 1:00 P.M. Saturday until 9:00 A.M. Monday. Banks conduct business from 9:00 A.M. to 12:30 P.M. Monday to Friday. In larger cities, the siesta is observed for an hour or two, but shops in smaller towns may not take a siesta.

The postal service is inexpensive and reliable. Chile is an excellent country for making collect telephone calls; its system is efficient and offers reductions for weekend calls.

Chile celebrates the following holidays: January 1, New Year's Day; Good Friday; May 1, Labor Day; May 21, Battle of Iquique; August 15, Feast of the Assumption; September 18, Independence Day; September 19, Army Day; October 12, Columbus Day; November 1, All Saints' Day; December 8, Feast of the Immaculate Conception; December 25, Christmas.

SECURITY. Some street crime exists in the larger centers of the country. Avoid exposing expensive items and keep your money and documents hidden, as pickpockets thrive in crowded areas. Stay alert to your surroundings. Outside major cities the atmosphere is relaxed and secure.

Politically, for the past seventeen years, Generalissimo Pinochet has purged the country of opposition. Recently, Chile has taken a bold but precarious step toward democracy. The volatility of the country's left-wing political parties has now stabilized. Occasionally, terrorist attacks occur on American institutions, particularly the Mormon Church, but the security risk for the traveler is small.

Drugs are an underground activity with little tolerance given by the authorities.

Security Rating: B.

CYCLING INFORMATION

BICYCLES. Chile has the best all-round bicycle shops, parts, and mechanics in South America. In Santiago, on the 800 block of Avenida San Diego, the latest Japanese and Italian components are available. These parts are moderately expensive, but the selection is great. In the central valley, parts are harder to find, but compared to Chile's neighbors, it's a gold mine. Northward to the desert and south of Puerto Montt, bicycles are uncommon; therefore, parts are scarce.

Chile is also one of the few countries on the continent where you can find any size bike tire: 26, 27, 28 inches, and 700C. Although the tires can be Taiwanese imports, the variety is great compared to other countries.

Chilean mechanics are knowledgeable, competent, and well equipped with proper tools. However, mechanics are reluctant to let customers use their tools for repairs. Their fees are reasonable.

ROADS. Chile's 78,000 kilometers of roads fall into three categories.

The primary road, running a length of 3,600 kilometers from Arica to Puerto Montt, is the Longitudinal or Pan-American Highway. The Pan-Am carries most of the country's traffic, including powerful, double semi-trailers and speedy, schedule-obsessed buses. Most of the highway is paved and well maintained. Rough sections occur, particularly where the concrete slabs have started to deteriorate. Shoulders on the highway vary from wide and paved to nonexistent. The Pan-Am is not a dangerous road if you maintain a high degree of visibility. An irritating aspect of the Pan-Am is that towns lie 2 to 5 kilometers off the road. After a hard day's riding, the 10-kilometer round-trip detour is unwelcome.

The second type of road is typified by the transversal routes connecting the Longitudinal Highway with cities, the Argentine border, and the Pacific Ocean. These roads rarely have dense traffic, but maintenance is poorer. The smaller the center, the less traffic and maintenance, but the more pleasant the bicycling.

The last type of road is the gravel and dirt routes found in the country's less accessible areas. Traffic on the secondary roads is usually light, excluding the Lake District's summer vacation period. Through parts of the Camino Austral and Patagonia, traffic is almost nonexistent.

Most roads heading to the Argentine border begin paved, but as the grades steepen they become unpaved, rougher roads. Grades over all unpaved roads can be exasperating, so a gearing ratio of 28-front, 34-rear is recommended.

South of Puerto Montt, the Austral highway is a rougher road, full of washboards, sand, rocks, and streams. At the beginning stages of the Austral highway, three ferry routes operate for only three months, starting their schedule the first weekend after New Year's Day. Outside this period, you can either take the highway and prepare to wait for a fisherman's help to cross; or to avoid the roughest, first 200 kilometers of the road altogether, take a year-round ferry from the island of Chiloé to the port of Chaitén, and continue ferry-free down the Camino Austral.

Farther south, in the Punta Arenas area, the main road is paved but poorly maintained, lapsing into gravel. Through the area the road crews have designed a system of paving only one side of the road, so that the gravel side is used for passing or for encountering oncoming traffic. On the island of Tierra del Fuego, road conditions are poor.

MAPS. There are three excellent map distributors. The first is the Chilean Auto Club, which produces an adequate country map but no large-scale departmental maps.

The second map producer sells good departmental maps that list accurate distances and regularly updated road conditions. Their smaller-scale *Ruta de Camineros* is confusing and worthless.

The Ministerio de Obras Publicas, the Public Works Department, distributes the best maps available. Providing excellent departmental maps, they've illustrated every turn in the road in their 1:1,000,00-scale map. The maps, when available, are free from the ministry in each departmental capital. The map's only fault is the lack of topography lines. Pass altitudes are given, but planning for terrain is difficult. The ministry's

Camino Austral map is updated yearly and is essential for its information on services, topography, and distances.

When bicycling in Chile, look for the *Turi-Tel* guides, available at any bookstore. These small guides describe each town, rate each road for scenic beauty, and contain small maps of specific areas. They produce four volumes: *Northern, Central, Southern*, and a *Camping* directory. They are excellent Spanish-language guides.

BIKE TRANSPORT. Traveling by bus is unpredictable. Regulations seem to vary depending on the company or number of passengers the bus already has. Even when they allow you to load your bike, the baggage personnel insist on having the handlebars turned and the pedals removed. To ease the entire process, tip the baggage handlers.

On the Longitudinal Highway, it is possibile to hitch rides from long-haul trucks. The best place to ask is at the service stations. Few trucks will stop when moving.

The government has suspended the train service north of Santiago. Now the only service runs from Santiago to Puerto Montt. Train travel is the most convenient option for transportation. Loading a bike is easy, but only certain trains have baggage cars, so you must ask which trains have baggage capability. There's only a nominal charge for bikes as baggage.

The archipelago contains a network of boat services connecting most ports and islands. From Puerto Montt to Punta Arenas there are small passenger boats and luxurious cruise ships. Prices for passengers and bicycles vary tremendously. For example, to cross Lago Todos los Santos in the Lake District, officials insist you pay the U.S.$8 passenger fare and an additional U.S.$8 bike fare. Other companies, such as Chacabuco, which connects the Isla de Chiloé to Puerto Aisén, do not charge for bikes.

If you consider taking the long-haul cruise from Puerto Montt to Punta Arenas, Navimag charges half the passenger fare, roughly U.S.$30–40, per bike. The company has the fare included in its fare schedules, so there's no other recourse.

COLOMBIA

Why should you visit Colombia? To start with, the people are warm, hospitable, and friendly. Their ethnic diversity ranges from European sophistication to native tribes untouched by Western civilization. Also tempting is a Colombian history that looks back on Spanish fortresses designed to keep the plundered Inca gold safe from Captain Morgan. Searching further back, there is San Agustín, a mysterious culture that left exotic

An ancient anthropomorphic statue in the San Agustín Archaeological Park

anthropomorphic sculptures in the tropical hillsides. The scenery is the most consistently intoxicating in South America. A multitude of mountains soar over the landscape, and at the tops of their passes you can look over hundreds of peaks stretching across the land. When you cycle in Colombia, terrain and nature become your masters, dictating your limits and defining your significance.

Yet permeating Colombia's beauty, interest, and friendliness is a dark side. Every traveler has heard horror stories of terrorists, thieves, tricksters, and drug dealers. To disregard the stories as inconsequential would be a mistake. Colombia is a potentially dangerous country in which to bicycle. In certain areas terrorists do bomb, kidnap, and kill; thieves do mug, rob, and snatch; and dealers do plant drugs on travelers. However, peace talks with terrorist groups, coupled with anti-extradition treaties with drug cartel members, have made Colombia safer. Try cycling in Colombia. Pack your adventure, don't forget your sense of caution, and enjoy a beautiful country.

CYCLE ZONES

The Caribbean Lowlands

TERRAIN. Most of the northern lowlands, divided by tropical rivers, are flat to gently rolling. The more you stay within these river systems, the flatter and easier the cycling is. For example, before entering Colombia's mountainous zone, the eastern stretch of the highway connecting Bogotá to Santa Marta is almost entirely flat. The western highway, from Medellín to Barranquilla, dips from one small valley into another. Compared to other parts of the country, the tropical Caribbean lowlands offer easy cycling.

SCENERY. Beaches and the Sierra Nevada wrap up the beauty of the lowlands. The beaches and the coastal islands far from industrial areas will lure you to them. The best beaches lie west of Cartagena, toward Panama. This small coastal road is an excellent route if you want to avoid the traffic on the Medellín–Barranquilla road. Shooting up from the Caribbean coast is the second gem of the area, the solitary peak of Santa Marta. It rises boldly to a height of 5,775 meters in less than 50 kilometers. The Sierra Nevada stands as a stunning, singular peak.

CULTURAL INTEREST. The Caribbean coast holds a moderate degree of historical significance. During the pre-Columbian era, cultures flourished and developed on the slopes of the Sierra Nevada. Cartagena, less than 300 kilometers from Santa Marta, was Colombia's capital after the Spanish invasion. Fortified by 3-meter-thick walls, its fortresses protected the Spanish plunder. Today Barranquilla, lying between Cartagena and Santa Marta, is Colombia's bustling seaport, intent on forgiving the past and turning its vision toward the future.

Only certain parts of the Caribbean lowlands will attract travelers.

WEATHER. The weather in the lowlands remains exasperatingly hot and humid all year. The wet season occurs from May to November, and the prevailing winds generally blow from the north.

Amazonas

TERRAIN. The terrain of the Amazon region is flat. Until you near the foothills of the eastern cordillera, the altitude doesn't vary. Traveling in this area can be enormously difficult. During the rainy season, roads disappear, and even in the dry season, the roads are dusty and rutted. Bicycling in this remote area requires meticulous planning.

SCENERY. The foothills of the eastern cordillera are on the extreme end of the Amazon basin. You can find undeveloped tropical forest if you venture off the main road and wait for the infrequent riverboats. Admittedly, to enjoy this area fully, don't go with a bike.

CULTURAL INTEREST. The points of interest are limited in Amazonas. You may find native settlements hugging the road, but their authenticity vanished once the road appeared.

WEATHER. Compared to the Caribbean coast, temperatures are lower because of a slightly higher altitude. However, the humidity is higher because of the lighter winds. The wet season lasts from April to October.

The Central Mountains

TERRAIN. The central mountain ranges form a giant V. The base of the V begins near the Ecuador border and extends northward, fading as it nears the Caribbean coast. Bisecting the two ranges is the Magdalena River, beginning near San Agustín and flowing for 900 kilometers to the northern coast.

The terrain is extreme. From deep in the Magdalena valley, you can climb 3,000 meters in only 40 kilometers, quickly reaching the treeless *paramó*. The central mountains are for cyclists who love to climb, want the raw challenge, and have the determination to achieve their goals.

Between the sharp peaks, inner basins sit at altitudes of between 1,000 and 3,000 meters. In the basins, villages snuggle and cities sprawl. Bogotá, the nation's capital, roosts at 2,650 meters.

The terrain lies in a predominantly north–south orientation, so cycling in this direction is easier than the strenuous cycling you can expect in an east–west direction.

SCENERY. The mountains hold by far the most beautiful scenery in Colombia. The exhilarating steepness of the peaks is incredible. Deep in the ranges, the mountains surround you with an endless array of peaks and chasms. Few summits reach beyond the snow line, yet the lush, green walls add to the area's mystery and feeling of infinity. The mountains of Colombia promote an awareness of terrain unattainable anywhere else in South America.

Bicycling in the "inner land," Tierradentro

CULTURAL INTEREST. The mystery of the mountains also manifests itself in the country's ancient cultures. The famous Incas never colonized as far as Colombia's inner mountains, and even today the cultures that once inhabited the area have yet to be understood. The clues remain: the mysterious statues of San Agustín, the burial caves of Tierradentro, and the stunning gold artifacts in Bogotá's Gold Museum. Their enigma continues to captivate.

Living cultures continue to dwell in the mountains. Combining ancient culture and living tradition, the artisan villagers maintain their identity though their works of art.

WEATHER. Altitude determines the temperature. At times, when you're sitting at 3,500 meters and the temperature has dropped to 5 degrees Celsius, it is hard to remember that you're only 5 degrees north of the equator. Typically, temperatures at altitudes ranging from 1,000 to 2,000 meters extend from 18 to 24 degrees Celsius. From 2,000 to 3,000 meters, temperatures range from 12 to 18 degrees, and above 3,000 meters temperatures remain below 12 degrees.

Temperatures remain constant all year; only the rains change. Two minor rainy seasons occur: the first, from March to May and the second, from October to November. Some precipitation falls year-round and no months escape the rain.

TOUR OF COLOMBIA

SAN AGUSTÍN

Distance: 465 km
Start/Finish: Popayán/Popayán
Season: October–March
Terrain: Mountainous
Scenery: ***
Interest: ***
Difficulty: Difficult

Km	Location	Scenery	Interest	Comments
00	**Popayán** (1,760 m)	***	**	
20	Crucero	**		No provisions
24	Totoró (2,570 m)	***		
22	Alto de Guanacas (3,130 m)	***		No provisions
45	**Inzá** (1,754 m)	***	***	Market Sat.
16	Jct. to Pisimbalá	***		No provisions
03	**Pisimbalá** (1,697 m) Tierradentro Archaeological Park	***	***	
03	Return to main road	***		
22	**La Plata** (1,054 m)	***		
31	Pital (921 m)	***		
05	Agrado (905 m)	***		
22	**Garzón** (890 m)	***	*	
28	Altamira 1,079 m)	**		
25	Timaná (1,030 m)	**		
23	**Pitalito** (1,290 m)	**		
37	Jct. to San Agustín	**		
06	**San Agustín** (1,690 m)	***	***	
06	Return to Jct.			
14	**San José de Isnos** (1,730 m)	***		
40	Abra dos Ullucos (3,773 m)	***		No provisions
42	**Coconuco**	***		
07	Jct. to Popayán	***		No provisions
24	**Popayán**	**	**	

GENERAL INFORMATION

GETTING TO THE COUNTRY. As Colombia encourages more tourists, airfares drop. This is most evident in the resort areas of the San Andres Islands and Cartagena. Colombia and Venezuela have become

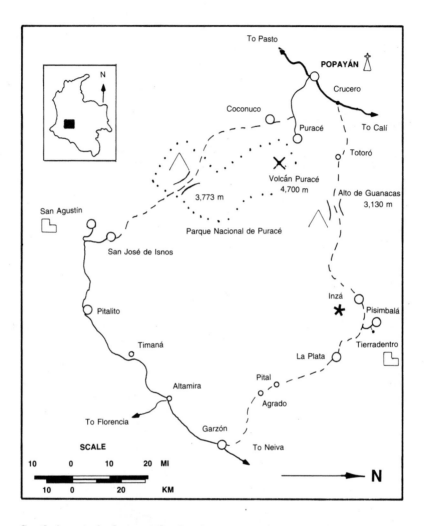

South America's cheapest destinations.

Because Colombia is the starting country for many South American tours, many flights now connect with Central America, North America, and Europe. All airlines flying into Colombia insist on your bike's being boxed. They waive any responsibility, stating that there's a good chance of theft if it's undisguised.

If you plan on traveling to Panama, see the "Getting to the Country" section of the Panama chapter.

Only one road crosses the border to Ecuador. Ipiales, busy but straightforward, sits high in the mountains. All entrance and exit formalities occur at this safe and simple border.

If entering Venezuela, you have two main routes and one minor route to consider. I recommend the crossing at Cúcuta.

Although the cycling is more difficult because of the crossing of the western cordillera, this route is safer, more beautiful, and more interesting than the coastal crossing at Maicao. For years the coastal crossing operated as a major black-market smuggling area. Recently, the police have curtailed this activity. Now Maicao has become notorious for narco-traffickers. The city is infamous for its crime, slime, and danger. The entire coastal section of Colombia is very dangerous for cyclists.

A third route crosses at Arauca, in the Amazon lowlands, but access is limited and the Venezuelan road reconnects with the main Cúcuta road.

If you want to go to Brazil, you have to either fly to Leticia or take your chances connecting with the infrequent riverboats, another adventuresome journey that's probably best taken without a bicycle.

DOCUMENTS. Check document requirements before buying a ticket to Colombia. Air travelers must have an onward ticket, despite pleas for an exemption because of a bicycle. Once in Colombia you can get a refund for an unused portion of a ticket if you persist and show proof you plan on leaving the country. Processing a refund can take twenty days, and the refund will be in local currency. If you used a credit card to buy the ticket, the process is simpler. The airlines will credit the refund to your account.

You must obtain visas before arriving at the border. Officials grant tourist cards at the border or through the airline. The Departamento de Aduana y Seguridad (DAS), the national security police, stamps your passport and tourist card that authorizes your length of stay, normally sixty days. You don't need any extra documents to bring a bike into the country.

While in the country, you must always carry identification with you. You can get an authorized copy of all your documents from DAS to carry in place of your originals. A good idea is to have photocopies of all your documents in case of theft.

When you leave Colombia, you must get an exit stamp in your passport. Most border crossings give the stamps, but at the Cúcuta crossing you must go to the DAS office in the city. No exit taxes are levied if you leave overland, but if you leave by air you have to pay U.S.$15.

If you have all the necessary documents, entering and leaving Colombia is easy. If you don't have the proper authorization, expect problems and delays.

ACCOMMODATIONS. Finding a place for the night is easy in Colombia. First, every town and city has a hotel, *pension*, or *residencial* providing high-quality service. Secondly, people are gratifyingly helpful. Most places provide soap, towels, toilet paper, and additional bedding at no extra charge. Some hotels allow you to use their stoves for heating water or cooking. Thirdly, Colombians understand security. The people will advise you take your bike into your room or provide a locked area to leave your bike. Lastly, prices are low. Colombia has some excellent values in South American accommodations.

Items to be aware of: First, pay up front for your room. Don't wait for the next day, as the price may rise overnight. Secondly, always keep your hotel room key. Do not leave it at the desk. Next, be wary of guides offering to show you various hotels. They expect a tip or a commission. Also avoid hotels catering to prostitution. They encourage a nasty criminal element, so the room's cheaper price isn't worth the extra risk. Finally, pay a little more for security in larger cities. If it doesn't feel safe, don't rent it.

Camping is uncommon in Colombia, but the paid camping spots that can be found—usually in tourist and resort areas—offer pools, cafes, and restaurants. Most sites charge per person and are ultimately no cheaper than a room.

Wild camping in the countryside is easy to find. Ask the locals' permission. Most people are obliging and don't mind your camping as long as you keep their gates closed. Don't camp near large cities. In remote areas stay out of sight of the main road.

FOOD. Colombia understands service. As in hotels, workers in restaurants are courteous and hard working. Waiting for service is rare.

You can find restaurants everywhere. The plate of the day, the *comida* or *almuerzo*, is universal. The meal starts with *sanoche*, a tuber soup, and is followed by a plate of rice, grilled meat, plantain, beans, and a small salad. A soft drink or fruit juice is also usually served. A variant, the *bandeja*, is the same meal minus the soup. Either special offers the cheapest and most nutritious dish of the day; ordering from the menu is twice as expensive.

The easiest place to buy your food is at supermarkets, which are in every city. You can buy small quantities, prices are well marked, and the variety is excellent. If you are in a smaller city without a supermarket, the general stores will stock a good selection of food.

With the proliferation of stores, markets have decreased in importance. Now they operate in dismal buildings, filled with hustlers and thieves. Smaller stores and supermarkets are much easier for shopping.

What kind of food to buy? An astounding array of fruit grows in Colombia. Visiting a supermarket exposes you to fruit you have never tasted, seen, or even imagined. But before buying the fruit, find out how it is used and whether it's ripe. Some fruits are used only for juices, while others can be awful if they're not ready for eating.

The most decadent pleasures await in the cafes. During a hard day of cycling, you can rest and indulge in heavenly pastries while drinking the best coffee in the world.

DRINKS. Except for Bogotá, treat the tap water everywhere. In more remote areas, the locals may use a stream or rain for their water supply. Therefore, use all water with caution. Purchased mineral water is very good but difficult to find. *Helados*, flavored ice water, is risky, as most ice hasn't been pasteurized.

The fruit juices are incredible. Cafes and restaurants have their seasonal specialties. Try as many as you can. Most fruits are simply puréed, while others are combined with milk, egg, honey, and other juices.

Colombia produces the world's best coffee. Everyone, from the glitzy cafe waiter to the flask-carrying vendor, sells it. Coffee is an obsession among Colombians. Coffee is served in various ways: *tinto* is a demitasse, *café negro* is a large cup of black coffee, *café perico* is a small coffee with milk, and *café con leche* is a large glass of milk with coffee added. Ask for your coffee unsweetened, *sin azucar,* as the coffee can be served horribly sweet.

Tea is also popular. *Té* is common black tea, and *aromática* is herb tea.

HEALTH. The four big diseases to watch for are cholera, yellow fever, hepatitis, and malaria. In the coastal lowlands and the Amazon, malaria prevails year-round, and chloroquine-resistant strains exist in the Amazon basin and Darién Gap. Hepatitis is widespread. Watch your hygiene and eating habits and have an up-to-date gamma globulin shot. You can get a booster in the clinics of Bogotá; make sure they use a clean needle and have kept the serum refrigerated.

PHOTOGRAPHY. Film in Bogotá is the cheapest in South America, so if you don't want to bring film with you, you can stock up here. You'll want to have lots of film; the scenery, the people, and the sites are eye-poppingly photogenic. Keep change handy for portrait shots. Ask to take a subject's picture. If he or she objects, don't take the picture. If the subject asks for a fee, arrange it beforehand. If not, freely snap away. If your subject demands money afterward, you'll have to let your conscience guide you. Additionally, you can use flashes at archaeological sites and at the Gold Museum if you pay an extra fee.

MONEY. When thinking of money, Colombians and travelers both think of security. When you enter banks, machine gun–carrying guards check your bags. When you change money, banks photograph you, your passport, and your traveler's checks. Banks are the safest, most reliable place to change money. Outside Bogotá, only the Banco de República cashes U.S. dollar traveler's checks. Bogotá does have *casas de cambio,* but use extreme care when leaving, as thieves could mark you. Banks are open from 9:00 A.M. to 3:00 P.M. and only from 9:00 A.M. to 11:30 A.M. on the final day of the month.

Rates for checks and cash are similar; the commission is only .25 percent. The small charges mean you should carry most of your funds in traveler's checks.

Do not use the black market. People on the streets may offer you a great rate, but you're taking a great risk. Criminals use an endless variety of methods to part you from your money.

Colombia uses the peso, circulating in bills and coins. Be careful with large bills, as forgeries abound. Put the bill up to a light and look for a silhouette in the large white area. Try to keep your small bills because everyone tries to get rid of their coins. When you give someone a large bill, you'll get a handful of coins, and you can quickly gather a heavy assortment of them.

The cost of living is low in Colombia. You can eat and sleep cheaply. From a traveler's point of view, the rate of inflation is tolerable.

Generally, shops are open from 8:00 A.M. to noon and then from 2:00 P.M. to 6:00 P.M. The length of the siesta varies between the coast and the highlands, and the smaller the town or the cooler the temperature, the less likely siesta will occur. This also applies for Sundays and holidays. For example, Neiva hosts a bustling market with intensive commercial activity on Sunday. Meanwhile, Pasto closes shop completely on Sunday. Generally, Sunday is a day of rest, and Colombians enjoy their leisure time.

Government offices are open the same times as general stores but are closed on Saturdays.

If you use the post for sending air mail or parcels, you must go to an Avianca office; they handle all international air mail. The mail system is efficient and inexpensive. Finally, receive mail at a specific address, not at a post office.

Colombia celebrates the following holidays: January 1, New Year's Day; January 6, Epiphany; March 19, Feast of St. Joseph; Good Thursday and Friday; May 1, Labor Day; June 29, St. Peter and St. Paul; July 20, Independence Day; August 7, Battle of Boyaca; August 15, Assumption; October 12, Discovery of America; November 1, All Saints' Day; November 11, Independence of Cartagena; December 8, Feast of the Immaculate Conception; December 25, Christmas.

SECURITY. Colombia has the unfortunate reputation of being the most dangerous country in South America. However, this is changing. Terrorist groups have started peace talks, drug cartels have compromised with the government, and criminals are no longer as violently desperate as they once were. While other countries' criminal reputations grow, Colombia's becomes more tranquil. Yet Colombia remains a country where you should keep a low profile and maintain a respectful attitude toward the locals. Always stay alert.

Traveling in the mountains is more dangerous if you use buses or trains than if you bicycle. Thieves are more apt to steal at bus and train stations. During the bustle and among the crowds, it's easy for a thief to snatch, cut, or sneak off with a piece of your baggage. If you travel by public transport in Colombia, watch your gear, particularly at stops. Never leave anything unattended.

In the mountains, thieves rarely use violence. They act cowardly, preferring to use deception to part you from your money. Common schemes include giving you drugged food or drink and posing as police. I was offered an incredible job on a cruise ship by an articulate English-speaking man. All I had to do was pay him to arrange my seaman's license and he would send me off to find my new employers. I never went to sea, however. If something or someone seems suspicious, do not comply right away. It could be a scheme. Remain slightly paranoid.

Compared to the thieves in the mountains, thieves on the coast are more desperate. Muggers using guns and knives are attacking cyclists more frequently. Cycling on the coast is perilous, with the most dangerous areas centering on Barranquilla and the border at Maicao.

Drugs cast a black shadow over Colombia. Every day the newspapers report on murders, kidnappings, bombings, or plane crashes, all directly attributable to drug trafficking. We've all seen movie clichés of the cold-blooded drug dealer who kills a rival for $50. But vicious drug dealers aren't Hollywood scriptwriter's fiction. They are real. Drugs are a deadly serious business. Don't respond to offers of "coke, cocaine, smoke, powder." Don't react positively, negatively, jokingly, or with contempt; any reaction on your part may elicit a threatening response. If police want to search your belongings for drugs, get their identification and try to get a witness, to discourage officers from planting drugs and then demanding a bribe and to dissuade robbers masquerading as police.

Guerrilla forces usually operate out of remote locales, so the chances of encounters while bicycling are also remote. Fortunately, and unlike the *Sendero Luminoso* of Peru, the terrorist forces have no quarrel with travelers. Guerrilla forces in Colombia may be polite, stopping you, explaining their manifesto, and then asking for a donation to their cause. Contribute.

Some terrorist groups do pose a real threat; get reliable information from embassies, tourist offices, bus drivers, and locals if you're visiting remote areas, particularly in these areas: east of the Andes except for Amazonas, the Antioquia department, the north coast, the northern Choco department, eastern Boyaca, eastern Caldas, northwestern Cundinamarca, rural Valle de Cauca, the Tolima department south of Espinal, and the cities of Cali and Buenaventura.

Security Rating: C.

CYCLING INFORMATION

BICYCLES. Bicycle racing is Colombia's national sport. You can find excellent imported Italian racing bikes, but this need for quality extends only to racing. Parts for touring and mountain bikes are rare. Except for racers, bikes in the country are either large three-wheeled cargo bikes or clunky roadsters. You may find some specialized mountain bike parts in higher-quality shops.

You can buy 26- and 27-inch tires, but check their diameter. Some locally made parts are of poor quality. Pay the extra and buy the imported parts, or anticipate and bring your own parts.

Mechanics are eager to please, viewing anything different as a challenge. However, this doesn't mean the mechanics are good. Outside major cities, mechanics lack the finesse and tools to do the job properly.

In Bogotá a multitude of bike shops crowds on Calle 13, from Carrera 16 onward. Most shops offer the basics, but good shops do operate in this area. Another shop specializing in more eclectic equipment is at 78-66 Avenida 13.

ROADS. Colombia boasts 38,000 kilometers of roads, but only 4,000 of them are paved. Road conditions vary from excellent toll roads with paved shoulders to narrow, muddy mountain tracks twisting endlessly up to the snow line.

Because of Colombia's topography, the major road system is shaped like a giant H. Many north–south routes along the valleys connect the lowlands and smaller, inner basins. A few east–west routes run between the two main cordilleras, but only two are paved.

Road grades vary. You can experience every type of grade—long and steep, long and gradual, short and gradual, and short and very steep—in this mountainous country. For example, *La Línea*, "the Line," is a heartsearing, 30-kilometer, first-category climb that challenges the racers of the Vuelta de Colombia every year. The pass though Puracé, on the other hand, covers the same altitude in 90 kilometers. On declines, be careful, because landslides, rocks, animals, and construction can abruptly stop a descent.

Colombia is undergoing a major reconstruction of its road system. Poor roads are being upgraded, and new roads to the more remote mountain villages are being built.

Most paved roads are toll roads. To avoid paying the toll, stay in the furthest right-hand lane. If you go through on the main lane, you might register on the scales and have to pay.

Finally, Colombia produces tons of cheap glass. As fewer bottles are recycled, they often end up smashed on the side of the road. Carry one or two spare tubes with you and ensure your tires are in good condition.

MAPS. ESSO and Texaco are supposed to sell country maps, but they don't stock them at their gas stations. You can get the best maps at the Corporación Nacional de Turismo and at the Instituto Agustín Codazzi. The CNT produces a very good map with a 1:1,500,000 scale. Although this is a small scale, it displays accurate distances, road conditions, and rough topography lines. The CNT in most provincial capitals sells city guides and gives away brochures and town maps. The Instituto Agustín Codazzi, which produces cheap, useful, up-to-date maps, operates in Bogotá, Popayán, Pasto, and Baranquilla. The *Mapa Vial and Artesanial*, at a scale of 1:1,500,000, is their best map even though it lacks topography markings. Not always in stock, the institute's maps are cheap.

BIKE TRANSPORT. Three types of bus service run in Colombia. As a rule, the simpler and more local the service, the easier it is to put your bike on the bus.

The first type of bus is the Boliviano Express. Complete with television and air conditioning, it's designed for the businessperson on long trips. The express is reluctant to take bikes because of the limited cargo space.

The *caminetas* are more basic but have larger cargo space than the express. If you pay a large extra charge, operators will load your bike.

Another type of vehicle, more truck than bus, is the cargo bus. Slow, informal, and full of adventure, it is open-sided local transport. An unlimited amount of cargo can be piled on the roof, but each piece is negotiated and paid for separately. In the back of the bus, oil-filled drums sway and bounce; on top, aluminum siding, goats, bags of coffee, bedroom suites, and bicycles are tied to the railing. Sitting atop the bus, you can watch your belongings and enjoy the views.

Everyone with a vehicle tries to make money with it. Truck drivers pick up any passengers along their route. Drivers will charge you for your bike, too, but you'll meet more local *campesinos*.

Because of Colombia's difficult terrain, it was the first country in South America to offer an extensive domestic air schedule. Airlines will expect your bike to be boxed.

The main railway line from Santa Marta to Bogotá will take bicycles for an extra charge.

COSTA RICA

Costa Rica has become a popular destination for ecotourism. The concept involves traveling to experience a country's raw ecological beauty through its parks and reserves. The tourist dollars are used to preserve the area's threatened natural beauty. In its compact 51,000 square kilometers, Costa Rica possesses thirty-four national parks and reserves. The parks' ecological diversity extends from dry savanna to volcanic fauna to flourishing cloud forest to beaches. For ecological exploring, Costa Rica is a treasure.

Politically, Costa Rica is a haven in a troubled region. What Costa Rica lacks in hair-raising political flammability it makes up for with stunningly beautiful scenery.

CYCLE ZONES

The Lowlands

TERRAIN. This area encompasses two sections, divided by the mountains near San José. The northern 220 kilometers of the Pan-American Highway is made up of sharp rolling hills, the road dipping into and out of the river valleys. The 316 kilometers of the Pan-Am through the southern lowlands are flatter, following more river valleys and plains.

SCENERY. Vast cattle ranches dominate the northern lowlands. Large rivers flow quickly and are ideal for swimming.

Cut by small rivers and streams, the roads of the southern lowlands ride abreast of the steeply rising Talamanca Cordillera. A very scenic ride follows the Corobuchi Valley from Buenos Aires to Palma Norte. The road hugs the river as it twists and turns, allowing the traveler to view the progression of flora and fauna as the altitude changes.

Rewarding national parks punctuate the region. Along the lowland highway, you can detour to Monteverde, a cloud forest clinging to the mountain's wall. A short distance away, at the dry savanna of Santa Rosa, you can see an abundance of wild animals. The remote peninsulas of Nicoya and Osa offer further excursions into other parks and uninhabited beaches. These and many other parks, well off the Pan-Am, are ideal for bicycling. You can wander independently, heading off alone to explore the bold scenery.

CULTURAL INTEREST. The lowlands are of limited interest. Little archaeological interest remains, and indigenous peoples are nonexistent.

WEATHER. The high temperatures are cruel. Typically, at 7:00 A.M. sweat will be pouring off you. The nights offer little relief, as the weather remains uncomfortably muggy. When cycling in the lowlands, wear a hat,

An orchid, one example of Costa Rica's natural beauty

drink frequently, and plan for long siestas. Winds generally blow easterly in the north and westerly in the south.

Meseta Central

TERRAIN. The big challenge of the central plateau zone is climbing into it. The Pan-American Highway ascends into the Meseta from two directions. In the north the Pan-Am rises in gradual stages through San Ramón, San José, and Cartago, climaxing in the Col del Muerte at 3,491 meters, the highest point of the Pan-American Highway in Central America. The southern climb into the Meseta is a steep, unrelenting 45 kilometers to the same crest.

Once into the Meseta, you encounter a series of gradual grades passing from one populous basin to another. Cycling difficulty is moderate.

SCENERY. The scenery is magnificent. Rising abruptly out of the basins, volcanic cones loom like ominous sentinels over colonial towns. Coffee plants, producing a carpet of green, cling to mountain slopes. The Meseta Central is a gorgeous area.

CULTURAL INTEREST. The colonial architecture is interesting. In San José the Teatro Nacional and the Palacio Nacional remind you of the grand colonial era. The capital also has great galleries, such as the Gold and National museums. Interesting spots don't often spring up to greet you in the Meseta, but they do exist in their unassuming glory.

WEATHER. The Meseta maintains a very comfortable climate, with warm, sunny days complemented by cool, refreshing nights. As in all mountainous countries, the higher the altitude, the cooler the temperature. At night the temperature at the summit of the Paso del Muerte can drop to 0 degrees Celsius. The rainy season runs from May to mid-November, and the winds blow from the northeast.

TOUR OF COSTA RICA

THE NATIONAL PARKS

Distance: 677 km
Start/Finish: San José/San José
Season: November–April
Terrain: Flat to mountainous
Scenery: ***
Interest: **
Difficulty: Moderate

Km	Location	Scenery	Interest	Comments
00	**San José**	**	***	
21	**Cartago**	***	**	
109	**San Isidro**	***		
29	Dominical	***		
24	Savegre	***		
18	**Quepos**	***		
(07)	Excursion to **Parque Nacional Manuel Antonio**	***		
25	Parrita	**		
44	**Jacó**	**		
30	Coyolar	***		
27	**Puntarenas**	***		
	Ferry to **Playa Naranjo** (daily, 0700 and 1600)	***		
07	Lepanto	***		
20	San Pablo	**		
05	Santa Rita			
20	Mansión	**		
12	**Nicoya**		**	
20	Santa Cruz	***		
16	Belén	**		
05	Filadelfia	**		
30	**Liberia**		**	
24	Bagaces		**	
22	**Cañas**	**		
50	Rancho Grande	**		No provisions
(25)	Excurion to Reserva Biológica Monteverde	***		
21	Esparza	***		
31	San Ramón	***		
13	Naranjo	**		
31	**Alajuela**	**		
12	**Heredía**	**		
11	**San José**	*		

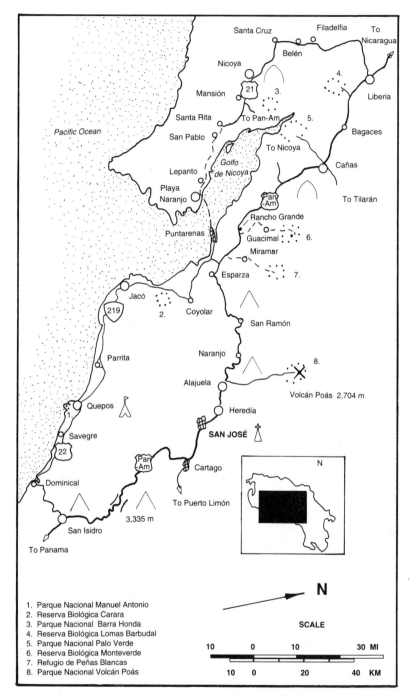

1. Parque Nacional Manuel Antonio
2. Reserva Biológica Carara
3. Parque Nacional Barra Honda
4. Reserva Biológica Lomas Barbudal
5. Parque Nacional Palo Verde
6. Reserva Biológica Monteverde
7. Refugio de Peñas Blancas
8. Parque Nacional Volcán Poás

N

SCALE

10   0   10   30 MI

10   0   20   40 KM

GENERAL INFORMATION

GETTING TO THE COUNTRY. Flying from Europe, you can connect through the United States. From the United States, you can reach San José via many American cities. San José also connects to all Central American capitals and to Ecuador, Colombia, Venezuela, and Peru. Leaving Costa Rica by air, you have to pay an airport tax of U.S.$5 and an 8 percent tax on all airline tickets bought in the country.

Recently, more charter flights are going to Costa Rica, so fares have become cheaper and there are more route options.

San José is an alternative to Panama if you plan to fly into or out of South America. A flight from San José to South America may cost more initially, but when you start figuring the extra taxes, the cost of living, and the visa fees for traveling in Panama, the cost to get to South America from either San José or Panama City is about the same.

The most common land route into Costa Rica is the Pan-American Highway, which connects to Nicaragua at Piedras Blancas and to Panama at the Paso Canoas crossing. Both crossings are straightforward, busy, and time-consuming. A second route crosses into Panama on the Caribbean coast. This crossing, at Sixaola, is not recommended, as it is filled with bureaucratic red tape and is out of the way (Sixaola lacks a road connecting it with Panama's interior).

DOCUMENTS. Westerners do not need visas. A valid passport and enough money to cover your intended stay are required. Onward tickets may be required if you arrive by air.

As you pass through customs, you will pay a small entry tax and then complete and pay for the bicycle's customs certificate. Vehicle insurance is unnecessary. Attendants will spray your bike tires to remove any contaminated animal manure. Officials also conduct a malarial inspection when you arrive overland. If you cannot show your antimalarial tablets and explain your regime to a border official, you have to submit to a blood test (which they'll do at the border).

ACCOMMODATIONS. Accommodations are more expensive and of a lower standard than other Central American countries. In Costa Rica most of the cheaper hotels, *pensiones*, are basic and noisy, and sometimes they restrict the hot water supplies. Generally, the lower-quality hotels are a poor value compared to those in other countries.

You can find camping spots in Costa Rican parks, and although the facilities in each park vary, always bring your own food and drinking water. Even if restaurants and food stores operate on the grounds, the prices are exorbitant. You usually pay to enter the park, and camping is either free or very cheap. Outside the parks, in San José for example, paid camping is as expensive as a hotel.

As with most of Central America, you face an overabundance of barbed wire and fence posts. To camp covertly you have to use your imagination. If you don't mind asking the locals, football fields and school yards offer safe and easy camping spots.

You can buy minor camping items, such as knives, GAZ stoves, and fishing tackle, in San José. You can find white gas and kerosene at hardware stores (*ferreterías*) and GAZ and kerosene at general stores (*almacenes*). Major camping equipment is uncommon because camping is not a local pastime. This may change in the future as the people become more environmentally aware.

FOOD. A variety of locally produced food is widely available. You can easily buy fruit, vegetables, bread, and beef, but imported food is expensive.

Restaurant meals are moderately priced, but small market stalls are excellent for cheap, filling meals.

While traveling, always carry extra food in case a village you planned for doesn't exist. With extra stocks you also have the freedom to stop at spots along the way, such as rivers perfect for swimming and parks filled with wildlife. It would be a shame to miss out on the country's pleasures because you lacked provisions.

Finally, some points about food expressions: "*Pinto con...*" means a breakfast with rice and beans; *gallo* is a filled empanada; and *casado* is a meal with salad, plantains, rice, and beans.

DRINKS. Whether you've been traveling through Latin America extensively or are new to Latin American bicycling, you'll be relieved to hear the water is safe to drink in all major cities. Costa Ricans are proud of their sanitation system.

Costa Rica is overflowing with small cafes called *sodas*, which serve *gaseosas* and *refrescos* (pop) and *refrescos naturales* (mixed fruit drinks). A huge variety of juices is waiting for you to try, from the basic pineapple (*piña*), papaya, and banana, to the exotic tamarind (*mozoté*) and barley (*cebada*), to the weird granadilla (*chan*) and roasted corn (*pinoliko*). Cheaper than pop, they are more fun to try.

The beer of Costa Rica is good, and if you order at a *barra*, it will be served with a choice of appetizers.

Check on the return when buying pop, as the container's cost may equal the contents. (A nonreturnable bottle is two to three times the price of a returnable one.)

HEALTH. Because Costa Ricans have a good sanitation system, they enjoy a high health standard. Costa Rica is the cleanest and healthiest of all Central American countries. Health services also are excellent. San José's medical labs will perform almost any blood, urine, or parasite test. San José is also a good spot for a checkup, as fees are reasonable and many English-speaking doctors and specialists work in the capital. Most drugs are available without prescription at pharmacies.

A year-round malaria risk exists in areas below 500 meters. You can obtain malaria pills for the length of your Costa Rican stay at the Ministry of Health in San José.

Milk products are safe to drink, but cook vegetables and peel fruit because of the use of "night soil" (human feces) for fertilizer.

PHOTOGRAPHY. Bring more film than you think you'll need. Slide and print film are expensive, and there are an incredible number of stunning mountain scenes, intriguing people, interesting animals, and beautiful plants to photograph. A zoom lens is handy for wildlife photography, and a macro is advàntageous for pictures of butterflies, orchids, and frogs.

The camera equipment in Costa Rica is limited and expensive. Print processing is common everywhere, and you can get slides processed in San José.

MONEY. The unit of currency is the colon, which is divided into centimos. Wide-open money exchanges, technically black markets, operate at borders. Don't accept the first price a money changer gives you. As you ask around, offers will rise. Banks are the easiest place to change cash and checks; however, they can charge outrageous U.S.$2 to U.S.$5 commissions. A discreet black market works in San José, where the rates are higher and the commissions lower. You will have to pay the runner who finds you. The black market is technically illegal, but there is little risk in changing money.

The cost of living is moderate. Prices are lower than North America but higher than other Central American countries, excluding Panama. The current economic situation is stable, with inflation at 20 percent.

Shops are open from 7:00 A.M. to 12:00 P.M. and then from 2:00 P.M. to 6:00 P.M. On Saturdays shops open only in the morning, and most major shops close Sunday. An exception is the supermarket in San José that's open from 8:00 A.M. to 6:00 P.M. Sunday. Small stores (*pulperías*) and cafes (*sodas*) open early and close late. Long-distance telephones operate daily from 8:00 A.M. to 10:00 P.M. Finally, bank hours are Monday to Friday 9:00 A.M. to 2:00 P.M.

The holidays of Costa Rica are as follows: January 1, New Year's Day; March 19, Feast of St. Joseph; Easter Friday, Saturday, and Sunday; April 11, Battle of Rivas; May 1, Labor Day; June, Corpus Christi; June 29, St. Peter and St. Paul; July 25, Guanacaste Day; August 2, Virgin of Los Angeles; September 15, Independence Day; October 12, Columbus Day; December 8, Conception of the Virgin; December 25, Christmas.

SECURITY. General personal safety is excellent. In San José you could run into minor problems with pickpockets and bag snatchers, but violent crime is rare. Never leave your bike unattended in San José, as a good bike is a valuable commodity, not an oddity. It's normal practice to take a bike into a store or *soda*.

The political situation is stable, and terrorist activity and hostility toward *gringos* are unusual.

Security Rating: B.

CYCLING INFORMATION

BICYCLES. Costa Rica has an excellent variety of bicycles. You can find BMXs (small "bicycle motocross" models), Mexican double-barreled dinosaurs, Italian racing machines, and high-quality mountain bikes. Components, even the latest developed, are easy to find for both racing and touring bikes, but touring equipment, such as racks and panniers, is limited. Imported parts are expensive, but you'll see equipment that you may never see anywhere else in Latin America. San José is a good place to stock up on hard-to-find parts. You can find 26- and 27-inch tires in bike shops and hardware stores.

Some towns in Costa Rica have more bikes than cars on the streets. Costa Ricans admire and respect cyclists, and bicycling is a popular pastime. Every weekend several races are held around the San José area, and in December the country stages the *Vuelta de Costa Rica*, an eleven-day, 1,500-kilometer race, hosting a large international field.

The best bike shops are in San José, and the best shops in San José are: Ciclo Ases on Calle 40 and Avenida 6, the best for the latest parts and equipment; Rudge on Avenida 8 and Calle 9, a big shop with a little of everything; and Ciclo Quiros on Calle 14 and Avenida 13, a small shop boasting the best repair facilities and the most friendly and helpful staff in Central America.

ROADS. The main road of Costa Rica, stretching from border to border, is the Pan-American Highway. Most secondary roads branch off the Pan-Am. Traffic is not usually a problem, as roads are well designed. There are good signs and distance markers all along the Pan-Am.

The worst section of this highway is from Liberia to San Ramón. This two-lane road is riddled with heat bumps and bordered with a cramped, gravel shoulder. Beyond San Ramón the road widens and is better maintained. You could avoid this rough stretch by going through the less traveled Nicoya Peninsula. Another rough section of the Pan-Am, which includes the Col del Muerte, the Pass of Death, stretches from Cartago to the Panama border. Intermittent sections of gravel and washouts reduce the road to one rough lane.

Most of the roads branching off the Pan-Am Highway are not paved. The most interesting parks (Monteverde, for example) call for side-trip excursions over rough roads.

MAPS. If you plan to stay on the Pan-American Highway, a good Central America map will suffice. The best maps are from the Instituto Geográfico Nacional. The 1:200,000 scale covers the Pan-American Highway in seven sheets, while 1:50,000 maps are also available for detailed exploring. You can find these maps at the institute or in San José at Lehman's or Universal bookstores.

If you plan to explore the national parks, try to find the excellent resource book *Costa Rica's National Parks* by Mario Boza. You can obtain free park information and maps at the SPN, the Servicio de Parques Nacionales, at Avenida 9 and Calle 17.

BIKE TRANSPORT. Buses will reluctantly take bikes if you go to the cargo department of the bus station. Expect to pay at least three times the amount of a passenger fare. Trains will take bikes without an argument. The bike, paid for by weight, travels in the baggage car of your train. Unfortunately, the earthquake in 1991 suspended train operations to Puerto Limón from San José. Hitching with a bike is difficult because of police patrols and strict laws prohibiting it.

ECUADOR

When you think of South America, the images that first come to mind are probably those of Ecuador. Ecuador is where volcanoes touch the sky, markets are a centuries-old tradition, and llamas are still used as beasts of burden. Ecuador is South America epitomized.

Ecuador is a high, mountainous country filled with dozens of volcanoes, some still spewing their smoke and steam like 6,000-meter chimneys. This area, the sierra, is inhabited by a rugged, proud Indian population that tenaciously clings to their culture by masking their *Mama Pacha* rites with Catholic saints and festivals. Here time has changed little. Tradition is as unshakable as the squat, earthquake-proof cathedrals. Yet the *campesinos*, suspicious of Westerners, share their culture only with travelers whose friendliness and understanding they feel they can trust.

Ecuador can be magic when you've committed yourself to its rugged terrain and fascinating people. Ecuador is the place to remove yourself from the *gringo* trail. Explore the tiny villages and weekly markets that have barely changed since the colonial period. Exploring this exotic country, you'll find everything you've dreamed about when you've dreamed about South America.

CYCLE ZONES

La Costa

TERRAIN. The coast of Ecuador presents the cyclist with a flat, monotonous area. The entire zone covers an area averaging 100 kilometers east to west by 700 kilometers north to south. The area, a large basin, funnels the water from the western side of the Andes down to the Guayaquil River delta.

North of Guayaquil, a moderate network of roads runs westward to the coast from the central river basin. You can take circular routes through the northern coastal villages, stopping at the northern coast's largest city, Esmeraldas, for any needed rest and relaxation. Take advantage of the surf; you will not find any more warm ocean water south of Guayaquil.

South, below the lowland capital of Guayaquil, the Andes begin to creep closer to the sea. On this narrow stretch of lowland, the Pan-American Highway slips between the towering Andes and the not-so-pacific Pacific. The Pan-American Highway, the area's only road, carries all international traffic.

SCENERY. Don't go to the western lowlands if you want beautiful scenery and unforgettable vistas. Signs of human activity are everywhere. With its highly cultivated land and flat, monotonous terrain, the coast is an area that you can pass through quickly and forgettably, allowing more time in the scenically stunning areas of the country.

CULTURAL INTEREST. The interest found in la Costa also pales in comparison to the rest of Ecuador. The coastal dwellers, mostly *mestizo* (half indigenous and half European), have long given up the ancient traditions of the sierra. Big money and fast commerce rule the coast. Guayaquil, the undisputed hub of this activity, has become a tawdry seaport and the country's least secure spot.

WEATHER. Simply put, the weather of the western lowlands is stifling year-round. The wet season, when the humidity is unrelenting, occurs from January to May.

The relative dry season on the coast is from June to October. This block of months is the best time for cycling in the lowlands because the humidity has greatly diminished, driver visibility has increased, and the chance of getting stranded by road washouts is minimized.

Winds in the area generally blow from the ocean and then gust up the mountainsides.

The Sierra

TERRAIN. Imagine the territory of the Ecuadorean Andes as a giant ladder. The eastern cordillera is the right support, the western cordillera the left support, and the ladder's rungs are the ridges between the mountain ranges. Between each of these thirteen rungs lies a basin containing a major city. The locals know the area as simply the sierra, and travelers know the zone by its more romantic name, the Avenue of the Volcanoes. The peaks running down this corridor rise to heights of over 6,000 meters. For cyclists wanting to dare the climbs, trails and shelters stagger up the sides of some volcanoes. Chimborazo is the most accessible.

Snaking down the Avenue of the Volcanoes, the Pan-Am continually climbs out of one basin to drop again into another. From some basins, rough spur roads head westward to the coast and eastward to the Oriente, the jungle region of Ecuador. On the spur roads to the coast, the mountainous terrain makes crossing against the grain of the Andes an arduous trip. The Pan-Am descends to the western coast from the city of Cajabamba. The road, poorly surfaced in sections, drops 4,000 meters during a 60-kilometer descent.

SCENERY. The Ecuadorean sierra abounds in stunning and varied landscapes. The basins, nestled between high passes and volcanoes, are occasionally semitropical and contain coffee plantations, extensive agriculture, and intense human activity. Other basins, higher in altitude, offer lonely vistas of volcanoes piercing the clouds.

Everywhere you ride in the sierra, these volcanic masses surround you. No matter how high you climb, the volcanoes loom higher, watching intently as you pass. Whether you're cycling in the high *paramó*, skirting over the volcano's shoulder, or directly challenging their mountainous trails, the volcanoes dominate your experience and never let you forget their presence.

The *paramó* offers another great cycling experience. This topographical zone, defined as the area of the highlands above 3,500 meters, is an austere world where the environment is pared down to sky, mountains, and a lone road, twisting between the mountains like a carelessly thrown rope. This stark scenery offers the cyclist the dramatic impact of being alone with the landscape.

CULTURAL INTEREST. The interest level of the sierra is high. To start with, the natives' awareness of tradition will humble you. Part of their tradition manifests itself in the weekly market, *el día del mercado*. Each city, town, and village has its traditional market day when the people gather, meet, and shop, striving to maintain their identity.

To interact at a town's market is worth the trip to Ecuador. Each market displays a different personality. For example, Otavalo offers beautiful, inexpensive handicrafts—a tourist's mecca. The Zumbahua market, essential to a tour of Ecuador, is rustic, noisy, and full of color. In one blood-soaked corner, butchers slaughter sheep, and in another odorous, dusty corner, locals barter for llamas. This is not a tourist market, so the locals are suspicious of strangers. Don't let this dissuade you; the authenticity of the market and its colorful traditions will lure you into a world of new sights, sounds, and smells.

Major Markets of Ecuador

City	Days	Interest Rating
Ambato	Monday	**
Guano	Tuesday	*
Guaranda	Saturday	*
Latacunga	Saturday and Tuesday	*
Machachi	Sunday	**
Otavalo	Tuesday and Saturday	***
Pujillí	Sunday	*
Riobamba	Wednesday and Saturday	***
Salcedo	Thursday and Sunday	**
Sanolqui	Sunday	**
Santo Domingo	Sunday	*
Saquisilí	Thursday	***
Zumbahua	Saturday	***

Another point of interest in Ecuador, often overlooked because of the attention generated by the markets, is the staid colonial churches. Built by the Spaniards with forced indigenous labor, the churches endure as low, squat structures reminiscent of the country's people. Occasionally, a facade may fly up in defiance of the earthquakes prevalent in this zone, but a church's appeal generally lies in its interior. Once your eyes have grown accustomed to the dim light inside, you will be awed by the gold, baroque excesses running riot throughout the altars and ceilings of the church.

WEATHER. As in most Andean countries, temperature is related to al-

A blind flutist plays a haunting tune in the Saquisilí market.

titude, not season. The higher you go, the colder and more windy it becomes. Nights in the sierra can be freezing, and in the *paramó*, even
colder.

Expect daily rain from October to May. The best time to visit the area is
between June and October, but rain can still fall any time of the year.
Good raingear is essential, as hypothermia is a distinct threat in the
mountains.

Generally, the prevailing winds of the sierra come from the southeast.
The wind blows from the Pacific and is funneled up the valleys and
chasms of the Andes.

TOUR OF ECUADOR

THE SIERRA

Distance: 861 km
Start/Finish: Quito/Quito
Season: January–December
Terrain: Mountainous
Scenery: ***
Interest: ***
Difficulty: Moderate to difficult

Km	Location	Scenery	Interest	Comments
00	**Quito**	*	***	
20	Sangolquí	*	*	Market Thurs.
14	Tambillo (Jct. with Pan-Am)	*		
18	**Machachi**	**		
25	Minitrac	**	*	NASA monitoring station No provisions
(20)	Excursion to Mt. Cotopaxi and Lago Limpiopango	***		No provisions
06	Jct. to Saquisilí	***		
09	**Saquisilí**	**	***	Market Thurs.
06	Return to Pan-Am	*		
04	**Latacunga**	*	**	
13	**Salcedo**	*	**	Market Sun.
27	**Ambato**	**	***	Market Mon.
19	Pelileo	**	**	Market Sat.
22	**Baños**	***	*	
68	**Riobamba**	***	***	Market Sat.
65	**Guaranda**	***	**	
26	Jct. to Mt. Chimborazo	***		
04	Pass (3,800 m)	***		
55	**Ambato**	***	***	Market Mon.
40	Return to **Latacunga**			
11	Pujilí	**	**	Market Sun.
24	Pass (4,000 m)	***		
27	**Zumbahua**	***	***	Market Sat.
(10)	Excursion to Laguna Quilotoa	***		No provisions
10	Pass (3,800 m)	***		
23	Pilaló	***		
11	Tingo	***		
69	**Quevedo**	**	*	
112	**Santo Domingo de los Colorados**	*	**	Market Sun.

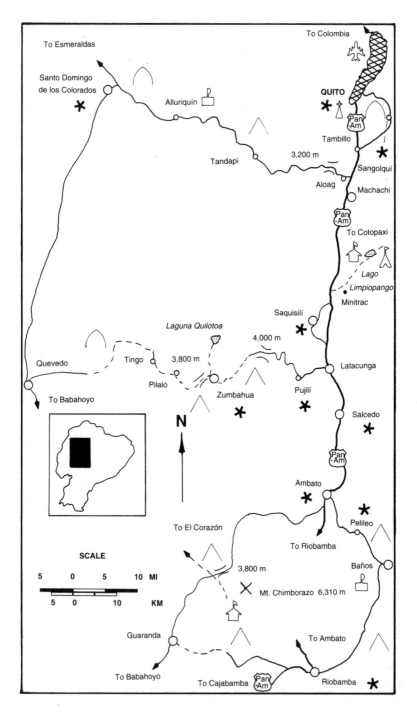

15	Alluriquín	**	
37	Tandapi	**	
42	Pass (3200m)	***	
10	Aloag	**	
15	Tambillo		
14	**Quito**	**	***

The Oriente

TERRAIN. The Oriente contains 36 percent of the country's area but only 5 percent of the population. The zone, found on the eastern side of the Andes, plunges from the sierra, forming a corner of the Amazon basin. The inhabitants of the area call this last mountain range *la ceja del selva*, the eyebrow of the jungle.

Stretching from the eastern cordillera of the Andes, the Oriente rates as a hilly region, but as you travel farther east, it quickly flattens to the jungle floor.

The main route of this zone skirts the jungle floor and undulates dramatically as it crosses against the grain of the Andean mountains. Climbs are unrelenting; you can expect 20-kilometer inclines, with the grades reaching a grueling 8 percent.

SCENERY. The views of the eastern cordillera are the best Oriente scenery. While you climb, vistas gradually come into view and then pass in a blur on the downhill.

Baños is the most beautifully situated town in Ecuador. Nestled in a spectacular basin, it offers the cyclist hot mineral baths, gorgeous waterfalls, and interesting hikes—it offers a break from cycling.

CULTURAL INTEREST. The Oriente is bursting with a pioneer spirit in the form of oilmen and prospectors who bring their brand of fast living to the area. The major towns supply the outlying Indian villages and prospecting regions. You should come prepared for a rough or friendly but always intense experience.

All the roads in this area, apart from the circular Baeza–Tena–Puyo road, end deep in the jungle. You could try cycling into the jungle, visiting mining camps, and then getting a ride back with a jeep or military plane. Some towns along the main Oriente road offer excursions by jeep and canoe deep into the jungle to visit indigenous settlements.

WEATHER. Rain is the biggest concern when traveling in this area. Unfortunately, rain can come any time of the year. What does change is the amount of rain. Even the "dry season," from November to February, gets an average of 15 centimeters of rain a month, while the greatest quantity of rain, an average of 24 centimeters each month, falls from March to October. Torrential rains can drop for days at a time, swelling the rivers and flooding the surrounding roads and villages.

The Oriente is a hot, humid region. The only escape from the climate is in the highlands; Baños, Puyo, and Baeza, perched above the jungle floor, catch the cool winds from the sierra.

GENERAL INFORMATION

GETTING TO THE COUNTRY. If your destination is Ecuador, you'll find countless flight combinations available. No matter where you buy airline tickets, you'll pay an 8 percent tax for domestic flights and a 10 percent tax on international tickets, as well as an additional U.S.$20 departure tax.

Overland to Ecuador from Colombia, the only road crosses at Tulcan–Ibarra. This route, the Pan-American Highway, handles all traffic.

When crossing from Peru to Ecuador, two overland border options exist. The first alternative, the Huaquillas–Zarumilla–Tumbes route, is the most common. It's through this rundown area, booming because of black-market merchandise, that most international traffic passes. This crossing is stressful, yet it offers flat, easy cycling. Paperwork and formalities are swift and trouble-free on both sides of the frontier. Disadvantages are the swirling intensity of human activity and the difficulty of locating the border control offices.

Undoubtedly, the greatest potential for trouble at this border is in dealings with people. Most of the inhabitants and officials apparently are smugglers and thieves. With this wide-open disregard for law and order, this border crossing is a sleazy, dangerous engagement.

When traveling in this area, it's important to keep your wits about you; be careful who you trust. Don't discuss your plans with strangers; immediately arrive, cross, and continue your journey in one day.

The other alternative for crossing by road into Peru is farther east, in the isolated Andean town of Macará. This hilly route is more arduous. You may find officials more suspicious of tourists' motives, and officials may even question why you are there. Subsequently, you'll need more time and possibly more money because of "hidden" expenses paid to the border guards.

From Macará to Sullana, the first major Peruvian town, is a long, lonely trip across the desert. The road becomes unpaved, and people become scarce in the northern Peruvian desert. Stock up with provisions and Peruvian currency in Macará. An advantage of the loneliness at this crossing is that the crime level and chances of an accident are reduced.

No international railways connect Ecuador to either Colombia or Peru. The road is the only way you can travel overland.

DOCUMENTS. Ecuadorean border formalities are simple. All nationalities except South American ones require a valid passport to enter the country, while only a few nationalities require visas. When entering Ecuador, you have to fill out two tourist cards. Regardless of how many days your visa authorizes, officials will allow you to stay only ninety days in a calendar year. Officials will not extend your visa beyond the ninety-day maximum.

You have to surrender your copy of the card when you leave the country. If at any point in your travels in Ecuador, you lose your card, expect a long, costly procedure to replace it.

Although the law requires you to have a ticket out of the country and

U.S.$20 per day for the length of your visa, officials rarely hassle tourists for either. If you do run into a snag, start by explaining your intentions and the idea of bike independence. You'll find perseverance, negotiating skills, gifts, and feigned ignorance all assets.

Documents or extra fees for crossing the border with your bicycle are not required. Normally, an official marks a notation in your tourist card under "Method of Travel."

ACCOMMODATIONS. Most towns and villages of Ecuador offer some type of accommodations. You'll discover that the variety of lodgings is dependent on the size of the town and the number of tourists the town attracts. For example, locations attracting tourists have higher standards and a greater variety of accommodations. Conversely, if tourist traffic is low and the town small, your choices may be limited to one or two places to sleep, which may offer only a roof and a lumpy bed.

Ecuadoreans use the terms *pensiones* and *residenciales* for local hotels. These lower-end hotels are usually frequented by Ecuadoreans traveling on some type of business. Each room's typical setup includes two single beds (double beds are rare), sheets, blanket, and token furniture; outside the room are communal toilets. Anything beyond these fundamentals may cost extra.

Ecuador's hotels offer an entirely hypothetical idea of hot water. All hotel proprietors in Ecuador will tell you they have hot water. Their assurances of hot water and their tempting descriptions of rolling steam and scorching temperatures persuade you to choose their hotel. Unfortunately, you learn their description of "hot" and yours are vastly different; "hot" may turn out to be barely tepid, steam is simply your breath, and scorching is a burning overstatement. To add to the abysmal situation, some hotels charge for the "privilege" of having a "hot" shower.

When you've experienced some rustic *residenciales*, the option of camping looks increasingly inviting. Wild camping is the only option. You can forget services such as hot showers or laundry facilities; and you won't find an area to pitch a tent that's safe, soft, and shaded. For the bicycle tourist, camping is a test of your independence, initiative, and ingenuity.

In the sierra, camping is easy and safe. The amount of open grazing land makes camping simple, while the friendly and unobtrusive people make it secure. The higher you rise in altitude, the more open land exists.

FOOD. Restaurants abound in Ecuador. Every town, village, and bus stop has some type of food stall where you can easily pick up a *plato del día* for a ridiculously low price. Ecuador is a country where it is possible to leave the camp stove at home and rely on restaurants, market stalls, and enterprising street cooks to satisfy your hunger.

Prices for meals are low, with the noonday meal, the *merienda* or *almuerzo*, offering the best value but the least variety. Lunch is the big meal of the day for everyone, and everyone eats the same thing. After traveling a while in Ecuador, you'll find the menus monotonous.

I'm sure some Ecuadoreans have eaten the same *almuerzo* every day of their adult lives. As a foreigner, you may crave some variety after a couple of weeks or months; when you've reached that point, you'll start experimenting in the more expensive restaurants. In them you'll find *churrasco,* a large meal consisting of a large steak, two extra fried eggs, and plantain, a dry starchy banana, used in the same way as potatoes. *Cuy,* the national dish, is spit-roasted guinea pig that you can find in moderately priced restaurants or at native fiestas. Before deciding to order one, watch the little rodents twirling around, paws and head intact, on the rotisserie. If that doesn't blunt your hunger, how about the fact that it's served *entero*? Receiving this gruesome plate only once, you may go back to ordering the *almuerzo*—again.

Restaurants are quick, efficient, and numerous, but another restaurant option is to buy food to go. Buy it, pack it in your pannier, and open it at your convenience. The *pollo asado* establishments, serving delicious roast chicken, and the *chifas,* Chinese restaurants, both offer takeout food.

Markets provide an exciting alternative to restaurants. Merchants accept bargaining for almost every item and in just about every circumstance. Even when locals clearly mark items or display them in small pyramidlike piles, you can try to get extra for the asking price. Don't feel embarrassed about bargaining; the locals embrace it as a lifestyle and business practice. Actually, they see you as not being too smart if you meekly accept their first asking price.

Almacenes, the general stores, is where you'll find yourself doing most of your food shopping. Here you'll find all the staples you need, including stacks of bagged rice and pasta, columns of canned goods, sugar-filled snacks, and fresh bread.

The hours vary. Some places may not open until later in the day or will close unpredictably during the afternoon siesta. These variables can make searching for food a frustrating, time-consuming chore. My advice is to buy your daily needs at the earliest opportunity and carry them with you for the day. Although this method adds to your day's weight, you won't go hungry or worry about where and when you'll next find food.

The *gringo*'s idea of the supermarket, shelves brimming over with goods, aisle upon aisle of choice, is a dream. Only in Guayaquil and Quito are there supermarkets, which are at least good for quick selection and variety.

Imported and specialized health foods are difficult to find anywhere in Ecuador, and when you compare them to locally grown items, they are exorbitantly priced. The exception is yogurt, which you can find at bakeries and *frigoricos,* the stores that sell refrigerated foods. Items imported to Ecuador include canned meats and fruit from Argentina, fresh fruit from Chile, processed foods such as peanut butter, and familiar name-brand foods. Realistically, with the amount of abject poverty in Ecuador, it's only a privileged minority that can be fussy about their food and can afford to pay for the extra effort needed to supply this market.

DRINKS. Treat all water. Water carried through faulty plumbing is a leading cause of most Ecuadorean illnesses.

The bottled mineral water found in Ecuador is easily obtained. The most popular brand sold in the country comes in two types, *sin gas* or *con gas*, without carbonation and with carbonation.

Cheap soft drinks, known to the locals as *colas*, can be found in every *almacen*, restaurant, and run-down truck stop in the country.

If you get tired of the tooth-aching sweetness of soda, market stalls offer some wonderful tropical juices. The local women make every conceivable type of fresh juice, from carrot to tamarind. You can have raw eggs or milk added, which are best with papayas or bananas. Find out, however, if the juices are *puro* (pure) or have water added.

Coffee is usually *puro*. When you order a *café*, it arrives in a small decanter of liquid concentrate. You add this to the glass of hot water and drink what tastes like a petroleum extract. Despite the proximity to Colombia, the world's leading coffee producer, the quality of Ecuadorean coffee is mediocre. Instant coffee is available but expensive.

Alcohol has always acted as an opiate to the impoverished masses of Latin America, and it is used no differently in Ecuador. Beer, for example, is always available and always cheap. The locals also use another, more potent—and even cheaper—anesthetizing drink, *guayusa*, tea mixed with *aguardiente* (literally, water with a bite). The drink is even more potent in the sierra, where you are already lightheaded from the effects of high altitude. Be careful or you could find yourself packed with an incredible hangover the next morning.

HEALTH. Ecuador doesn't offer any special, exotic Latin American diseases. Conversely, it also doesn't rank as a healthy country.

Common to all of Ecuador are amoebic dysentery, hepatitis, and typhoid.

Carry a treatment of Mebendazol for worms and Flagyl for amoebas. Both drugs can be obtained without a prescription in just about any pharmacy in Ecuador.

When you arrive in the lowlands, the health risks increase. Apart from the usual intestinal problems, the greatest lowland hazard is malaria. It exists universally in both rural and urban areas throughout the year in zones below 800 meters. The Oriente has a higher malaria risk than the coast and contains the more dangerous chloroquine-resistant mosquitoes. Another risk in the Oriente is yellow fever.

In the early months of 1991, the Andean countries, most severely Peru, suffered an outbreak of cholera.

MONEY. The major currency of Ecuador is the sucre, divided into ragged bills and forgettable coins. Yet, despite the currency's forlorn look, Ecuador is one of the few countries in Latin America operating with a free-market economy. You can buy and sell any major currency—Deutsche mark, English pound, or American dollar—subject to availability. If you're planning to travel to other countries or have money sent from home, Ecuador is an ideal place to restock with American dollars.

You can accomplish all your transactions in Quito and Guayaquil. Outside these cities, you'll find lower rates of exchange and fewer banks. For example, in the Oriente it's almost impossible to exchange even cash; stock up on sucres before leaving Guayaquil and Quito.

Changing money in the two major cities of Ecuador is a straightforward procedure. The safest and most reliable method is to go to *casas de cambio*. They usually have their buying and selling rates prominently displayed in their windows. Transaction fees are small, and apart from a small difference between traveler's checks and hard currency, they don't charge a commission for changing money. They might charge a small fee when changing traveler's checks into hard American currency. If you shop around, you'll discover the fees and rates are consistent from one place to another.

The small price you pay to receive hard currency is worth the investment if you're traveling into either Colombia or Peru. Both neighboring countries have higher exchange rates for American dollars versus traveler's checks. But remember that despite great deals, Colombia and Peru have immense crime problems; carry only as much cash as you can afford to lose.

Some *casas de cambio* require you to show the original bill of sale in order to convert traveler's checks into dollars. Therefore, keep the original receipts for your checks in case the exchange house wants them.

Changing money at the houses is always easier and faster than at the banks, which usually have long lineups, inefficient service, and higher commissions. Banks are useful, though, if you want to receive money from home. Ecuadorean banks offer one of the best places in Latin America to receive money if you have an account at an affiliated international bank. If you use this method, expect a delay of a week or two for the bank to complete the transfer. To avoid disappointment and starvation, don't procrastinate transferring funds.

The sucre is on a gradual downward slide. This constant devaluation isn't drastic enough to minimize the amount of currency you exchange. Ecuador had economic problems from 1986 to 1989, and the government legislated severe economic restrictions, none of which greatly affected the traveler. The changes have done nothing to help the local laborer who continues to work for a hundred dollars a year.

For the native Ecuadorean, living isn't easy. Prices are high, goods limited, and wages low. For those with money, the cost of living is very low. Hotel rooms start at a couple of dollars a night, and meals at a dollar and a half. For the bicycle tourist, it's easy to spend a lot of time in the country without worrying about finances.

When you enter or leave Ecuador, figure out the exchange rate beforehand, as you will find deals with the border money changers. However, their number and persistence can overwhelm you, so keep your wits about you and shop around for the best rates. Don't accept a ridiculously high rate; it's probably a setup for you to get robbed.

The markets of Ecuador offer the tourist a handicraft paradise. Most towns have only one specific market day, but some larger centers also host a secondary market during the week. Try to plan your trip around the markets, either to shop or to enjoy their color and traditions.

As a rule, the larger the market, the later it starts and the longer it stays active. For example, the Saturday Otavalo market, the largest tourist-oriented market in Ecuador, doesn't bloom until 8:00 or 9:00 A.M., while the smaller, intimate market of Zumbahua begins at dawn and starts to break up around 10:00 A.M.

Business hours for regular shops vary, depending on whether they're in the sierra or the lowlands. Shops found in the cities of the sierra are open from 8:30 A.M. to 12:30 P.M., close for lunch, and reopen from 2:30 to 4:30 P.M. Monday to Friday. Most shops are open from 8:30 A.M. to 12:30 P.M. on Saturdays, and almost everything closes Sunday unless it's the town's market day.

In the lowlands, particularly the commercial capital of Guayaquil, hours are seasonal, allowing for a longer siesta during the hotter summer season. From May to December, shops are open from 8:30 A.M. to 1:30 P.M. and from 2:30 to 6:30 P.M. Monday to Friday; from December to May, store hours are 8:30 A.M. to 1:30 P.M. and 3:30 to 6:30 P.M. Monday to Friday. Most shops of the lowlands close for the entire day on Saturdays.

All government offices in the country are closed Saturday and Sunday. Banks in Ecuador are only open from 9:00 A.M. to 2:00 P.M. Monday to Friday.

Holidays, treated like Sundays, are as follows: January 1, New Year's Day; May 1, Labor Day; May 24, Battle of Pinahincha Day; July 24, Simon Bolivar's Birthday; August 10, Independence Day; October 12, Columbus Day; November 1, All Saints' Day; December 25, Christmas.

The postal service in Ecuador is generally reliable. Letters and postcards are expensive to send, yet large, registered parcels are comparatively cheap.

SECURITY. Despite the country's history of unstable governments, Ecuador maintains an average security record. The political situation has improved over the years, and even though the military still watches the process of democracy intently, the threat of military violence is small. Because of the stable politics, no guerrilla movements operate. Very small, semi-active splinter groups exist, but the chance of encountering them is negligible.

The people of the sierra are traditionally honest and hardworking, and it's the rare traveler who encounters any serious criminal problems. Sierra Ecuadoreans aren't materialistic, and the people have a sense of respect for each other and for tourists.

Unfortunately, the inhabitants of the coastal lowlands and Quito are less honest in their dealings with travelers and each other. Awash in consumer goods, the area attracts criminal activity. This situation, limited to the coastal lowlands, makes travel here riskier than in the rest of the country. Yet when weighed against the cocaine-induced problems of its neighbors, every part of Ecuador is safe.

Ecuador is an anomaly among the Andean countries. The growing of coca leaves and their use among the inhabitants is illegal. Unlike Peru and Colombia, farmers aren't growing the crop, workers aren't processing the leaves, runners aren't smuggling coca paste, and drug barons aren't corrupting everyone they contact. Drug-related violence, therefore, is small.

It's rare to have anything stolen outside of the two major commercial centers of the country. This doesn't mean you should travel with your eyes closed, but it's possible to relax in Ecuador.

Security Rating: C in Quito and Guayaquil; A in other areas.

On the tranquil road to Laguna Quilotoa

CYCLING INFORMATION

BICYCLES. The bicycle tourist traveling through Ecuador can find three categories of bicycles: First, the three-wheeled tricycle used by the locals for transporting cargo. Second is the one-speed Chinese roadster. Looking like an Art Deco bicycle with its slick black moldings and heavy steel frame, the bike has style but no feasibility for the cyclist. The final category is the cheap, multispeed racing bike. This item, "top of the line" for Ecuador, is similar to a North American department store special. Characteristics of this style include shoddy construction and poor-quality components.

Finding replacement parts for a high-quality touring bike is almost impossible. Ecuadoreans can't afford anything even moderately expensive, and the high import duties on foreign goods eliminate the demand for expensive imported items. Avid Ecuadorean cyclists go to Colombia to buy equipment. You should do the same if you need any replacement parts or repairs.

Despite Ecuador's lack of bicycle variety, bikes are widespread. The populace uses them for riding around town, going shopping, or shuttling between their farms. Every town has a bike store and repair shop. Surprisingly, most shops' focus is to do fancy paint jobs; fluorescent colors are fashionable. Mechanics lack mechanical ingenuity and will find a triple chainwheel or an index shifter baffling. Even one-piece cranks are unknown. You must repair your bike independently.

Replacing tires is also difficult. The most common size of tire is 28 inches. Cheap 27- and 26-inch tires are available, but forget replacing 700C tires.

If you become absolutely desperate for parts and you can't wait until you leave the country, the best city to look for replacements is Guayaquil. Bicycle shops in this city get more imports than Quito, which because of its terrain has little demand for bikes. This pattern extends throughout Ecuador. The flat, lowland agricultural centers have a greater demand for bikes, parts, and mechanics than the mountainous sierra, where locals perceive bikes as status symbols used only for quick trips around town.

If after exhausting these possibilities, you still have problems finding suitable parts, a place that may help is a small shop at 628 Casilla in Ambato that rents mountain bikes to foreigners. The owner rents them for travelers to coast down to Baños and beyond, and then return by bus. No one guarantees the store can help, but anything is a possibility when you're desperate.

ROADS. Half the country's 17,000 kilometers of roads remain open year-round. Other routes are muddy dirt tracks prone to mudslides, floods, and earthquakes. Between these two types, road conditions range from poorly maintained decrepitude in the Oriente to the well-paved, well-traveled Avenue of the Volcanoes. If you don't know the state of an upcoming road, talk to returning bus drivers.

Don't trust traffic lights. Even if they work, they have so much dust and grime on them no one can see their lights. So everyone speeds through intersections, challenging anyone's right-of-way, another manifestation of *machismo*.

Most cities use cobbles rather than blacktop. Their quick deterioration starts from the curb outward, so you'll run over gaps and rim-bending potholes as you dodge traffic on the roads. Cars and buses won't give you any space, carts occasionally take up the inside lane, and pedestrians hop on and off the sidewalk to avoid crowds. Be careful.

Most main roads are continually upgraded and downgraded, depending on the economy, weather, and motivation of the road workers. Most maintenance is done with manual labor, so repairs are of poor quality. The Pan-American Highway is generally well maintained and provides a paved shoulder. An exception is the area surrounding Quito. This section is usually in rough shape because of the shortage of main roads running into the capital.

Most of the traffic in Ecuador travels on the Pan-Am. Most of the Pan-Am's length snakes along the Avenue of the Volcanoes. Generally, outside the Pan-Am the higher you rise in altitude, the less traffic you'll meet. The most competition for space and oxygen comes from *collectivos*, the small buses that ply their way between every village and town of Ecuador. Since you're certain to encounter them on any trip on the Pan-Am, be visible and wear a dust filter.

As a final note, police roadblocks always occur at the bottom of a hill. Despite your wish to pass them in an unidentified blur, stop.

MAPS. You can buy the best maps of the country in Quito at the Instituto Geográfico Militar, on top of the hill on the eastern side of El Ejido Park. You have to submit your passport to get a visitor's pass.

The *instituto* makes and distributes maps of varying scales, the best of which is the 1:1,000,000 even though it lacks distance markings. You can buy a small *mapa vial* that shows these markings but lacks topography lines. Maps are not expensive, so buy the most helpful. If you plan to do some trail riding, buy the smaller 1:200,000 and 1:50,000 maps.

The institute will not have all parts of the series you want, but it usually has the larger, more popular maps. Some larger bookstores in Quito and Guayaquil catering to foreigners may have copies of the *instituto*'s maps in stock.

Not all maps are up to date. New roads are built, old ones deteriorate, and towns disappear. New editions of maps are rare, so don't implicitly trust a map if you go to obscure areas of the country. Double-check with locals to find out the situation.

Apart from the *instituto*'s maps, maps found in Ecuador are useless, though colorful.

Tourist offices in some larger towns also may provide verbal information, sketchy maps, and reading material for travelers. They're also a good place to check for cheap accommodations, sights, personal guides, maps, printed information, and inter-tourist communications.

BIKE TRANSPORT. Ecuadorean public transport is convenient, cheap, and easy. Most of the people can't afford to own a car, so they use buses and trains. The drivers expect everyone to pay a bit more for cargo, and it's a good idea to settle the entire fare, bicycle included, before starting. Most charges for bikes amount to about 30 to 50 percent of the passenger fare.

The fastest and most convenient method of getting to a destination is by *collectivos,* little buses that scurry to and from every city, town, and village. The conductor loads your bike on top of the bus (unpack it first) and then ties it down to avoid losing it on the mountain roads.

Always watch your bike until everything on top is packed—not so much to deter theft as to prevent anything heavy from being loaded on top of the bicycle. Fifty-kilo bags of rice bouncing on top of your bike can damage your wheels.

Trains work on the same principle as *collectivos,* which won't be a surprise when you see an Ecuadorean train: it's usually the shell of a bus nailed to the train's flatbed. Passengers climb in and take a seat while the conductor lashes everyone's cargo to the rooftop.

Ecuador's main train route runs from Riobamba to Quito and is more interesting than the road. The train usually takes much longer, stopping at every village and hut along the track, even halting for a passenger appearing out of nowhere.

GUATEMALA

Guatemala is made up of three historical and cultural levels. The first level, the ancient Maya, built vast metropolises, flourished, and died out in the Petén region. Today you can see their beautiful, mysterious cities as beautiful, mysterious ruins. The second level of Guatemala's history, the living native world, descended from the ancient Maya. The native world also combined small aspects of the Western world. The third cultural level, the Hispanic-American world, had its colonial beginnings in the city of Antigua. Later, Antigua prospered, serving as the capital of Central America until its devastation by earthquakes. Now the *mestizos*, centered in Guatemala City and the coast, repress their native blood and live in the twentieth century.

At Tikal, a Mayan pyramid soars into view.

CYCLE ZONES

Petén

TERRAIN. The Petén is the vast lowland area neighboring Belize and the Mexican province of Chiapas. You can expect to find flat to rolling terrain along the Petén routes until you hit the foothills of the Sierra Madre.

SCENERY. The beauty of the Petén lies in its jungle. The birds, the animals, and the plant life are innumerable. Here, you'll luxuriate in the shade of a *ceiba* tree as you watch toucans and listen to howler monkeys. You can still experience virgin forests in isolated areas and national parks. Sadly, with road construction comes devastation and deforestation. Along the roads, the jungle has been stripped for pasture and agriculture.

CULTURAL INTEREST. Despite the extreme climate and tropical diseases, the Maya settled, developed, and expanded their city empires throughout the Petén. During the height of Mayan development, the civilization constructed the ceremonial centers of Tikal and El Ceibal. In this period, the Maya Classical, Tikal had hundreds of temples serving a population of 50,000. Today the Parque Nacional Tikal surrounds these extraordinary ruins. Other sites throughout the Petén, more difficult to access, are in various stages of excavation, but are worth the effort if you have time.

The Petén is a difficult area to cycle. Unpaved roads, combined with a lack of provisions and the tropical climate, challenge every cyclist.

WEATHER. Winds from the northeast predominate. The temperature and humidity are high year-round. It's important to plan around the wet season, April to October. The Petén roads become impassable because of thick mud and road washouts.

Sierra Madre

TERRAIN. The mountains of Guatemala form a rectangular block from Mexico to El Salvador. A chain of active volcanoes makes up the sierra's backbone. Traveling through this area, you'll face constant climbs and descents. You'll commonly reach passes over 2,500 meters high. Cities alone average 2,200 meters.

SCENERY. The mountains and volcanoes are stunning. The black cones of active volcanoes exhale blasts of steam and sulfur. Inactive cones become crater lakes, producing the most intoxicating scenery in Central America. Growing on the mountainsides are pine forests and jungle growth. Just about every road in the Sierra Madre is worth pursuing.

The major sources of difficulty in the mountains are the grade and length of climbs. The major roads through Guatemala's mountains are paved and carry a reasonable amount of traffic. If you are in shape, this zone poses a moderate challenge.

CULTURAL INTEREST. The Sierra Madre is one of the few places in the Western Hemisphere where most of the population is *indígena*, or na-

At the Sololá market, the people maintain a strong sense of culture and tradition.

tive. Through the centuries, the European culture has only grazed the native way of life. Although Maya traditions now mingle with Catholicism and European morality, the *indígenas* maintain a strong identity. This pride, this determination, keep their culture intact and make the area fascinating for the traveler.

To experience this fascination, visit the markets. Each center has a market day when the surrounding villages converge to sell their goods. Chichicastenango's Sunday market, with its colorful religious element, is the most famous, but for the most intense event, visit the less frequented markets, such as Sololá.

WEATHER. Temperatures are springlike, providing moderate days and cool, comfortable nights. Altitude more than season determines temperature. The rainy season is from May to October. Trade winds from the Pacific arrive from the southwest.

TOUR OF GUATEMALA

THE SIERRA MADRE

Distance: 706 km
Start/Finish: Ciudad de Guatemala/Ciudad de
Guatemala
Season: November–May
Terrain: Mountainous
Scenery: ***
Interest: ***
Difficulty: Difficult

Km	Location	Scenery	Interest	Comments
00	**Ciudad de Guatemala**		**	Market Sat.
32	San Lucas Sacatepéquez	**		
13	**Antigua Guatemala**	**	***	Market daily
11	Parramos	**		
06	**Chimaltenango**	*		Market Sun.
15	Patzicía	**		Market Wed., Sat.
11	**Patzún**	**		Market Sun.
29	Semetabaj	***	**	Market Tues.
08	**Panajachel**	***	**	Market Sun.
	Ferry excursion to San Pedro la Laguna (Tues., Fri., Sun. 1300)	***		
	San Pedro la Laguna	***	**	Market Sun.
(18)	**Santiago Atitlán**	***	**	Market Fri.
(15)	San Lucas Tolimán	***	**	Market Tues., Fri., Sun.
(31)	**Panajachel**			
08	**Sololá**	***	**	Market Tues., Fri.
12	Los Encuentros	*		
17	**Chichicastenango**	**	***	Market Sun.
12	Santa Cruz del Quiché	**	*	Market Thurs.
44	**Totonicapán**	**		Market Thurs., Sat.
11	**San Cristóbal Totonicapán**	*	*	Market Sun.
61	Malacatancito	**		
18	**Huehuetenango**	*	**	Market Thurs., Sun.
04	Chiantla	*	**	
20	Aguacatán	***	**	
38	**Sacapulas**	***	**	
13	Jct. to Nebaj			
(24)	**Nebaj**	***	**	Market Thurs., Sun.

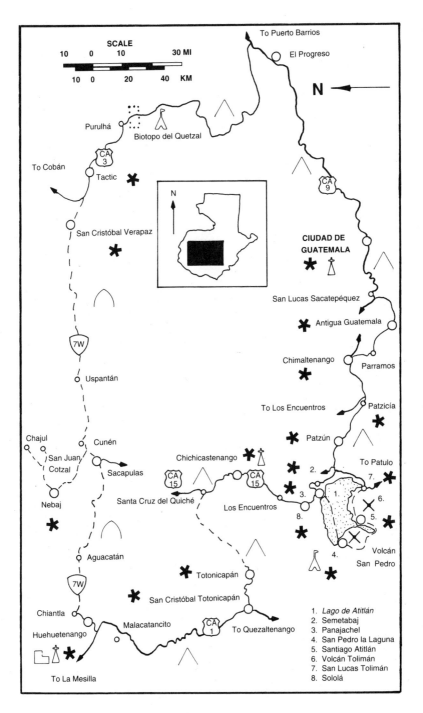

SCALE
10   0   10   30 MI

10   0   20   40   KM

To Puerto Barrios

El Progreso

N

Purulhá

Biotopo del Quetzal

CA 3

To Cobán

Tactic

San Cristóbal Verapaz

N

CIUDAD DE
GUATEMALA

San Lucas Sacatepéquez

Antigua Guatemala

Chimaltenango

Parramos

7W

Uspantán

To Los Encuentros

Patzicía

Chajul

Cunén

Chichicastenango

Patzún

To Patulo

San Juan
Cotzal

Sacapulas

CA 15

CA 15

2.

7.

Nebaj

Santa Cruz del Quiché

Los Encuentros

3.

1.

6.

5.

8.

Aguacatán

Volcán
San Pedro

4.

7W

Totonicapán

Chiantla

San Cristóbal Totonicapán

Huehuetenango

Malacatancito

CA 1

To Quezaltenango

To La Mesilla

1. *Lago de Atitlán*
2. Semetabaj
3. Panajachel
4. San Pedro la Laguna
5. Santiago Atitlán
6. Volcán Tolimán
7. San Lucas Tolimán
8. Sololá

(11)	Jct. to San Juan Cotzal			
(07)	San Juan Cotzal	***	**	
(07)	Return to Jct.			
(12)	Chajul	***	**	
(23)	Return to **Nebaj**	***	**	
(24)	Return to Jct. to Cunén			
05	Cunén	***	**	
25	Uspantán	***	**	
61	**San Cristóbal Verapaz**	***	**	Market Tues., Sun.
22	**Tactic**	**	**	Market Thurs., Sun.
15	Purulhá	**	**	
04	Biotopo del Quetzal	***		
82	Jct. to Ciudad de Guatemala (Hwy. CA-9)	**		
14	**El Progreso**	*		
71	**Ciudad de Guatemala**	*		

The Coast

TERRAIN. The coastal portion of Guatemala lies between the mountains and the Pacific Ocean. The main road, CA-2, runs from Mexico to El Salvador along a mainly flat plain traversing hundreds of rivers and streams. From Ciudad Tecún Umán, at the Mexican border, to Mazatenango the terrain is hilly.

The CA-2 is the quickest, least problematical route through Guatemala. If you want to skip the interesting and beautiful areas of the country, the coast offers the easiest cycling in the country.

SCENERY. The coastal forest and scrubland have succumbed to agriculture and grazing. It is a densely populated region where the people make full use of the fertile land. Unfortunately, the intensive farming has stripped the area of natural beauty. Now the coast is the least beautiful area of Guatemala.

CULTURAL INTEREST. The Maya never settled on the coast, preferring to expand north to the Yucatán, west to Belize, and south to Honduras. Any remains of ancient cultures have surrendered to the destructiveness of man and nature. The *indígenas*, preferring to stay in the mountains, still shun the area, depriving the zone of ethnographic interest. The coast is the least interesting area of Guatemala.

WEATHER. From the southwest, trade winds blow off the ocean and across the plains. As in the rest of the country, the wet season, which is very wet here, extends from May to October. Temperatures remain steady, but the humidity levels of the rainy season make cycling uncomfortable.

GENERAL INFORMATION

GETTING TO THE COUNTRY. Guatemala City is connected to the rest of the world via either the southern United States or the Caribbean. Few direct flights arrive from Europe. Tourism is catching on in Guatemala, which means there's more demand for cheap charter flights. Guatemala City has flights to most capitals in Central America. No direct flights connect to South America; you must fly through Panama. If you buy international tickets, you have to pay an additional 13 percent tax.

If you are headed to Belize, you can cross in two ways. The only road crosses through Melchor de Mencos, a rough journey, made increasingly perilous by robbery and guerrilla activity. Check the situation before embarking on your journey. The second method is by boat. From Puerto Barrios on the Caribbean, you can take a boat to Punta Gorda in Belize, a good alternative if you want to avoid the hazards of the Petén. Ensure your documents are in order.

From Mexico four routes cross into Guatemala. The first, La Mesilla, is the most interesting and scenic but, because of the terrain, also the most difficult. If you want to explore the Chiapas region of Mexico, Mesilla is the best crossing. El Carmen, the less used second route, now has more dangerous guerilla activity. Avoid this crossing. The third crossing, Tecún Umán, is the fastest, busiest, and easiest. The last route connects the Petén to Mexico. You first have to cross a rugged 160-kilometer road to El Naranjo, on the San Pedro River. From there, you take an eight-hour boat upriver to the Mexican town of La Palma.

Going into El Salvador, you have four options. The first choice slides along the coast at Alvarado. Expect plenty of traffic but decent roads. The other three routes are mountainous and more difficult. The shortest but roughest is Valle Nuevo. San Cristóbal Frontera is the most scenic, and Angunatu is convenient if you want to miss the Guatemalan highlands yet still enter El Salvador. Each crossing will depend on where you are in Guatemala and where you want to get to in El Salvador.

If you cross into Honduras, the most obvious crossing is at El Florido. Although the road is rough and steep, the exceptional ruins of Copán are worth the effort.

DOCUMENTS. Everyone needs passports. Nationals of British Commonwealth countries need to obtain visas before arrival. Other nationalities require only tourist cards. You can obtain extensions for either at the *migración* office at 12 Calle and 8 Avenida in Zona 1 in Guatemala City.

When you enter the country, officials charge you 1 quetzal for the card and entry. Overcharging is widespread, especially at the Belize border. The locals accept the obvious graft, but with perseverance you don't have to. Extra documents are not required for your bike.

ACCOMMODATIONS. Hotels, *casas de huéspedes*, and *pensiones* are cheap and abundant. Rates for rooms are supposed to be posted in the rooms, but they are usually out-of-date or simply ignored.

The costs for rooms are low, so don't settle for the first room you see. An extra dollar can bring a surprising difference in quality, so search and compare.

Guatemala has no youth hostels, but private houses provide room and board. This is a good alternative if you plan a lengthy stay in the country. The best town for finding room and board is Antigua, where tourists flock to learn Spanish.

Paid camping exists around resort areas, such as Lake Atitlán and

Amatitlán, and in national parks, such as the Quetzal Sanctuary. Most camping sites are rustic, simply a cleared area and a pit toilet. Paid camping is only worth the trouble if no other accommodations are available. The exception to this is Tikal, where camping is the best way to experience the jungle.

Approach wild camping with caution. Where guerrillas are active, camping may be risky. Locals will inform you of the dangers of camping in certain areas. Ask for help if you must camp in an uncertain area, as the locals can also provide security.

Finding a clear spot in the mountains is usually easy. Most mountains have enough trees to provide cover. However, camping in the Petén is trickier, as the jungle provides few clearings.

FOOD. Food costs are cheap everywhere in Guatemala. Markets, general stores, supermarkets, and restaurants all offer cheaper prices than Mexico or Belize. Markets run only in the morning, and food stores are open from 8:00 A.M. to noon and from 2:00 to 6:00 P.M. You can find food stores at every city, town, and road junction.

Restaurants are also cheap and easy to find—just don't expect a variety of dishes. The *plato del día* may be the only choice. Try to choose places with sanitary conditions. At restaurants you can also buy takeout tortillas.

Two difficulties you should remember are that finding food can be difficult in the Petén and isolated mountain areas, and that food, such as tortillas, bread, and leftovers, spoils easily in the tropical heat.

DRINKS. Treat all water. Bottled water is difficult to find outside main population centers and tourist areas. *Agua mineral* is club soda. *Aguas* are soft drinks, *refrescos* are small bags of juice, and *liquados* are fruit juices mixed in a blender.

The national beer is below average. *Aguardiente* is made from sugarcane and is the national liquor. Alcohol mixed with *gringos* seems to ferment hostility in the locals.

HEALTH. Follow usual hygiene, cooking, and food preparation precautions. Cholera has reached Guatemala, and amoebic dysentery is endemic. For the Petén, your yellow fever inoculation should be current. A chloroquine regime against malaria should be taken for travel in all areas below 1,500 meters, especially for the Petén.

Be careful of extreme variations in temperature. In Quetzaltenango temperatures can drop to 0 degrees Celsius; yet, after a quick 45-kilometer downhill, you are on the 40-degree coast.

PHOTOGRAPHY. The colorful scenes in the markets and the ancient traditions of the people will tempt you to take pictures of everybody. Remember the *indígenas* are naturally shy. Some may charge you a small posing fee. Be discreet.

Camera equipment and slide film are exorbitantly priced. Print film is cheaper. You can develop both prints and slides in the capital.

MONEY. The unit of currency is the quetzal, divided into centavos and abbreviated as *Q*. Banks in most cities change either dollars or traveler's checks at the free-market rate without a commission. Banks are open daily from 9:00 A.M. to 3:00 P.M.

A tiny black market operates at the borders. If you are in the capital, exchange houses offer a slightly better rate than banks.

The cost of living is low. A dollar can stretch a long way.

Guatemalans are not late-night people. Most shops and towns close at 6:00 P.M. daily, including Saturday and Sunday. Government services and large stores are closed Saturday afternoon and Sundays except the post office, which closes at 7:30 P.M. on Saturday. Postal rates are cheap, and delivery is reliable if you send parcels registered.

The following are the major market days of Guatemalan towns. Monday: Antigua and Comalapa; Tuesday: San Pedro Carchá, Sololá, Patzún, Toliman, and Sumpango; Wednesday: Momostenango and Patzicía; Thursday: Chichicastenango, Antigua, Patzún, Huehuetenango, and San Martín Jilotepeque; Friday: Sololá, Santiago de Atitlán, and San Francisco el Alto; Saturday: Patzicía, Santo Tomas Chiche, and Sumpango; Sunday: Chichicastenango, Huehuetenango, Momostenango, Nahualá, Panajachel, Patzún, Zunil, Palín Quiché, San Cristóbal, Cantel, and Sumpango.

Guatemala celebrates the following holidays: January 1, New Year's Day; January 6, Epiphany; Holy Week; May 1, Labor Day; September 15, Independence Day; October 12, Discovery of America; October 20, Revolution Day; November 1, All Saints' Day; December 24–25, Christmas.

Every settlement has a patron saint day when everything closes so that the townspeople can venerate their saint and rejoice. If you are lucky, you may run into a town's celebration.

SECURITY. Unfortunately, the security situation in Guatemala is substandard. Criminals in the capital and tourist centers are focusing more attention on travelers, particularly in Guatemala City, Antigua, Panajachel, and Chichicastenango. Buses have also been robbed on the Flores–Belize road and the Flores–Rio Dulce route.

Encounters between guerrillas and the army are occurring in the Petén, northern El Quiché, Huehuetenango, Sacatepéquez, and Escuintla. The roadblocks and overall tension could affect you. The good news is that the guerrilla forces aren't targeting tourists, but you should be cautious in these areas. Don't travel at night and always carry identification with you.

Security Rating: C.

CYCLING INFORMATION

BICYCLES. Guatemalans have discovered the mountain bike, and the old Chinese one-speed isn't the standard it is in other countries. Although most of the bikes are of inferior quality, it's possible to find higher-quality bikes and parts. Every sizable town will have 26-, 27-, and 28-inch tires. Prices for tires and parts are cheaper than in Mexico or Belize, and the availability is greater than in Honduras.

Each small town has a *reparación de bicicleta* shop, although it could be only a shack with a hand-painted sign. Don't expect much help for advanced repairs. You can find parts, tires, and equipment at parts stores called *repuestos* or at hardware stores. If you run into problems, the country is small enough that you can catch a bus to the capital.

Guatemala City is an oasis for parts and repairs. Bicycle stores are well stocked with the best components, and intricate repairs, such as wheel building, are possible. Prices for parts and labor are similar to prices in the United States.

ROADS. Guatemala contains 18,000 kilometers of roads. Only 3,000 are paved. The good news is that most main centers are connected by paved road; choosing an unpaved road is just that—a choice. There are good unpaved roads that are better than some paved roads. Lastly, getting off pavement takes you away from the "*gringo* trail" and into the more remote regions of the country.

Once on the unpaved secondary roads in isolated regions, expect rough conditions, varying from thick dust and thicker mud to large rocks and larger potholes. Yet the challenge and rewards of these routes are worth every bit of effort.

Driving habits in Guatemala are atrocious. Buses swerve in and out of traffic, and trucks trundle along exhaling choking amounts of exhaust. Luckily, traffic is light because there are few private vehicles in the country, and most drivers prefer to travel at night. The busiest stretches of road are between Guatemala City and Puerto Barrios, Highway CA-2 along the coast, and the road between Escuintla and the capital.

You'll find that in areas where guerrillas are active, townspeople have organized self-appointed paramilitary groups to defend themselves. When you enter these towns, you must stop. Be courteous and cooperative.

MAPS. The best place to buy maps is the National Geographical Institute, Avenida las Americas 5-76, Zona 13 in Guatemala City. You can find maps with scales varying from 1:1,000,000 to 1:50,000. If you can't buy certain maps because of military restrictions, the institute will let you copy what you need. The institute is open from 8:00 A.M. to 4:30 P.M. Monday to Friday.

If you can't obtain any of these maps, Texaco produces a reasonable map of Guatemala. Although it lacks topographical detail and the Petén roads are inaccurate, it is the best alternative. You can buy the map at bookstores and tourist offices.

Lastly, don't ask the locals for distance information. Since most travel by bus, their sense of distance is poor. Typical answers from locals can range from 50 to 150 kilometers for the same stretch of road.

BIKE TRANSPORT. First-class buses will take a bike if they are short of passengers. Second-class buses will take animals, produce, furniture, and anything else as normal cargo. Your bike is just another piece of cargo and rarely will it be a problem. Expect to pay about 75 percent of the (cheap) passenger fare for your bike.

Trains aren't worth the trouble.

Truck transport exists, but you have to pay for it.

HONDURAS

Honduras is a destitute country. Every facet speaks of poverty. Economically, its per capita income is less than $700. Politically, the Honduran government is corrupted by outside interests. Historically, Honduras has only one Mayan site of interest; others have been forgotten or destroyed by invaders. The country is 90 percent *mestizo,* struggling people without a traditional sense of culture. Despite its poverty, Honduras is an unpretentious country with its own merits. The Bay Islands, for example, provide beautiful, accessible, and uncrowded beaches; Copán, the brilliant Mayan ruins near the Guatemalan border, was the Maya's Athens.

TOURING INFORMATION

TERRAIN. Honduras is a mountainous country, but its average altitudes don't reach the lofty heights of Guatemala or Costa Rica. Long river valleys, such as the Sula, slice a hundred kilometers deep into the highlands. Following these valleys, the main roads gradually climb to the mountain plateaus. Inner plateaus and basins average 900 meters in altitude, but passes rarely rise above 1,500. Bracketing the mountain zone are two narrow coastal areas. Honduran terrain shouldn't impede your cycling.

SCENERY. The scenery of Honduras is pretty but not spectacular. The forest-covered mountains, bisected by streams and rivers, are satisfying. The best of these spots is Lago de Yohoa on the main San Pedro Sula–Tegucigalpa highway. Richer Hondurans use the charming area as a resort.

The Bay Islands are a beautiful spot to relax. From La Ceiba, on the Caribbean coast, reaching the islands is easy.

CULTURAL INTEREST. Hondurans are predominantly of mixed blood. Their *mestizo* traditions focus on agriculture and natural resources. Their culture has no weekly markets, no colorful customs, just a daily existence weakly modeled on Western capitalism. Sadly, the people lack a unifying identity.

You should see Honduras' two historical sites. Ignored and rustic, the colonial city of Comayagua has dwindling historical importance. Comayagua was the capital for 333 years, and its decaying cathedral and colonial architecture are interesting. The highlight of Honduras is the magnificent Mayan ruins of Copán. If you plan to go to Guatemala, take the road passing the site.

You might not have too much interest in Hondurans, but Hondurans will be intensely interested in you. Whenever you arrive in a town, people will swarm. With the lack of ordinary tourists, locals treat bicycle tourists like aliens.

WEATHER. Honduras is so hot that even the breezes feel ovenlike. Temperatures in the 35 to 40 degrees Celsius range are common. The mountain areas get cooler, but the sun is relentless everywhere. Try to get most of your cycling done early in the day so you can escape the heat and winds. Prevailing winds blow from the northeast, increasing in speed in the afternoon and occasionally bringing rain in the evening. The wet season is generally from May to October, while on the coast, the rain arrives earlier in the year. Downpours usually occur at night, raising the humidity level for the next day.

GENERAL INFORMATION

GETTING TO THE COUNTRY. All flights to Honduras from Europe and the United States connect through Miami. Tegucigalpa, San Pedro Sula, and La Ceiba have international airports with direct flights to Mexico City, Belize City, and Guatemala City. You must pay a 10 percent tax on all international tickets bought in Honduras, and foreigners cannot buy international tickets with the local currency.

To cross into Guatemala by road, you have two options. The first is via Agua Caliente. This paved route is risky because of sporadic guerrilla activity. The second route is through La Entrada. Incorporating a short, unpaved, steeper section, it's the route of choice for its relative safety and its proximity to the ruins of Copán.

To El Salvador, two main routes cross the border; both require caution. The first, crossing through military zones, sits in the highlands. Land mines are still buried in the area, so do not venture off the road. The second crossing is on the Pan-American Highway. This crossing is also dangerous because of cross-border bandit groups, yet it is the easiest way to enter El Salvador.

Entering Nicaragua, you should stay with the three main crossings closest to the Pacific coast. Los Manos, the farthest north of the three, is straightforward but poorly provisioned. The El Espiño route meanders. You have to head north only to intersect with the Managua–Los Manos road going south. Taking this way is fruitless. El Triunfo, the Pan-Am crossing, is the easiest of the three routes, and if you want to stay on the coast, it's also the shortest route.

Most borders are only open until 5:00 or 6:00 in the afternoon. Finally, because of the political situations of Honduras' three neighbors, check with an embassy or other travelers on each crossing status.

DOCUMENTS. Most nationalities need passports and visas. You can obtain a visa at the border, but it's cheaper to get one at a consulate. If you don't need a visa, you will need a tourist card that costs U.S.$3. If you arrive by air, officials may ask for an onward ticket or proof of sufficient funds, neither of which are concerns if you arrive overland by bicycle.

Be forewarned: Honduran border crossings are the most corrupt in Central America. Officially, you must pay an entry tax of U.S.$2 and an exit tax of U.S.$1. In reality, you'll pay more than that. As you start the crossing process, officials will give you a slip of paper that must be stamped by five different officials (immigration, vehicle authorization, transit tax, fumigation, and quarantine). You have to buy each stamp from the respective official. No one fumigates, no one checks your bags—they're only interested in collecting the "tax." Beyond the scrap of stamped paper, you also need to buy a driving permit, worth about U.S.$3, from the armed forces. A permit can have more than one bike put on it. Costs for all procedures increase on the weekend. When you exit Honduras, you must repeat the process.

ACCOMMODATIONS. Most hotels in Honduras are of a low standard. Hotels, *pensiones*, *hospedajes*, and *hotelitos* are the same. When choosing a room, check for water rationing. The landlord may be reluctant to allow clothes-washing because of drought or concern about the water bill. There may also be a limited period when water is available. Another factor to be aware of is Honduran couples renting hotel rooms by the hour. It is unsettling to watch the parade of couples discreetly trying to enter and leave the hotel while you sit on the patio. The bright side to this is that double beds are very common. Each room has a private cold shower, and landlords have no problem with keeping a bike in your room.

Honduras has no youth hostel facilities.

No paid campsites exist in Honduras. You might find a primitive official spot in the national parks or the Lago de Yohoa area.

Wild camping is difficult. Farmers have fenced most of the land for grazing or timber cutting, so finding a clear spot takes time and patience. If you ask permission from locals, however, they will usually agree without hesitation.

White gas is unavailable. You can find *kerosina*, kerosene, at gas stations, while GAZ cartridges are occasionally available at hardware stores, *ferreterías*.

FOOD. Most of the food is grown locally. Food shortages occur in rural areas and you have to accept whatever is available. You may enter a town hoping for cookies, bread, and a cold beer, but may find only moldy buns, tomato paste, and warm pop. Additionally, food storage is a problem in rural areas, so you should carefully check fresh and frozen food for spoilage. In Tegucigalpa you can find supermarkets, but imported food is difficult to find everywhere.

Restaurants offer the usual set lunch, the *comida corriente*. Don't expect anything grand. A good, common meal is the *pollo frito*, deep-fried chicken served with salad and tortillas (don't eat the salad). The chicken is also excellent to take on the road for a later lunch. Finally, a common restaurant trick is to give you an English menu quoting higher *"gringo"* prices. Simply and knowingly ask for the Spanish menu.

DRINKS. Bottled water is difficult to find except as *refrescos* (soft drinks). Don't drink untreated water, including ice cubes, shaved ice drinks, and juice in plastic bags, as amoebic dysentery is endemic. *Refrescos* and beer are both common, but at times hard to find cold.

HEALTH. If you're going to the north coast, get inoculations against typhoid, tetanus, and yellow fever before arriving in Honduras. Hepatitis is also common, so a gamma globulin shot is useful. While traveling, ensure you have Mebendezol for worms and Flagyl for amoebas. Cholera is also spreading through Honduras, and malaria is prevalent along the north and south coasts and the Bay Islands. Take precautions for both. Finally, be careful of dehydration. The heat and exertion can lead to heatstroke, so always watch your water supply, especially in the dry season.

PHOTOGRAPHY. Film is cheap if you purchase it with money exchanged at black-market value.

MONEY. The unit of currency is the lempira, divided into 100 centavos. Banks in Tegucigalpa will exchange money at the official rate. Outside border areas and the captial, don't go to a bank for exchange because if they do change your money, they do so at loan-shark rates. A parallel market operates in the capital and at the borders. The parallel rate is as high as 75 percent over the official rate. You can obtain the best rate with American dollars and traveler's checks. Normally, checks are accepted at a lower rate. Don't have money sent to you in Honduras; it is a bureaucratic nightmare and you'll receive only the official rate in lempiras. Buying American dollars is extremely difficult.

The cost of living is low, and the current inflation rate is a reasonable 10 percent.

Shops in rural areas will open and close earlier than shops in larger cities. Government offices are open from 7:30 A.M. to 3:30 P.M.; the post office and telephone, from 7:00 A.M. to 8:00 P.M. Both are expensive.

Holidays are as follows: January 1, New Year's Day; April 14, Day of the Americas; Holy Week; May 1, Labor Day; September 15, Independence Day; October 3, Francisco Morazan Day; October 12, Discovery of America; October 21, Army Day; December 25, Christmas.

SECURITY. Street criminals, notably robbers and pickpockets, are increasingly common in Tegucigalpa. Don't leave your gear unattended or your bicycle unlocked. Outside the capital, the risk decreases. The biggest security threat is from the guerrilla and military groups. With the *Contra* still hiding out in small numbers in Honduras, the northeast remains unsafe. Along the El Salvador and Nicaraguan borders, rural areas have unexploded land mines, so don't venture off the main roads. You get used to the strong military presence, as every corner seems to have a soldier with a machine gun, and every road has an *alto reportese* post.

Security Rating: B.

CYCLING INFORMATION

BICYCLES. Honduras imports most of its bicycles from Guatemala. Some mountain bikes are available, but parts are almost impossible to find. With the huge trade imbalances that Honduras faces, bike parts are a low priority, so you should go to either Guatemala or Costa Rica for parts. You can find 26- and 27-inch but not 700C tires.

Good repair shops are nonexistent outside the capital. The small shops that do exist specialize in fixing flats. Don't trust the expertise of mechanics, as it is likely that you'll get a part returned in worse shape. Mechanics seem to consider a hammer a precision tool. In Honduras do your own bike work. The only acceptable store for parts is Debisa on Avenida Mendietta and Calle 2, across from the Presidential Palace in Tegucigalpa.

ROADS. Honduras has 17,000 kilometers of roads, of which 2,000 kilometers are paved. Luckily, the seven paved roads are the main thoroughfares through the country, so traveling on rough roads is by choice. The seven roads are the Pan-American Highway connecting El Salvador and Nicaragua; its connection to Tegucigalpa; the road from the capital to El Paraiso, on the border with Nicaragua; the road from the capital to Juticalpa, in the northeast; the Tegucigalpa–Puerto Cortés road; the road from San Pedro Sula to El Ceiba, along the Caribbean coast; and the route that runs from San Pedro Sula to Copán.

If you stay on these main roads, the conditions are manageable. The traffic intensifies along the Tegucigalpa–Puerto Cortés corridor. Away from these routes, the roads are satisfactory, with decent grades and the odd short, rough section. Most climbs don't surpass 15 or 20 kilometers in length. Bicycling conditions in the cities are atrocious. The capital has terrible traffic and roads, while smaller towns have cobbled streets.

Honduran roads are manned by checkpoints signaled by *alto reportese* signs. Few people ever stop, they just slow for the speed bump, honk their horn, wave merrily at the guard, and away they drive. Since you are an anomaly, do not take chances: ensure the guard sees you and doesn't want you to stop for questioning.

MAPS. Maps are hard to obtain. The tourist office map is useless, the Texaco map is difficult to find, and the AAA map details only distances. Getting a good map is a concern, because at times villages and provisions are separated by climbs on difficult roads. If you are in the capital, you can buy a good map from the Instituto Geográfico Nacional. Take your passport, go between 7:30 A.M. and 3:30 P.M., and prepare for a hassle.

BIKE TRANSPORT. The trick in finding a bus for bike transport is to look for one with a roof rack. Inexplicably, conductors are reluctant to use the lower luggage compartment for anything except luggage or boxes. Expect to pay 75 percent of the passenger fare per bicycle. Watch how they load the bike, as I've seen folding cots stacked and tied atop bikes.

Hitchhiking is possible on the main roads if you look desperate.

MEXICO

Mexico is an adolescent. It's at a point in its development that it wants independence. Yet to progress, Mexico requires the guidance and resources of its neighbors. So the country stumbles, making novice mistakes and then learning from them.

Adolescence also permeates Mexico's social order. The country lives for the moment. Its people enjoy themselves, work when they have to, and save their worries for *mañana*. *Machismo* is exhibited everywhere. The men revere women but haven't the maturity to value them. The women, accepting the social order, wait for their prince to rescue them.

Mexico's beauty, history, and people are its true wealth. Mountain vistas, tropical resorts, and fascinating deserts fill the land. The land hosted the first great civilizations of the Western Hemisphere: the Olmec, Teotihuacán, and Toltec societies. Now you can visit the pyramids, ballcourts, and altars they left behind. The language, clothing, crafts, and festivals of each culture have been handed down to its descendants: the Tarascans of Michoacan, the Tzeltas and Tzotzils of San Cristóbal de las Casas, and the Maya of the Yucatán. Each group resists "Mexicanization," attempting to live by simple farming.

Despite Mexico's growing pains, it has great potential. The people are resilient and honorable and their land is vast and rich.

CYCLE ZONES

Baja California

TERRAIN. The Baja land mass is the narrow, long peninsula of Mexico that dangles from the border of California, U.S.A., and stretches to a latitude of 23.5 degrees, the Tropic of Cancer.

Road conditions in Baja vary. Highway 2, running from Tijuana to Mexicali, is a nightmare of transport trucks, high-velocity buses, and extra-wide recreational vehicles. Stay off this road as much as you can.

The other paved roads are less traveled. Highway 1 extends the 1,692 kilometers from Tijuana to Cabo San Lucas, crossing over the peninsular divide seven times. Fortunately, each successive climb is less arduous, as the mountains diminish farther south. Highway 1 is generally well maintained. As you go farther south, the road carries less traffic, mostly rocketing buses and American motor homes. Highways 3 and 5 are the only other paved roads of note. For most traffic both roads are one-way trips because the pavement ends at San Felipe on the Gulf of California coast.

There are no circular routes if you limit yourself to pavement. Thirty-four kilometers south of San Felipe, the hard, smooth surface unceremoniously ends and the fun begins. The tracks and unpaved roads of Baja present isolated beauty, the reason for cycling in Baja. On the back roads of Baja, washboard sections will make you nauseous, you'll pass sections of sand so deep you have to carry your bike, and you'll encounter rocky sections, chiseled out of the side of mountains, that can crack rims, shear bolts, and shake the fillings out of your teeth. These are some of the toughest roads in Latin America, and no amount of description will prepare you for them.

SCENERY. The Baja desert is not full of the desolate sandy dunes that may come to mind when imagining the African Sahara or the Middle East. Life fills Baja California. There is a saying among the inhabitants of this part of the world, "Everything in the desert bites, stings, or scratches." You'll discover forests of cardon cacti, looking like 10-meter-high inverted chandeliers, rising off the desert floor. Their spiny bases mingle with smaller porcupinelike cholla cacti to produce a chaotic mass of needles and spikes.

The vegetation of Baja alone is worth the trip. For example, one of the weirdest plants in the world, the cirrio, grows in only one latitudinal zone of the peninsula. These limbless trees, bleached white by the unrelenting sun, twist and turn in the sky like a surreal plant imported from Venus. When it rains, small green branches erupt from the trunk, and a large, orange blossom blooms from the tree's tip.

Scorpions and snakes have their seasons. Scorpions come out after it rains and crawl into small crevices at night. So watch where you put your feet and hands, especially in the morning. Rattlesnakes are prevalent during the intense heat of the summer, when they have a habit of lying on the road at night to enjoy the asphalt's absorbed daytime heat. Tarantulas can be common any time of the year, yet this hairy spider's bite is not poisonous, just painful.

These land pests may seem threatening, but the sea, easy to get to from just about anywhere on the peninsula, holds its quiet wonders. Crabs, clams, and fish are abundant, and the locals catch and eat every type of marine life. Dolphins frolic about near the shores of some beaches, and near Loreto you can watch the giant blue whales arrive in the bay to mate between December and February.

Adding a final touch to the bewitchment of Baja's natural history, the sunsets and the infinite number of stars in the night sky are exquisite. The dust captured in the air refracts and lengthens the last rays of sunlight to produce intense shades of pinks, reds, and purples that gradually fade to black. As you watch the night sky becoming darker, the number of pinpoints of light expands to infinity, and the Milky Way splashes across the heavens. From far in the distance, you hear a coyote howl, and the sound grips your heart. The isolation in Baja fills you with melancholy.

CULTURAL INTEREST. The people of Baja are of two types. The first are those who live an austere, independent life, trying to scrape out a living from the land and sea. You'll see them in the *campos* tending a small plot of land or taking care of lonely resorts until the tourist season starts.

The second group works in the tourist trade. The locals loathe tourists but are forced to endure them. Most of this resentment arises from the tourists' disparaging attitudes. Yearly, the Baja people confront thousands of motor homes, each packed with American food, a microwave to cook it in, a color television, and an air conditioner. The tourists cruise up and down the highways of Baja without really encountering a Mexican, without eating a local meal, and without feeling the desert air. Locals feel used and insulted by these *gringos*.

The first people of Baja were nomadic tribes that roamed the area, scavenging for food, water, and shelter. Later a few Spanish expeditions, notably Cortés, arrived and searched for gold. They left quietly after finding there wasn't any wealth to exploit. Following Cortés and his gold lust, Jesuits and Franciscans were the next invaders to fall upon Baja. These two groups had the greatest impact on the indigenous people of the area. The Jesuits were the first to organize and teach the Indians about agriculture, stock raising, art, and, of course, God. Despite these advances, epidemics and internal dissension killed thousands of natives.

With the expulsion of the Jesuits, the Franciscans bore the cross of missionary zeal and then followed the same pattern of cultural imperialism and genocide. Today there are still Franciscan missions in many Baja towns. Small and solid, the churches draw people to town for weekly communion.

Although these churches don't rank as architecturally significant structures, you can feel the area's history by visiting them. Immerse yourself in the missions' past and ponder the motivation of their keepers. Some churches are open to visitors, while other churches closed decades ago and now sit stoically among the cacti and sand.

WEATHER. Baja is a desert—blasting sun, high temperatures, and moisture-sucking winds. While traveling in this area, it's vital to carry lip balm, sunscreen, and sunglasses. Don't underestimate the power of the Baja sun any time of the year. Although days are intensely hot and bright, at night heat dissipates quickly, so warm sleeping equipment is essential as well.

The amount of rainfall you can expect in Baja depends on your location and the time of year. Rainfall increases the farther down the peninsula you travel. San Felipe averages about 4 centimeters a year, whereas Guerrero Negro receives about 30 centimeters. If you are on the west coast, you may see more rain than on the east. Cities such as Tijuana, San Vincente, and Santo Tomas receive 20 to 30 centimeters of rain a year. Mexicali and La Paz, on the western coast, receive 13 centimeters. Most rain falls from January to March, with sparing rain from September to December and nonexistent precipitation from April to August. Watch for washouts caused by downpours.

The winds of Baja blow in from the body of water that is closest. On the western side of Baja, the wind comes off the Pacific, blowing from the northwest. On the eastern side, the winds blow from the Gulf of California, in a northeastern direction. Be aware of the *churrabusco*, a strong storm system that can reach hurricane proportions and last for up to two days. An impending *churrabusco* begins with very calm conditions, but then a fine dust develops in the air. This dust becomes thicker higher in the atmosphere, changing the sky color from a clear blue to an opaque brown. Watch for these conditions; if they occur, start looking for shelter.

Central Mexico

TERRAIN. I define central Mexico as the area from the Pacific coast to Mexico D.F. (Districto Federale), and from the Tropic of Cancer to the southern coastline.

The area consists of a series of high basins nestled between walls of mountains. The basin's main city acts as a distribution and collection center for its outlying agricultural villages. Each basin is like its own city-state, a largely self-contained area with a hub that provides government and business services and a surrounding countryside that supplies food and resources. This arrangement has been the standard for centuries and continues today. Old foot and mule trails, connecting the basins, have been replaced by twisting paved roads.

A ride through central Mexico usually begins by traveling the length of the basin, climbing over the pass, and quickly dropping down into the next basin. Climbs of 20 to 30 kilometers are common.

Altitudes of these basins range from 1,000 to over 2,500 meters. Toluca, just outside Mexico D.F., sits at a cool altitude of 2,600 meters, the highest of the zone.

SCENERY. The profusion of mountains and the exquisite lake region combine to make this zone the most beautiful in Mexico. The peaks and volcanoes patched with pine forests are reminiscent of an alpine country, but the occasional agave and cactus remind you you're in Mexico. The small plots of land that have been deforested for growing corn, tomatoes, and watermelon alternate with untouched swatches of trees, creating the image of a patchwork quilt spread across the slope.

South of Guadalajara and stretching to Toluca is the most picturesque area—Michoacán. Adding local color to the scene, small indigenous settlements surround the region's lakes. Michoacán is where the lakes are more spectacular, the mountains more scenic, and people more interesting. The area is lightly visited by tourists, who usually have resorts or archaeological sites on their minds. Because the area is rural in character and expressways connect Guadalajara and Mexico City, the amount of traffic on the local roads is small, making it even more enjoyable to cycle through.

CULTURAL INTEREST. With the lack of tourists in central Mexico, a bicyclist will attract plenty of attention. Generally, the people are friendly and inquisitive. In the areas where tourists are more common, however, the locals are understandably more suspicious.

The people who live in Mexico's central area are mainly native. They practice labor-intensive farming methods, growing maize in any available space of land that will hold their plants. The area also produces excellent craftspeople, particularly weavers and potters.

A detail of a door in Morelia

As is common throughout the less-developed world, the people of the area either confront living in rustic conditions by hoping the next harvest is bountiful or by joining the rural exodus to the metropolises of Guadalajara and the capital. In the eighteenth century, the *indigenas'* lifestyle was virtually crushed by the colonial rulers. History repeats itself, and today a way of life is being left behind like it was hundreds of years ago.

Pre-Columbian ruins still exist in this area. Foundations of buildings and fortresses dot the lake area. Ruins such as Ixtlán del Rio and Tzintzuntzan date back to the pre-Aztec Tarascan period. The Aztec era is represented by the ruins of Tenango and Calixtlahuaca. Some ruins are situated beside the road and are easy to reach by bicycle. Few are officially guarded, so the locals use them for pasture. If you get a chance to camp on a terrace of one of these ruins, you will feel as though you are grazing immortality.

As the Spanish conquered the area, they founded cities such as Guadalajara, Uruapan, Toluca, and Morelia. The cities' colonial architecture is worth seeing.

It's worth spending at least a week in Mexico City. Start at the Museum of Archaeology and trace the past of the Tehoucan, Mayan, Olmec, and Aztec peoples. Following the trail of ancient history, travel outside the city, where the ruins of Teotihuacán sit as vestiges of past gods. Return to the city and visit the colonial Plaza Mayor, one of the grandest in the world. Modern architecture and art are shown at the University of Mexico, in the Poliforum Cultural Siquerios, and throughout the city streets in the murals of Orozco, Siqueros, and Rivera.

The only precaution to take when visiting the capital is to wear a smog filter when you're cycling. In recent years air pollution has gone beyond dangerous levels, and the authorities discourage any type of physical activity. There's a perpetual brownish green haze in the air of Mexico City.

WEATHER. From June to September, only about 75 to 100 millimeters of rain falls in central Mexico. The rest of the year is dry, with sunny, cloudless skies.

Temperatures vary according to altitude. The state of Sinaloa, on the western coast, is hot and humid year-round. In Nayarit and Jalisco, the altitude rises and the temperature gets cooler during the day. Nights are noticeably cooler, so you should bring a set of warm clothing. Between Guadalajara and Mexico City, the altitude becomes even higher, and although the days aren't cooler, the nights are cold. We experienced frost the times we camped at the top of mountain passes.

The wind patterns of the area result more from terrain formations than from pressure systems. Wind tends to be funneled through a basin.

TOUR OF MEXICO

MICHOACÁN

Distance: 802 km
Start/Finish: Guadalajara/Mexico D.F.
Season: October–May
Terrain: Mountainous
Scenery: **
Interest: ***
Difficulty: Moderate

Km	Location	Scenery	Interest	Comments
0	**Guadalajara**		***	
53	**Chapala**	*	*	
08	**Ajijic**	**	**	
17	**Jocotepec**	**	*	Market Sun.
45	Tizapan el Alto	**		
44	**Sahuayo**		*	
09	**Jiquilpan**	*	*	
17	Villamar		*	
24	Tangamandapio			
15	Jacona			
05	**Zamora**			
15	Tangancicuaro	**		
14	Chilchota			
07	Carapan	**		
39	**Paracho**	**	*	
48	**Uruapan**	*	*	
29	Tingambato			
33	**Pátzcuaro**	***	***	
17	Tzintzuntzan		*	
07	**Quiroga**		*	
15	Iratzio			
27	**Morelia**	**	***	Market Thurs., Sun.
67	Paso de Mil Cumbres (2,886 m)	***		
32	**Ciudad Hidalgo**	***	*	
19	**Tuxpan**	**		
28	**Zitacuaro**	***		
49	Villa Victoria	*		
52	**Toluca**	*	**	Market daily
32	Paso de las Cruces (3,995 m)	*		
35	**Mexico D.F.**		***	

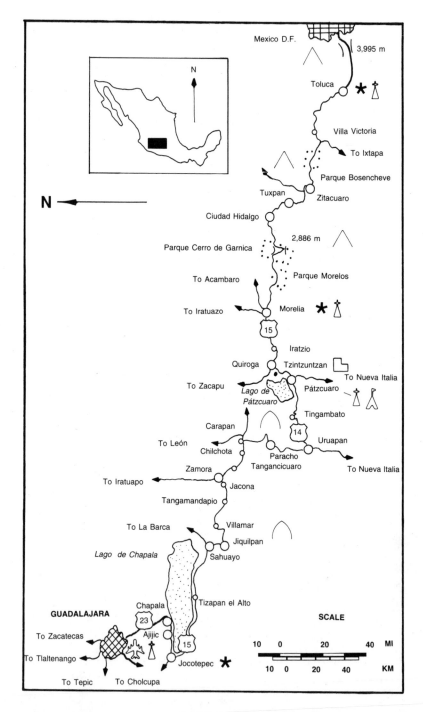

Southern Mexico

TERRAIN. Southern Mexico is the area from Mexico City to Palenque, making up the four states of Puebla, Guerrero, Oaxaca, and Chiapas. Although small, the area is intense.

The southern area of Mexico is the most physically demanding section of the country to bicycle in. Although it doesn't have mountains as high or traffic as intense as central Mexico, its terrain and climate combine to provide a challenge.

The terrain pattern divides into three sections. From the capital to Pueblo, there is a short mountain stretch, where the road climbs and drops steeply. The first section ends with a 40-kilometer drop from the Pueblo valley to the Oaxaca valley. There are no provisions on this road. It's lonely and isolated, so prepare your provisions with the expectation you won't find anyplace to resupply.

The second stretch covers Tehuacán to Tehuantepec and consists of valley riding mixed with 20- to 30-kilometer drops. This isn't as severe as in central Mexico but the climbs and drops are continuous, making it difficult to catch your breath and develop a rhythm.

The third terrain section runs from Tuxtla Gutiérrez to Palenque, where the road becomes more mountainous and severe. Once you've crossed the main pass out of San Cristóbal, heading to Palenque, a long descent passes through various vegetation zones until you reach the tropical plains of the Yucatán.

SCENERY. The light of the area makes taking photographs of the scenery worthwhile. The hues of red, gold, and brown in the mountains seem to glow in the early morning. Conversely, the vegetation, butterflies, and flowing water of the lush tropical valleys add their photogenic exquisiteness.

Agua Azul and the Sumidero Canyon are the two jewels of the area. Agua Azul, situated between San Cristóbal de las Casas and Palenque, is a series of cataracts and waterfalls that glow in a powder-blue color. You can relax, swim, and camp for a small fee.

The Sumidero Canyon is one of the deepest canyons in the Western Hemisphere. A thousand meters deep, it seems to rise from nowhere. From Tuxtla Gutiérrez you can ride to the top of the canyon and enjoy its grandness.

CULTURAL INTEREST. Despite the hazards, difficulty, and scarcity of people, the area's human interest makes up for its negative factors. From Pueblo to San Cristóbal, the mountain areas of this region are scattered with small villages populated by indigenous people. They still follow a culture centuries old that's filled with distinctive costumes, traditions, and speech. Many people of the villages can't speak Spanish. They trade in weekly markets where each group brings their produce to sell and barter. The Oaxaca valley and the San Cristóbal highlands are the two major enclaves of these indigenous peoples. You can explore both areas by mountain bike, but of the two, San Cristóbal is the more interesting. Get directions and a map before heading out. A good place to find out more information is at the Na Bolom Museum at Vincente Guerrero 33. Always remember to ask permission before taking photographs of people in their villages. Some of them are very superstitious, and tourists have gotten themselves into trouble by shooting first and asking questions later.

The Oaxaca valley was the cradle of a past, dominant civilization that predates the Spanish and Aztec. The valley of Oaxaca is strewn with ruins. You can start at one end of the valley and stop every 10 kilometers along the road to view more archaeological digs and restorations until you arrive atop a flattened mountaintop that holds some of the most impressive ruins in Mexico—Monté Alban. The view of the valley from the mountaintop is worth the ascent.

WEATHER. The second half of southern Mexico's difficulty equation is its climate. Central Mexico contains dizzying climbs, but the climate is always tempered by the constant high altitude that keeps the temperature low. The Yucatán, on the other hand, suffers incredible heat and there is little in the way of climbs. In southern Mexico you have short climbs and drops added to hot temperatures. The wetter valleys of this region produce papayas and bananas; if the valley is dry, huge candelabra cactus reach for the sky and exalt in the sun. The heat feels relentless. The Pacific side of the mountains produces hot and dry conditions, giving the impression that you're in an oven. The Caribbean side holds hot and humid conditions that make you feel like you're in a sauna. Both conditions are uncomfortable, exhausting, and motivation-sapping.

Yet this heat doesn't penetrate the mountains. Passes will still get nightly frosts, so you need warm clothing. Perched at 2,000 meters, the cold and wind bite deeply.

The wind of south-central Mexico is dependent on which side of the continental divide you're traveling on. Winds are strong from the north-northwest if you are north of the divide. If you're on the south side, the winds come from the southwest. Still, the Isthmus of Tehuantepec winds produce very difficult cycling conditions. The isthmus funnels the winds that are produced by the differences in air pressure between the Caribbean and the Pacific.

The wind through this area ends about 40 kilometers past the intersection with Ventosa. Abruptly, the wind stops and the quiet that prevails is calming after the turbulence of the past 70 kilometers.

The dry season of the area is similar to central Mexico. Dry and cool from November to April, that's the best time to cross through this area. Another advantage to crossing in the dry season is you minimize the risk of hurricanes and other damaging storms.

The Yucatán

TERRAIN. The Yucatán is the large, flat peninsula that spreads out from the southeast portion of Mexico like a fan-shaped tail. If you arrive from the mountains of Chiapas or the *selva* of Tabasco, you'll notice a sharp change in landscape, vegetation, and people. The land is flat, the vegetation dry shrub, and the people simple. Yet the land is very easy to

The Templo de las Inscripciones *in Palenque*

bicycle through, and the archaeology sites are numerous and intriguing.

You'll find the terrain nonthreatening. The land is flat to slightly rolling. *Puuc*, the Mayan word for hilly, is also the name given to the entire Mayan archaeological area. This isn't a reference to the terrain but to the dozens of Mayan pyramids that lie in rubble, covered in shrub and populated by iguanas.

SCENERY. The Yucatán is a large limestone plateau. Because of the flat, scrubby nature of the land, the natural scenery is boring. Iguanas dash about to add excitement, but beyond that, the dry, hot, and monotonous scenery doesn't offer much: no surface streams, no babbling brooks, no shimmering ponds. Rainwater is cached in underground cavities the locals call *cenotes*.

CULTURAL INTEREST. The many ruins, cleared, restored, and maintained, are the area's highlights. If you enjoy learning about ancient civilizations, this is the area. Some smaller sites are a short distance off the main road and the regular tourist's itinerary, so try to see them if you're in the area. Other sites—Palenque, Uxmal, Chichén Itzá, Tulum— are grand, impressive, and crowded.

The area is a magnet for tourists. Resort-seekers from Cancún and Isla Mujeres take day trips by tour bus to these main attractions. If you want to avoid the crowds, try to get there early.

The Mexican government encourages the development of resorts and welcomes foreigners with cash and spending power. Still, the people are displeased. With the influx of capital and jobs, they may be better off financially but not spiritually. The locals see millions of affluent tourists come into the area, throw their money around, and treat the locals as servants. Resentment has deepened, and the locals display hostility toward tourists. From November to March, these attitudes worsen as the tourist season builds. Try not to take the locals' disposition personally. You may be sneered or hissed at, but don't get angry. Maintain the attitude it's their country and you're a guest.

Speaking Spanish helps defuse the hostility. Although many locals involved in the tourist industry speak English, they will look at you more kindly if you can talk to them in their language.

Off the main roads of the Yucatán, speaking Spanish may not always help. In the small rural villages, tradition runs deep. Mayan is still the mother tongue of many locals, particularly the females who don't involve themselves in business. You can find women in their traditional dress of white blouses and black skirts weaving tourist wares on their large looms. You can usually find someone who speaks Spanish when you need to.

WEATHER. Rainfall arrives from the direction of the Caribbean during the months of June to September. You'll find the east side of the peninsula wetter and the vegetation more lush than the west side.

The wind follows the contours of the coast. Starting from the southern point of Chetumal, the wind moves northward on the east side of the peninsula, cuts across the top moving westward, and then southward on the land's western side.

With the combination of the wind and very high temperatures, it is important to drink constantly. Temperatures in the area can reach 35 degrees Celsius in the shade. Try to take your siesta between noon and 2:30 P.M., the hottest part of the day.

TOUR OF MEXICO

THE YUCATÁN

Distance: 896 km
Start / Finish: Cancún/Cancún
Season: October–May
Terrain: Mostly flat; slightly hilly between
Muna and Oxkutzcab
Scenery: *
Interest: ***
Difficulty: Easy

Km	Location	Scenery	Interest	Comments
00	**Cancún**	***	*	
58	Villa Guerrero			
24	Jct. to Chiquila			
06	Nuevo X-Can			
(47)	Excursion to **Cobá**	**	**	
07	X-Can			
36	Chemax			
30	**Valladolid**	*		
35	Chichén Itzá	*	***	
05	Piste			
17	Dzitás		*	
25	Jct. to Cenotillo			
29	**Izamal**		**	
11	Citilcúm			
07	Tekantó			
31	Tixkokob			
21	**Mérida**	**		
18	**Umán**			
15	Yaxcopoil		*	
31	Muna		*	
16	Uxmal	*	***	
14	Santa Elena			
12	Kabah		**	
02	Left at Jct.			
05	Sayil		**	
04	Xlapak		*	
04	Labná		*	
18	Loltún	**		
10	**Oxkutzcab**			
49	Tzucacab			
23	Santa Rosa		*	
10	Dziuche			
20	José María Morelos			
23	Jct. to Chetumal			
18	Jct. to Launa Kana			

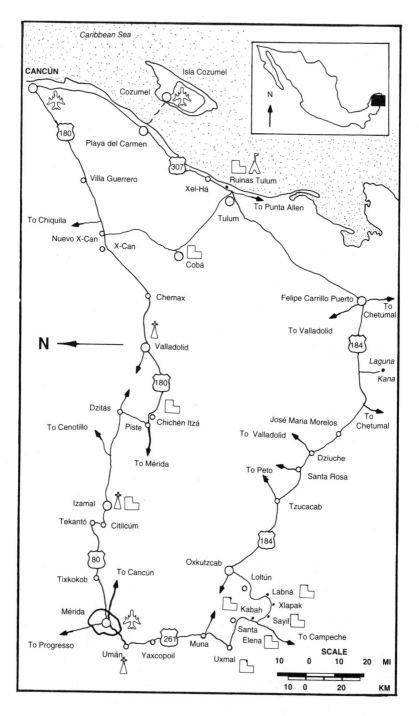

(16)	Laguna Kana	**	*
40	**Felipe Carrillo Puerto**		
95	**Tulum**		
(44)	Excursion to Cobá	**	**
03	Ruinas Tulum	***	***
14	Xel-Há	***	
49	**Playa del Carmen**	**	
	Ferry to **Cozumel**	***	
	(five departures daily)		
66	**Cancún**		

GENERAL INFORMATION

GETTING TO THE COUNTRY. You can reach Mexico City from at least two dozen cities in the United States. Most have two or more flights daily. It's easy to book connections between major cities in the United States and Mexico.

From Canada flights run twice a week from Montreal, Toronto, and Vancouver. Canada isn't as well serviced, but connections are possible if you have a specific departure date.

From Europe, Amsterdam, Brussels, Frankfurt, London, Madrid, and Paris each have two to five direct flights a week. From other cities in Europe, you will need to stop over in North America.

The Asian rim connects to Mexico City through Tokyo, Melbourne, and Sydney. Australia connects through Hawaii, so plan an extra day or two stopover. Australia–Mexico flights are also exorbitant. It may be cheaper to fly to Los Angeles or San Francisco and travel onward from there.

Direct flights connect Mexico City to two points in South America: Quito and Lima. Quito is a good option if you want to miss the turmoil of Central America and the risks of Colombia.

By rail three access points connect Mexico to the United States: Nuevo Laredo–Laredo (Texas), Ciudad Juarez–El Paso (Texas), and Nogales–Nogales (Arizona). From anywhere in the North American rail system, you can travel southward and make direct connections to Mexico City. The train trip from North America is long and tiring, so plan for a couple of recovery days when you arrive.

Buses offer less comfort than trains but are quick and convenient. They travel everywhere in Mexico, and catching a bus at a border point is simple. Each town has a terminal with a destination board. Arrive with your bike boxed and you are ready.

If you plan on arriving by road from the United States, I recommend crossing at one of the smaller border towns. You will find fewer problems, fewer formalities, and less traffic. Here people are more relaxed, the atmosphere more sedate, and the situation more manageable. Later you'll have opportunities to experience the big-city Mexican throngs properly. After you do, you'll wonder why you wanted to visit them in the first place.

Another point to consider when choosing your northern entrance route is to think about the amount of traffic the road carries and the road's condition. Major routes are ghastly for cycling. For example, Highway 15 is suicidal. Narrow and poorly surfaced, this artery shuttles all the international traffic between the western United States and Mexico. Be safe and stay off the main international routes.

Entering Guatemala from southern Mexico, you'll find one main road route, one minor road route, and one river route. The main route is the Pan-American Highway. Crossing at Tapachula is the fastest, flattest, but least interesting route. There are also long stretches along this route without provisions.

The minor road, more interesting than the Pan-Am, crosses the border at Ciudad Cuauhtemoc. The highlands of Chiapas in Mexico and Huehuetenango in Guatemala are worth the effort to visit. The highest point on this road is the section from San Cristóbal de las Casas to Comitán de Dominguez. The first 90 kilometers contain some steep grades. If you are not in a hurry and you are in shape, take this route. You can skip this steep portion by avoiding San Cristóbal and crossing from Tuxtla Gutiérrez to Comitán via Venustaino Carranza. For conditions on the Guatemalan side, see the "Getting to the Country" section of the Guatemala chapter.

The most difficult and adventurous route has little to do with altitude. There isn't even a road. From Palenque you can travel to Tenosique, then to El Pedregal, on the border between the state of Tabasco and Petén province. A daily boat travels the river between El Pedregal to El Naranjo in Guatemala. This is a great alternative if you want to visit the Petén jungle and archaeological zone, but it is very difficult riding on the Guatemalan side.

Entering Belize, the border crossing is simple. Be sure you have your documents, including necessary visas, in order before arriving at the crossing. Authorities on the receiving side are thorough because of the area's drug trafficking. The route between Chetumal and Orange Walk is flat, paved, and untroubled. Traffic is light, people are friendly, and the provisions are plentiful.

DOCUMENTS. All tourists entering Mexico need tourist cards. North Americans need proof of citizenship (a passport, a citizenship card, or a birth certificate) to obtain a card. Most European nationals require a passport when applying for a tourist card, which you can get at any Mexican consulate, Mexican tourist office, or border. The card, normally valid for six months, can be extended through the Jefe del Departamento de Migración, Secretaria de Gobernación in Mexico D.F. They may ask for a doctor's note as proof of your inability to travel or evidence of financial means before issuing an extension.

The card is free, so don't pay a dollar for it at the border. You can refuse to pay and demand to see the *jefe*.

If you are entering Baja California and are planning to continue to the mainland, make sure that you obtain your card at the border. Both states, Baja Norte and Baja Sur, are duty-free zones, so officials do not normally issue tourist cards. This is especially important if you are entering at a smaller crossing.

ACCOMMODATIONS. Mexico offers a great variety of accommodation choices. Resorts such as Acapulco and Cancún offer five-star hotels. Other cities will have accommodations of some type, and towns will have small *quartos economicos* catering to Mexican travelers. The variety and condition of hotels deteriorate as you move away from the big cities and tourist areas. You'll find little variation in comfort between hotels in the same price category. If you see one hotel at a given price, you've seen them all. You should base your decision on the location and degree of security.

The cheaper range of hotels also offers more conveniences for the bicycle tourist than more expensive places. Most cheaper hotels have laundry facilities to hand-wash your clothes, are never fussy about storing bikes, and have an honest, family attitude that promotes security.

In some areas of Mexico it's very difficult to find accommodations of any type. Baja's isolated oases have limited spots to rent a room. In southern Mexico you will not find accommodations less than a day's ride apart, particularly between Oaxaca and Tuxtla Gutiérrez.

Expensive areas to find a room include Baja California, Mexico City, and the Yucatán. Baja is difficult because of the area's remoteness, Mexico City because of the demand, and the Yucatán because of the locals' mentality toward tourists. Few bargains are available in these area; if you want economy, you have to sacrifice comfort.

I don't recommend using the few youth hostels that exist in Mexico. Besides insulating you from the locals, they are usually away from the center of town. Their varying operating hours and seasons make them unreliable.

There is scattered paid camping in Mexico. Most organized spots are parking lots for trailers, with connections to electricity, water, and maybe even sewage facilities. The cost is high, considering the cost of a hotel room. Paid camping is not worth the trouble. Two exceptions, however, are Agua Azul, which doesn't have a hotel, but is worth a prolonged stay, and Palenque, where a campground with a place to swim offers a cheap alternative in an otherwise expensive town.

The feasibility of wild camping depends on the area. In Baja it's ridiculously easy. Pick a time, get out of sight of the main road, and set up camp. Central Mexico is more of a problem because of the agricultural restrictions and the population density. The people living off the land use every patch of it for farming. They cultivate impossible slopes, scraping out a living wherever they can. This does not leave a lot of area to camp in. Southern Mexico is fairly easy. Check out a riverbed or piece of desert. Three reliable spots we found throughout Mexico were the cleared area around microwave stations, football fields, and abandoned rock quarries.

If you find it difficult to find a cleared spot to camp freely, ask whoever is around for a suggestion. Ask the *jefe* or *comisionario* of the local farming cooperative. Ask at lone farmhouses. Ask the guard at the small archaeological zone. Ask at gas stations and truck stops. People are friendly and very accommodating. Just don't ask on the outskirts of big cities or places you don't feel comfortable; use your common sense.

If you need camping equipment, you won't find much, in either equipment or parts. Mexican importers don't stock parts. You either buy the whole unit or nothing.

Gas stations are a good place to find cooking fuels. Most of the PEMEX stations carry leaded, unleaded, and diesel fuel; some have kerosene. GAZ cartridges may be available in large sports stores and the sports section of large department stores. Don't count on a steady supply of the canisters. Mexicans call white gas *gasolina blanca,* and it is available at paint or hardware stores, *tlapalterias.* This supply is also unreliable.

Baja has its own fuel peculiarities. Although you can find gasoline at frequent spots along the main roads, you should buy unleaded and bring along a filter. No one filters the gas, but everyone waters it down, and at times the attendant will hand-pump it from a large drum. White gas, exclusively used for stove fuel, is only available in La Paz, at the sports store at Revolution 1190 and Degollado, beside the large department store.

FOOD. You'll find restaurants of all types. World-class dining starts at U.S.$85 a head, but there are also 25-cent taco stands on the roadside. In large cities the availability is limited only by your budget. If money isn't a concern, it is not too difficult to pick a satisfying restaurant.

When planning meal stops on the road, try to determine the size of the village and the amount of traffic it probably sees. This will determine the variety and quantity of the restaurants. You may encounter areas where there isn't a large amount of traffic, and if there is a restaurant, its set meal will be available for only a couple of hours. Plan ahead for isolated areas such as Baja, southern Mexico, and the Yucatán.

Restaurants open early and close late. They start with a list of dishes to choose from, along with a set meal of the day. As the day progresses, the list becomes smaller until there is simply nothing left, and then they close shop. The local term for the set meal of the day is either the *comida corrida* or *el plato del día.* The meal can comprise a variety of things that the cooks prepare, based on the local specialties or what is in season.

You can buy food at supermarkets, corner stores, and markets. In supermarkets the prices are fixed, the variety is excellent, and the convenience is unparalleled. You can find supermarkets in moderately sized cities. I recommend them. An *abarrote* is a small corner store that is run by a shopkeeper as a private business. The selection is adequate and prices more expensive than the supermarket. You can usually find an *abarrote* in any village along your route. Selection will be smaller and prices higher in the smaller towns.

Markets are the most expensive option for buying food in Mexico. Found in the larger cities, markets are made up of a large population of independent businesses specializing in fruits, vegetables, meats, or dry goods. If you want to experience a traditional part of Mexican culture, go to a market. Most tourists visit the markets looking for handicrafts, so the locals will take more of an interest if you're buying food. Locals like shopping in the markets because they can barter and interact socially. The market helps you live the Mexican experience; the supermarket is for convenience.

In Baja you will find provisions to be your main priority. Empty roads stretch for hundreds of kilometers, kilometers where food and water don't exist. You quickly learn that food and water are precious. Plan to have a carrying capacity of at least 15 liters of water per person. When calculating the amount of food and water to stockpile, find out from the locals about the current road conditions. Unpaved roads will batter you physically and mentally, so anticipate that your daily distances will be reduced. Six kilometers an hour on some roads is excellent time. In planning, also keep an emergency supply of easy-to-prepare food with you in case you have mechanical problems or underestimate the wind or road conditions. At times, people and traffic are rare.

DRINKS. I would treat all tap water in Mexico. Although you can smell the chlorine in the water, don't trust it.

You can get water in several ways. You can find bottled water only in certain areas of Mexico, and prices and availability are a function of the number of tourists. An interesting way to get your water is from the ice factories that you can find in central Mexico. (The water is pasteurized before being frozen.)

Some water suppliers will sell you water cheaply if you have your own container. In southern Mexico if you want to buy water, you will have to pay the market rate.

In Baja bottled water, soft drinks, and beer are available at every gas station, truck stop, and store. You'll never have a problem buying drinks at even the smallest settlement or truck stop.

The Yucatán's water is the most dreadful in Mexico. Nature collects and stores its rainwater in large limestone caves. The lime dissolves into the water, which accounts for the heavy mineral taste in the public water supply.

Soft drinks (*refrescos*) are available everywhere in Mexico. They are easier to find than bottled water in any small village, restaurant, or hotel. The cheapest spot to buy the coldest soft drinks is at the liquor store. If you don't want to pay for the bottle deposit, they will give you your drink in a small plastic bag tied at the top with a straw. Plastic is much cheaper than glass in this petroleum-rich country.

Mexico produces great beer. Like soft drinks, you can find beer everywhere in Mexico.

HEALTH. Except for a few specific risks, Mexico is a healthy area to travel in. You should get vaccinations for typhoid, polio, and tetanus before you arrive.

If you plan to bicycle on the Pacific coast, Gulf of Mexico coast, in areas of central or southern Mexico below 1,000 meters in altitude, or overnight in rural Yucatán, maintain a chloroquine regime for malaria. The major resort areas, such as Puerto Vallarta, Acapulco, and Cancún, are risk-free, but if you are staying overnight away from cities, take medication.

Cholera is on the rise. Avoid raw shellfish and pay close attention to food preparation.

Mexican insects can be horrible. Mosquitoes are a problem on the coast, below 1,000 meters, and in the Yucatán. You should carry insect repellent. Repellent is also useful against ticks. They usually infest dry, grassy places, so check your clothes and body in those areas.

Mosquitoes and ticks may be annoying, but the worst insect is the "no-see-um." These are small gnats that must be entirely jaw. Though they're almost invisible, they swarm by the hundreds and have a ferocious bite that leaves chunks of skin missing and welts around the bite. They attack the softer skin of the neck, arms, and eyelids. The gnats are usually found around cattle pastures and water sources. Insect repellent works for a short time and so does covering up vulnerable areas. Finally, if everything fails, be reassured that they do disappear after sunset and hydrocortisone cream reduces the itching.

MONEY. The major unit of currency is the peso. You'll find the American dollar is the most accepted form of foreign currency. Banks in large cities accept other currencies, but the chances of finding such a bank are low and the rates lower.

At large hotels and in all of Baja California, you can use either dollars or pesos. You will still be better off changing dollars into pesos, as the official rate is higher than the seller's rate.

The best place to change currency in Mexico is at a bank. The official rate operates throughout the country. There is little difference between changing traveler's checks and hard currency. The only circumstance in which the form of money may make a difference is in smaller banks of the outlying cities. They may not accept checks at the official rate, or they may only accept one brand of check. They may also have restricted hours for changing money.

Normally, banks are open from 9:00 A.M. to 1:30 P.M. daily except holidays and weekends. Try to plan to exchange money at reasonably sized towns. Finally, inflation is low, so don't worry about the amount you change at a time.

Large hotels, restaurants, and large department stores will also change dollars for pesos, but their rates are lower than the banks'. Some stores will accept dollars at the higher bank rate if you are making a purchase.

Numerous money exchange facilities operate at the borders.

I would not change money on the streets of Mexico. The difference between the official and black-market rate is small, and anyone who is offering you an unbelievable deal is trying something suspicious.

Credit cards have limited usefulness in Mexico. Only larger establishments accept them. Obviously, they are good for emergencies, for cash advances, and for major purchases, such as airline tickets.

Buying American dollars in Mexico is difficult. Most banks are reluctant to sell dollars to tourists, and the exchange rate to buy dollars is very high. Guatemalan quetzals and Belizean dollars are not accepted outside their respective border towns.

Opening times and siestas for stores and government offices vary greatly. As a rule, the larger the city, the later the stores open and close. In smaller towns they may open with the sun, close two hours for lunch, and close again when the sun sinks. Another rule is that the hotter the temperature, the longer the siesta.

An artisan paints a pot in the market of Zamora, Michoacán.

Most shops close on holidays. On Sunday the smaller stores may open for a couple of hours. Museums and archaeological sites are open Sunday and closed Monday.

Mexican shops close on the following holidays: January 1, New Year's Day; February 5, Constitution Day; March 21, Birthday of Benito Juarez; May 1, Labor Day; May 5, Commemoration of the Battle of Puebla; September 1, the President's annual report to the nation; September 16, Independence Day; October 12, Day of the Race; November 20, Revolution of 1910 Anniversary; December 25, Christmas.

Abarrotes, which are family run, seem to open and close randomly. Some open late and close early; some take a siesta; others work through to 5:00 P.M. and then close for the day.

Government offices are usually open from 8:00 A.M. to 5:00 P.M. Monday to Friday. You'll find post offices open Saturday, but services are staggered, so you may not get exactly what you want when you want it. For example, if you want to ship a parcel out of the country, the post office requires you to have it cleared at customs first, usually at a different location with different hours than the post office. Postage rates are high, but service is reliable.

Long-distance operators are available until 9:00 P.M. every day; expect a lineup.

The handicrafts of Mexico will tempt you. The variety of material and creativity of design are unequaled. Each region has a specialty. For example, some excellent handicrafts include silver from Taxco, weaving from San Cristóbal, pottery from Pátzcuaro, and basketwork from Oaxaca. Bargaining for handicrafts in the market is the normal tradition, but try to be reasonable so that you're not exploiting the craftsperson.

Film is readily available, at about the same prices as in North America.

SECURITY. Wherever we traveled in Mexico, people were always warning us about the robbers and thieves on the roads. Yet, wherever we went, people would greet us with friendliness, or at worst, indifference. We never ran into an uncomfortable situation and never felt threatened. Locals and tourists told us second-hand stories. Whether we camped in villages, left our bikes in the care of museum guards, or strolled through the busy streets of Mexico City, we felt comfortable and secure.

This isn't to say that you should walk about with money hanging out of your pocket or your flashy camera bouncing against your chest. If you take normal traveling and camping precautions and stay alert in large cities, you should not have any problems.

Presently, the political situation is very stable. Occasionally, an upstart terrorist group detonates a bomb or kidnaps a businessperson, but it's rare for a bicycle tourist to be involved.

A minor drug problem exists. Smugglers use remote areas to grow marijuana, and with the government crackdown, joined by the U.S. Drug Enforcement Agency, foreigners are unwelcome in the remote regions.

Security Rating: A outside cities; C in cities.

CYCLING INFORMATION

BICYCLES. If you do not plan to bicycle in the remote areas, a good touring bike is adequate. If you are going to be riding unpaved roads, of which there are only a few in Mexico, then a mountain bike is essential. In either case be sure that you have sufficiently low gearing for the mountain stretches that fill Mexico.

Two accessories I would highly recommend are tire savers, which pick up and shuck off the thorns and needles from your tires, and a rear-view mirror. Many of Mexico's main roads are shoulderless, giving you very little room to bicycle. When you have to cycle on these roads, it's important to be aware of the traffic coming from behind you. There will be times when you have to ditch yourself onto a narrow, soft shoulder.

Bicycles are not popular in Mexico. With the inexpensive price of gasoline, everyone tries to drive a car. Only the poor and children ride bikes. High-quality bike parts, therefore, are difficult to find. A contingent of racers bicycle in the Guadalajara area, which is the best area to find parts. High-quality Japanese and Italian components are three times the American or European price. Touring parts are impossible to find, and the largest freewheel size is twenty-eight teeth. The most common tire size is 28 inches; 27- and 26-inch tires are less common but available with some searching.

If you have a desperate need for a part or repairs, I'd recommend traveling to the United States to find exactly what you need, rather than suffer the frustration of trying to find what you want in Mexico.

Mexican mechanics are geniuses when you need something repaired. They have an intuitive sense of how things work. Welders and machinists, whom you can find through the tourist office, are available at very low cost to fix or rebuild parts that you would normally throw away. The low labor cost involved can make it worthwhile to have a part fixed until you can get a replacement shipped or you arrive in a country that has much better equipment, for example, Guatemala.

Bike shops in Mexico City are usually small stores selling assorted equipment. Most bikes are sold from department stores that don't sell parts or do repairs. Small bicycle shops are inadequate for the touring cyclist. They have neither the experience nor parts to fix high-quality touring bikes.

This is where you can find bike shops in the following areas: In Baja California, a basic shop operates in La Paz, at the corner of Ramirez and Hidalgo. In central Mexico in Guadalajara, there's a good shop at Independencia Sur, near Cuauhtemoc. There's also a repair shop near Obrego and Licencia Verdia. In central Mexico, Mexico D.F., go to 1 D. Guerra and Bucarrelli, or to San Pablo and Jesus Maria. Two wholesale stores operate at Las Cruces and Regina. They will sell if you act desperate. In southern Mexico, in Puebla, at the intersection of 4 Poniate and 7 Norte is a good shop, as well as several others in this area. In southern Mexico there is a basic shop in Oaxaca at las Casa and Ordaz.

Finally, before entering Mexico, have your bike in sound mechanical condition and carry tools and spare parts—in other words, be self-sufficient. You'll find very little in the way of either tools or parts outside major cities.

ROADS. Always think of safety and security while cycling in Mexico. On busy stretches of highway, you can judge Mexican driving habits by the number of dead animals on the shoulder. You will see bloated cows, flattened dogs, and twisted burros rotting by the side of the road.

The roads on the mainland range from twisting mountainous roads to six-lane expressways with a bike path. Seven factors I've found relevant to cycling in Mexico: the first, the vicious speed bumps outside every town and village. Locals call them *vibradores* or *topes*. The second is animals on the road; donkeys, cows, and horses meander freely. Thirdly, trucks without tarps cause grain, gravel, and corn to sweep into your eyes. Another caution: road heaves in the road, caused by intense heat turning the asphalt soft and then shifting under the pressure of vehicles. A fifth factor, the roads in small villages turn into overflowing market streets. Number six, late Sunday afternoons are a bad time to travel because of the drinking and driving among the locals. Finally, be visible. Mexican drivers think they're saving on their car batteries by not using headlights. Dusk, foggy conditions, and rain are dangerous times to bicycle.

MAPS. Maps for Mexico are easy to find inside and outside the country. The American Automobile Association (AAA) produces excellent strip maps covering specific areas such as Baja California, central Mexico, southern Mexico, and the Yucatán. Although their topography lines are indistinct, the maps are accurate about provisions and distances.

For Baja a good map is essential. AAA produces the best map and guide to the peninsula. They detail every highway, track, *campo*, and riverbed (*arroyo*) on the peninsula. Don't go to Baja without the AAA map and guide.

On the mainland, the PEMEX map is a hefty, sixty-page booklet covering every road and village that exists or was once planned to exist. The accuracy is questionable on some details, but it's an excellent information source on what to expect for terrain and major villages. The map also has twenty-one excellent city maps.

The scale of the tourist office's map is too small for anything except general route planning. It seems as though you can find it at any tourist office in the world.

An agency within Mexico where you can buy large-scale maps for backcountry riding is the Centro Deasseoria y Distribucion de Informacion Estadia y Cartógrafia. You can find it at Balderas 71 Mexico 1 D.F.

BIKE TRANSPORT. Thousands of buses run in every direction, heading toward every destination. Your ability to get your bike on a bus will depend on the bus's need for passengers, the class of bus, and your persistence. Expect to pay about half a fare for each bicycle. Try to load and unload it yourself. You will have to take the bike to get tagged at the cargo depot.

Major trains will accept bikes more readily than buses, but security is more of a concern. You will also pay more for the bike than on buses.

Hitching a ride is the easiest method of all. Although not as reliable as buses or trains, trucks scurry on the roads in large numbers. Mexicans are curious, friendly people, and getting a free ride on a truck is always informative and fun.

NICARAGUA

Nicaragua is a battered, struggling country. For the past century, its people have been treated as government pawns. In the 1920s, the United States ordered its Marines into Nicaragua to protect American banking interests. From the thirties through the seventies, the Somoza patriarchy dictated everyone's lives. In the eighties, the Sandinistas overthrew the Somozas and their American yoke. The nineties have brought a fragile democracy that tries to balance left-wing military ideals against affluent repatriates and landless *compañeros*. Through each past political upheaval, the people have suffered, and they manifest this suffering in hostility toward *gringos*, a term synonymous with *Yanquís*.

Nicaragua holds few intrinsic rewards for the cycle tourist; food is scarce, the scenery hot and dull, and the people suspicious. Despite the country's poverty, its latent hostility, and broken government, Nicaragua affects the traveler. Bicycling, you receive a profound sense of poor, resilient people who have lost their sense of destiny. You'll learn a lesson in Nicaragua, whatever your political views.

TOURING INFORMATION

TERRAIN. Terrain divides Nicaragua into three main areas. The first, on the Caribbean Sea, comprises the Mosquito Coast and the surrounding river plain. Recovering from the incessant encounters between the military and the *Contra,* the area is closed to travelers as the military winds down. If you do manage to secure access to the region, most transport is conducted by riverboat. Few roads cross the area.

The second area of the country is the Isabelia Mountains, lying on the country like a triangle. One point of the range begins in the south, near Costa Rica, and then fans northward to the Honduran border. Ultimately, this range culminates in the lofty peaks of Guatemala, but the peaks lie low in Nicaragua. The roads' altitudes rarely pass 1,000 meters.

The third area is the coastal strip bordered by the volcanic chain and the Pacific Ocean. This flat, agricultural area has the two largest lakes in Central America, Lake Nicaragua and Lake Managua. Bicycling through this strip is easy.

SCENERY. The scenery is monotonous. Nicaragua has a few highlights: the sight of a perfectly shaped volcano rising out of the plain, the waves of Lake Nicaragua rhythmically caressing the shoreline, and the stoicism of the parched northern mountains. The landscape offers no grand vistas or breathtaking sights.

CULTURAL INTEREST. Nicaragua was a backwater country until the Sandinistas overthrew Somoza in 1979. The leftist government made

Having fun with the boys on the steps of a church in León

worldwide headlines and became the preoccupation of the American government. Traveling through towns, you'll witness shell-shocked buildings, scarred by bullets. Downtown Managua is a postapocalyptic scene, with only skeletal remains of buildings. Today Nicaragua's interest for travelers is the vestiges of this decade-long experiment of military socialism.

WEATHER. Hot! Hot! Hot! And even hotter and more humid during the rainy season from June to October. The low mountains provide little relief from the heat. The southeast winds will cool you unless you're traveling that way.

GENERAL INFORMATION

GETTING TO THE COUNTRY. TACA (Transportes Aires de Centro America), flies through Houston, Miami, and New Orleans. The only direct flights from Europe originate in Moscow. Aeronica flies to Mexico City and most Central American countries.

From Honduras you can cross on three viable roads. Do not cross north of Los Manos because of the political tension and the risk of encountering unexploded land mines. The two most northerly crossings, at El Espiño and Los Manos, leave you at virtually the same point, Choluteca, Honduras. Los Manos is the most direct route into the Honduran heartland. You have to be cautious at both crossings; there have been an increasing number of robberies. The southern route along the Pan-Am is the shortest, safest, and most commonly used route.

The only route into Costa Rica is the Pan-American Highway; it's straightforward.

DOCUMENTS. Most nationalities need visas. Yet, with the quickly changing political climate of the country, check before arriving. You can obtain most visas at the border. For your bike you'll need a driving form, obtainable free at the border. A bike license quickens the process. Expect to spend a protracted time, usually from two to eight hours, because border officials are thorough.

ACCOMMODATIONS. The word *hotel* can mean anything from the luxurious Hotel Managua to plywood-partitioned, cell-like rooms with a bare cot. The terms *pension* and *hospedaje* refer to the lower end of room selection that offer an unsterilized view of the Nicaraguan lifestyle. Accommodations are generally inexpensive, but it's worthwhile to spend extra cordobas for the difference in quality.

Hotels in Managua, Nicaragua's capital, are exceptions. Few of the hotels accept the local currency, demanding only American dollars. If you don't have them or don't want to spend them, you'll pay an exorbitant amount in cordobas.

Outside Managua the hotel selection ranges from very limited to nonexistent. This poor selection may force you to use earplugs for the loud noise and make you wish you had nose-plugs for the communal bathroom. Finally, Nicaraguan hotels are an authentic adventure unto themselves, providing great stories of local guests, squalor, and six-legged roommates.

A few paid camping spots exist outside the main cities of Managua and León. The question is, why would you want to pay to camp in these locations in the slums and suburbs? Paid camping is not worth the expense and bother.

Camping gear is impossible to find, being relegated to army use. Actually, if your camping gear looks like "army surplus," for example, by being khaki-colored, officials could confiscate it at the border. Finding white gas and GAZ cartridges is impossible, although, with difficulty, you can find kerosene at gas stations and some *tiendas.*

Wild camping is difficult, as people fence the land for either cattle grazing, agriculture, or military uses. Rural areas along the Honduran border may have undetonated land mines. It is important to ask the locals about camping before wandering through the countryside.

FOOD. The food the Nicaraguans produce locally is inexpensive; there just isn't enough of it. Fruit, vegetables, eggs, and chicken are the easiest to find. In the small *pueblos,* staples such as rice, sugar, and meat can be difficult to buy. Imported food is very expensive.

Most small towns in the mountains don't have food stores or restaurants, so planning for your meals is important. This is less of a problem along the coastal strip.

Most restaurants and food stores open late and close early. If you plan an early start, buy your breakfast the night before, or if the hotel you are staying at has a *comedor*, arrange your breakfast the previous evening.

Bring as much specialized food with you as possible. I was in one supermarket in Estelí where I saw a few cans of Russian mackerel, Bulgarian peas, a small mound of 5-kilo bags of rice, and row upon row of ketchup. The ingredients were a challenge to my cooking imagination.

DRINKS. Treat all water. Try to keep your water supply full; it is easy to drink 10 to 12 liters of water in the heat of the day. Obtaining water is not usually a problem, as many houses have a water supply.

Soft drinks, *gaseosas*, are expensive. Fruit juices (*refrescos*), which are made with ice water, are delicious but risky to your health. *Refresquitos* are bottled fruit juices that are safe and tasty but more expensive than pop. As in most Latin American countries, regardless of the state of their economies, beer is available everywhere. The national brand is poor.

HEALTH. You should get typhoid, tetanus, and polio shots. The sanitation system in rural areas is poor, and the *compañeros'* personal hygiene is abysmal. When the locals are desperately trying to survive with what little they have, hygiene and health are secondary. Intestinal parasites are endemic; carry worm and amoeba medication. Malaria is prevalent from June to December in areas below 1,000 meters except for the heavily urbanized areas. There have been outbreaks of cholera in Nicaragua.

Rats are a very serious problem in Nicaragua. Carefully watch where you camp, as they swarm at night. I was cycling into León at dusk as hundreds of rats began scurrying through the ditches and onto the road. They were being pulverized by cars whose drivers felt that running over as many as possible was a civic duty.

Government services, such as hospital care, ambulances, and medicine, are rare. Be as medically self-sufficient as possible and be cautious when cycling, eating, and drinking everywhere in the country.

PHOTOGRAPHY. You cannot buy slide film or photography equipment or have processing done in Nicaragua. You can buy print film with American currency in the lobby of Hotel Managua. Bring what you need; remember it is illegal to take pictures of military zones and personnel.

MONEY. There was once the cordoba, then the nuevo cordoba, and now the cordoba oro. Nicaragua faces an inflation rate of 13,000 percent, so currencies are devalued and change quickly. Don't overstock cordobas because of inflation and the lack of goods. You must pay for tourist services and imported items, when they exist, with American dollars.

A flourishing black market has become more open. Black-marketeers, called *coyotes*, are easy to find. Although you may be offered fantastic rates of exchange, unless you plan to stay in the country for a long period, stick with a minimum of cordobas.

Most shops don't have a major reason for opening. The money is valueless, stocks are depleted, and customers are few. Ask around in small towns, as most stores don't advertise. Store hours are from 11:00 A.M. to 5:00 P.M.; banks, from 9:00 A.M. to noon and from 2:00 to 4:00 P.M.; and government offices, from 7:00 A.M. to 4:00 P.M.

National holidays are: January 1, New Year's Day; Thursday, Friday, and Sunday of Holy Week; May 1, Labor Day; July 19, Day of the Revolution; September 14–15, Independence Days; November 2, All Saints' Day; December 7–8, Days of the Immaculate Conception; December 25, Christmas.

SECURITY. Crime is increasing in Nicaragua. The desperation caused by the economy and the canceling of social programs has driven people to crime. Armed bandits have multiplied in the mountain regions of the Honduran border. Fortunately, most problems occur on or near public transport. When you bicycle, don't hang things off your bike, as the children run alongside and try to grab what they can.

The locals in the north hold an anti-*Yanquí* prejudice. Rarely does violence occur; instead, there's just a latent hostility experienced in everyday encounters. Remember, every *gringo* is a *Yanquí.*

Politically, you should not become involved with the everyday politics of the country. Roadblocks and demonstrations occur in Managua, and since you're seen as a target, avoid them.

Security Rating: C.

CYCLING INFORMATION

BICYCLES. Cycling is primitive in Nicaragua. Most bikes are of low quality and are imported from Mexico, complete with steel lever brakes and 2-kilo chainguards. Aside from 26- and 28-inch tires, which are available at general merchandise stores, parts are impossible to find.

You'll see hand-painted *Se Reparan Bicicletas* signs dotted around towns. Most mechanics' knowledge of quality touring bikes is nonexistent, their tools basic. You need to know how to repair your bike and rely on your own ingenuity.

ROADS. Nicaragua has 15,000 kilometers of roads; 1,600 are paved. The essential roads, the Pan-American Highway and the Managua–Los Manos route, are completely paved. Other roads are in rough condition (filled with potholes, heat-bumps, and patches of gravel—you must be careful) because the government has no funds for their upkeep.

Mountain roads are well graded, and most climbs are under 15 kilometers in length. Outside the major cities, you'll find little traffic, and drivers are used to bikes, oxcarts, cattle, and pedestrians on the road. Traffic moves slowly, and drivers give plenty of room. Finally, few signs are posted, so traveling without a map, especially in Managua, is frustrating.

MAPS. In Managua, Intourismo produces an expensive, inadequate map of the country and a good map of Managua. The Ministry of Culture, if you can find it, occasionally has good maps for sale. Try to bring a map with you, as it is difficult to find one in Managua and absolutely impossible out of the capital.

BIKE TRANSPORT. The whole transportation system is meager. People wait for hours to try to get on a bus or hitch a ride on a truck. People stuff themselves into any available space, hanging out of doors and windows. Gasoline is expensive and parts are unobtainable, so local transport is scarce. Getting a lift with a bike is tough. If you do find a bus or truck, expect to pay two to three times the passenger fare.

PANAMA

Panama is the least interesting country in Latin America. The scenery is insignificant, and the cultural interest is negligible. The country is expensive, and the crime rate is increasing. The country lacks a definitive reason for travel. Panama's main purpose is business; from the Panama Canal to unrestricted bank laws to the militarily defined Canal Zone, the country exists to serve the international community.

For the traveler, Panama is a psychological and physical bridge connecting North America to South America. Outside Panama City, the Bridge of the Americas spans the trench separating the continents, the Panama Canal.

Although no road runs through the Darién Gap, the mass of jungle, river, and swamp buffering Colombia and Panama, Panama remains a crossroads of the world. From Panama you can escape to anywhere in the world, and in Panama you can escape from anywhere in the world.

TOURING INFORMATION

TERRAIN. Geographically, Panama is separated into two lowland areas. The first zone, west of Santiago, is the foothills of the Tabasara Mountains. This section of grazing and agricultural land will come as a surprise if you expect easy, steady cycling; instead, it presents hilly, more difficult cycling.

The second zone, east of Santiago, extends to the end of the Pan-American Highway. This area, consisting of flatter lowlands than in the west, has easier cycling.

SCENERY. The scenery of Panama is at its most lush and pleasant west of Santiago. The rolling hills offer verdant views over tropical valleys. East of Santiago, the scenery is flat, monotonous pasture.

CULTURAL INTEREST. Most of Panama's economy revolves around the revenues it receives from the Panama Canal. The canal, representing most of the country's Gross National Product, also represents Panama's main interest point. Beyond the locks, only two other areas will interest you. Tucked into a corner of Panama City, a few old walls remain from the colonial period; and on the inaccessible Pacific coast lives a small tribe of *Cuna* natives who make a living posing for photographs. Panama's interest to the traveler is small.

WEATHER. Panama's seasons divide into wet, May to December, and dry, January to April. The rainfall in the west is very predictable, both monthly and daily. The mornings are hot and humid; then from noon to 3:00 P.M., the clouds build into large thunderheads. First drops begin to fall around 3:30, and by 4:30 you are in the middle of a solid, tropical

How can the driver possibly see where he is going? A typical local bus in Panama City

downpour. By 7:00 P.M. the sky begins to clear. East of Santiago, this rainfall pattern is less predictable.

Prevailing winds are from the south.

GENERAL INFORMATION

GETTING TO THE COUNTRY. Panama City is a world crossroad, not only because of the famous Panama Canal shipping route, but also because of the huge number of connecting airlines from around the world.

Overland, coming from Costa Rica, the only viable border crossing is at Paso Canoas. The crossing is easy and straightforward. Another overland route crosses at Sixaola, on the northern coast, but it's impossible to continue inland by road.

If you plan to go on to or arrive from Colombia, the easiest, quickest, and cheapest method is to fly; but the procedures are complicated. Panama and Colombia both demand that you have a ticket out of the country, so you need to buy an onward or return ticket. The best way to do this is to charge the ticket on a credit card. You can then credit your account if you want to refund the unused portion of the airline ticket. If you can't credit the flight, you may have to wait from days to weeks for a cash refund. Secondly, airlines in Colombia and Panama require you to box a bicycle to reduce the chances of it being stolen en route. Airlines are usually relaxed about weight limits if they know you have a bike and you have no more than one other piece of baggage.

The Darién Gap, separating Colombia and Panama, is a formidable piece of low-lying jungle. People have crossed it on foot, bicycle, and motorcycle. There was even a British engineering unit that tried to cross by jeep—they didn't succeed.

Crossing the gap is a major undertaking. Among the dangers inherent in this expedition are the threat of accident and illness a long way from medical facilities. Narco-traffickers operate in the area. You will need to carry your equipment over difficult sections. During the rainy season, the gap is impossible to cross because the rivers flood and the route disappears. The trip between Yaviza, Panama, and Turbo, Colombia, can take seven to ten days, and because of the extra provisions and canoe ferries entailed, the journey is more costly than flying.

Admittedly, I haven't crossed the Darién and would only recommend it to the adventurer who craves challenge and excitement. Just know what you are getting involved in.

DOCUMENTS. Most nationalities require a passport and visa to enter Panama. If you arrive overland, an onward ticket is unnecessary, but you must pay a U.S.$4 vehicle permit tax and a $1 fee to have your bike tires fumigated. Receipts are given for each. Keep the vehicle permit accessible, as it is examined at every road checkpoint. The driving permit you receive at Paso Canoas is valid for only three days. You must obtain an extension at the customs office located on the main square in David, submitting photocopies of your passport, entry stamp, and vehicle permit. The extension is free, but expect to waste half a day for processing of the paperwork.

If you are proceeding to Costa Rica, you need an exit permit to export the bicycle out of Panama. Again, this is obtained in David. You don't require an exit permit if you leave by air; however, you have to pay a U.S.$15 airline departure tax.

When entering with a bicycle, officials may ask for proof that you own your bike. Show them a bike license or "official-looking" papers with serial numbers.

ACCOMMODATIONS. Considering the high cost of food in Panama, the cost of hotel rooms is reasonable. The lower-quality rooms are cheap and offer the best value. As the quality of rooms increases, the prices rise dramatically.

When renting a room, always request a working fan. This may cost fractionally more, but it greatly increases your sleeping comfort. Note that only one hotel and one paid camping spot exist in the 240-kilometer stretch between Santiago and David. East of Santiago, accommodations are easily found, while the cheapest and safest accommodations in Panama City are near the Presidential Palace in the San Felipe District.

Paid camping is rare in Panama. Two sites operate, but they are well off the main road. You can camp wild in Panama, but camp near someone's home and always ask permission. At night criminals roam the roads, looking for thieving opportunities. As you get closer to the Canal Zone, be even more careful.

Kerosene and GAZ cartridges for stoves are available at hardware stores (*ferreterías*). White gas is not available.

There is a meager selection of camping equipment in Panama City at the Army and Navy store on Via España, east of the Plaza Cinco de Mayo.

FOOD. Food is expensive in Panama. With most revenue coming from the Canal and service industries, few people produce food. Most food is imported from the States, which is why prices are higher than in North America. For a poor country, the variety of food is phenomenal. You can buy peanut butter, granola bars, processed cereals, and any type of canned soup or vegetable. Supermarkets maintain sufficient stocks, but to buy the locally produced food you have to visit a market. Milk products, rice, and pasta are the cheapest products. Fruit and vegetables are limited and expensive.

Restaurants are the best value for the money. Easy to find, restaurants use locally grown food and serve moderately priced meals. Some specialties of Panama include *ropa viejo*, shredded beef mixed with vegetables and served with rice or plantain, *tamales*, mashed yucca stuffed into a banana leaf, and *sancocho*, a traditional stew of chicken and vegetables.

Prepare for the stretch of road between David and Santiago, as food there is scarce.

An excellent treat found on every street in Panama is the shaved-ice dessert. These cones of ice, flavored with one of a dozen different syrups and topped with condensed milk or sugarcane molasses, are safe, delicious, refreshing, and cheap.

DRINKS. Water is safe to drink in the Canal Zone; otherwise, treat all tap water. Mineral and bottled water are difficult to find, but soft drinks and beer are available everywhere. Panama produces excellent 1-liter cartons of fruit juice.

HEALTH. Cholera has surfaced in Panama. You should be inoculated against yellow fever. Malaria has been eradicated east of the Canal Zone, but west of the Zone, toward the Darién Gap, chloroquine-resistant strains of malaria prevail throughout the year.

PHOTOGRAPHY. Although the Canal Zone is entirely duty-free, the price of photography items is more expensive than in North America or Europe. You can buy film more cheaply in Colombia or Costa Rica than in Panama. Processing is easily done in the capital. It's forbidden to take pictures of military zones and border areas.

MONEY. Panama uses the American dollar for its currency. However, they call it the balboa, after the explorer who discovered the Pacific. Because of the free trade of every major currency in the world, exchanging, buying, transferring, or wiring money is unconstrained and easy. However, Panama hasn't recovered fully from the asset freeze put on by the American government when President Noriega was in power, and there are monetary points to understand. First, when you exchange traveler's checks, compare various banks' commissions; they vary greatly in their charges. Secondly, some banks may not cash some types of checks, so you might have to search for the correct bank. Because of the political and criminal climate, you can't buy some types of traveler's checks. On credit card transactions, you'll have to pay an additional 5 percent tax. Panama is a generally worry-free country for financial transactions.

Operating hours are usually from 8:00 A.M. to 12:30 P.M. and from 1:30 to 6:00 P.M. Food stores (*abastecedores*) open earlier and close later. Banks are open from 9:00 A.M. to 1:00 P.M.. Postal rates for letters and postcards are expensive, but registered parcel service is efficient and surprisingly cheap. Panama also has excellent telephone communications.

Panama celebrates the following holidays: January 1, New Year's Day; January 9, National Mourning; Shrove Tuesday; Good Friday; May 1, Labor Day; October 11, National Revolution Day; November 3, Independence Day; November 4, Flag Day; November 10, First Call of Independence; November 28, Independence from Spain; December 8, Mother's Day; December 25, Christmas.

SECURITY. The Canal Zone is a dangerous area. Yet, with caution, you can travel safely. In the Zone, the worst part of the country, stay in after dark, keep your valuables hidden, do not talk to people while you have your belongings with you, and only trust people in uniform. The rest of Panama is surprisingly relaxed, the people friendly.

Politically, things are tense in Panama. The United States' removing its presence from the Canal Zone, the continuing political influence of foreign governments, and the longstanding corruptness of its politicians all produce tension. The people are angry. There is deep hostility to *Yanquis*, so you should not discuss politics with people and avoid political demonstrations. Recently formed terrorist organizations have bombed political targets.

Some of the country's people are deeply involved in drugs. From growing to smuggling to money laundering, some Panamanians are nefariously entangled with drug cartels.

Security Rating: D.

CYCLING INFORMATION

BICYCLES. Panama is not a bicycling country. People in Panama believe they are above bicycles; only the poor ride them. In a country where the latest audio and visual equipment is sold, high-quality bicycles are rare. Mountain bike parts and touring equipment are nonexistent. Tires (26- and 27-inch) are available. Basic replacement parts, such as bearings and races, and basic cycling clothing are available on Via España at Calle 45. Another shop, offering basic equipment, is on Via Fernandez de

Cordoba at Calle El Dorado. These Panama City shops have repair facilities that are fast and reliable for basic repairs requiring specialized tools.

ROADS. Panama does not produce oil. Rather, concrete is a major export commodity. Subsequently, the roads of Panama are constructed from large slabs of concrete laid end to end. The entire Panamanian portion of the Pan-American Highway is made of these slabs. When the concrete is in good condition, cycling along it's fine. When the concrete has deteriorated, large gaps open between the slabs, making cycling difficult. Cycling is even more dangerous because of the high volume of traffic combined with the lack of shoulders and the narrowness of the roads.

Traffic in the Canal Zone and between Panama City and David is intense. Large transport trucks, delivering imported goods, speed down the narrow, two-lane roads, creating strong blasts of air. Drivers are atrocious and oblivious to bicycles.

Only one road, from Colón to Panama City, crosses the width of Panama. In the capital the traffic is rapid and dangerous, with hundreds of buses dodging in and out of traffic to pick up passengers. Another very dangerous area to bicycle is on the road over the Bridge of the Americas; use the sidewalk instead. Finally, if you want to avoid the climb between Remedios and Santiago, take the old road north of Tole, at kilometer post 329, through Sanja.

MAPS. Good maps are hard to find outside Panama City. If you intend to stay on the Pan-Am, however, a basic map will suffice. You can find the best map of Panama at the Instituto Geográfico on Via Tommy Guardia and Usa Simon Bolivar, near the University. They have scales varying from 1:500,000, covering Panama in two large sheets; to larger scales of 1:250,000 and 1:50,000, essential for crossing the Darién Gap; to an excellent city map at 1:12,500.

It is impossible to find maps for South America here.

BIKE TRANSPORT. You can put a bike on a bus if you arrange the passage with the driver beforehand. Fares are moderately expensive, and there should be no extra charge for the bike.

Hitching with a bike is difficult because of the large number of military checkpoints and the transports that are sealed by customs before leaving the Canal Zone.

PARAGUAY

Traveling in Paraguay is like visiting a past era, one of rustic values. When you bicycle along the country's roads, you see a steam locomotive chugging on its tracks, you pass a horse-drawn cart lumbering on the road while oxen drag a plow slowly through a field.

Yet forward-looking Paraguayans rush impatiently, trying to keep up with other Latin Americans. In partnership with its neighbors Argentina and Brazil, Paraguay is building some of the largest hydroelectric dams in the world, and the country's free-market economy has turned its border cities into South America's largest duty-free shopping spot. Those Paraguayans wishing to keep their traditional values and uncomplicated lifestyles seem destined to be overwhelmed by progress.

CYCLE ZONES

Mesopotamia

TERRAIN. Mesopotamia lies between the Rio Paraná and the Rio Paraguay. The northern section of this area, high Mesopotamia, is flat; however, the farther you travel south, the more hilly the terrain becomes. Long climbs are rare here; the roads just pitch and roll slightly. In the far south, along the Argentine border, the terrain rises and drops unceasingly.

A cart full of brooms on the bank of the Paraguay River.

A forgotten statue at the ruins of Trinidad

SCENERY. Forest covers 50 percent of the zone. Wooded hills are plentiful in more remote regions, but along the main roads, agricultural development has denuded the land. You'll find pleasant scenery in Mesopotamia. If you are looking for quiet bicycling conditions, the zone offers an alternative to the busier roads of Argentina and Brazil.

CULTURAL INTEREST. Southern Mesopotamia offers a nifty cycling opportunity. The people in the area enjoy a lifestyle based on agriculture and handicrafts, maintaining a solid identity through their native language of Guaraní and their folk art. Townspeople create their crafts, not for materialism but for a sense of pride. Each village specializes in a craft handed down through generations of artisans. You can look for *ñanduti* lace in Itauguá, woolen blankets in Centú Cué, and pottery in Caacupé.

Farther south, in the departments of Misiones and Itapua, Jesuit ruins punctuate the land. When exploring them, tramping through fields and evading cattle, you will experience the ruins as they were left centuries ago. Yet, more for Paraguayans than travelers, the government is slowly restoring and rejuvenating the ruins.

WEATHER. The summers are blistering. Common daily highs reach 40 degrees Celsius, with little nightly respite because of the humidity caused by the thunderstorms. The best cycling months are from May to October. These winter months are cooler and drier.

TOUR OF PARAGUAY, ARGENTINA AND BRAZIL

MESOPOTAMIA AND MISIONES

Distance: 1,101 km
Start / Finish: Asunción/ Asunción
Season: October–March
Terrain: Flat
Scenery: **
Interest: **
Difficulty: Easy

Km	Location	Scenery	Interest	Comments
00	**Asunción**	**	*	
12	**San Lorenzo**	**	*	
07	Capiatá	**	*	
10	**Itauguá**	**	**	
07	Ypacaraí	**		
17	Caacupé	**		
18	Eusebio Ayala	**		
23	San José	**		
32	**Coronel Oviedo**	**		
46	**Caaguazú**	**		
112	**Juan O'Leary Sanatorio**	**		
79	**Ciudad Presidente Stroessner**	*	**	
03	**Foz do Iguaçu** (Brazil)	***		
(32)	Excursion to Hotel das Cataratas	***		
05	**Puerto Iguazú** (Argentina)	***		
23	Cataratas del Iguazú	***		
63	**Wanda**	**		
57	**El Dorado**	**	**	
32	**Montecarlo**	**		
48	Puerto Rico	**		
73	**San Ignacio**	**	***	
16	Santa Ana	**		
21	Candelaria	**		
24	**Posadas**	**		
04	**Encarnación** (Paraguay)	**		
(28)	Excursion to Trinidad	**	***	
52	**Coronel Bogado**			
71	Santa Rosa	**	*	
20	San Ignacio	**		
29	**San Juan Bautista**	**		
35	**Villa Florida**	**		
53	Quiindy	**		
46	**Paraguarí**	**		

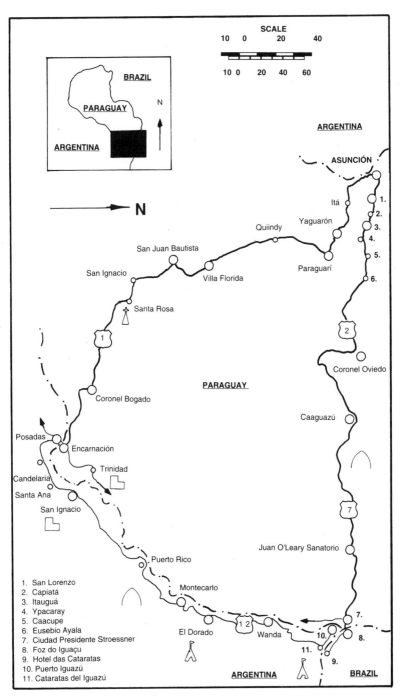

15	**Yaguarón**	**
12	Itá	**
36	**Asunción**	**

Chaco

TERRAIN. The Chaco is the vast, uninhabited area stretching from the Rio Paraguay to the Bolivian border. The zone slopes gradually; from its lowest point, 70 meters at Asunción, it rises to 400 meters at the Bolivian frontier. Besides this gradual rise, the terrain is flat.

SCENERY. Westward from Asunción, the Chaco is a level, marshy area filled with birds and animal life. The swampland becomes drier as you travel farther northwest; the middle Chaco is a scrubby landscape. Near the Bolivian border, the landscape fades into desert. Animals such as birds, jaguars, and reptiles dominate the area. The Chaco offers little scenic grandeur, but it does offer many possibilities to see wildlife.

CULTURAL INTEREST. The Chaco is one of the most isolated areas of South America. People living in this area, among them ranchers wanting autonomy and ex-Nazis desiring anonymity. Recently, with the building of the Trans-Chaco Highway, small settlements have arisen out of the barrenness, but they peter out as the land dries up.

In the center of the Chaco, Mennonite farmers have settled into a self-sufficient way of life. They've built communities that live without outside disturbances.

Farther north and away from the main road, indigenous groups maintain a nomadic lifestyle, living off the land and eating whatever they hunt and gather.

WEATHER. Chaco summers are intensely hot. The land provides little shade or wind. In the summer months, rain falls, making the dirt roads impassable. Winter months are cooler, more comfortable, and, as in Mesopotamia, the ideal months for traveling.

GENERAL INFORMATION

GETTING TO THE COUNTRY. Reaching Paraguay from Bolivia is accomplished only through struggles on both sides of the border. If traveling this route, get instructions at respective consulates and ensure you have your documents in order before leaving La Paz or Asunción. The Trans-Chaco is seldom used, and officials in the area are suspicious of foreigners.

I don't recommend crossing overland from Bolivia. The Chaco of Bolivia and Paraguay contains many perils: exhaustion, exposure, poor roads, and poisonous snakes. You would need complete self-sufficiency. A much better alternative is to circle the Chaco through the more accessible, less demanding routes in Argentina and Brazil.

Three crossings connect Paraguay and Brazil: two roads and one river. The most popular land route is via Brazil's Foz do Iguaçu and Paraguay's Ciudad del Este. As the main conduit for goods between the two countries, this route is heavily traveled. The road is in good condition, with some sections divided into a four-lane highway.

Farther north is the road connecting Pedro Juan Caballero with Ponta Porâ. From the Paraguayan border, a passable dirt track crosses the flat rangelands of northern Mesopotamia. After sending an offshoot toward Concepción, the rough road continues to about 100 kilometers before the intersection with the international Asunción–Iguazú route. This route holds some interest if you want to see more of Paraguay and you don't mind the rough conditions.

The third method of entering Paraguay is via Corumbá in southwestern Brazil. Twice a month a large riverboat journeys downriver to Asunción. Although the trip is long, the wildlife, scenery, and interest level are high. For traveling into either country, this route provides an excellent journey.

From Argentina two routes exist. Which one you choose depends on which country you want to stay in longer. The first crossing, in a far northern corner of Argentina, immediately deposits you in Paraguay's capital, Asunción. This busy route carries much of the international traffic between the two countries.

If you would prefer to travel more in Paraguay, take the second Argentine crossing at Posadas–Encarnación, which is the easier of the two crossings.

DOCUMENTS. All non–South Americans need passports, but visa requirements depend on political winds, so check them beforehand. Everyone receives a tourist card upon paying the U.S.$3 fee. Semiliterate soldiers seem to have fun filling the card in for you.

The tourist card should specify you are traveling by bicycle. This documentation is the only requirement you need for your bike—you don't have to pay for any other fees, licenses, or permits.

Some border crossings, particularly those with Brazil, close on weekends. Although locals cross freely to shop, officials are not officially on duty. However, paying them "overtime" may help your passage. Also, if you plan on traveling on the Trans-Chaco Highway, get instructions, permission, and stamps at the respective embassies to reduce border problems and delays.

ACCOMMODATIONS. Few quality hotels exist in Paraguay; most hotels range between basic and mediocre. Despite this low quality, most towns possess accommodations of some description. Prices are reasonable; just don't arrive in the country with high expectations of five-star service.

A few paid camping sites operate in Paraguay. An excellent camping facility operates outside Asunción's center, near the Botanical Gardens. Other camping sites spring up along the resort area of the Rio Paraná, enticing tourists with resort activities.

Camping wild is safe. In the south the locals use most of the land for farming, but where the locals aren't farming, the wooded hills offer excellent, free camping spots.

When camping in the Chaco, marshy areas in the south make it difficult to locate a site. Farther north the cacti and poisonous snakes make camping a challenge. You must have camping capability for traveling in the Chaco, as distances between *paradors* are beyond a day's bicycling.

Gasoline is easy to find but of poor quality. (Most gasoline is mixed with alcohol, producing a less flammable fuel.) Pure cane alcohol, *naftalcol*, is imported from Brazil and works as well as white gas. You can find GAZ cartridges in Asunción's camping stores, which also stock poor-quality camping equipment imported from Brazil and Argentina.

FOOD. Some of Paraguay's food supply is locally produced, and some comes from the food-producing giants of Argentina and Brazil. Fruit, vegetables, and meats are grown in every area of Paraguay. Relative costs of the locally produced food are low, but imported food prices rely on the current economic conditions of its neighbors, so prices for imported foodstuffs fluctuate daily.

Food is plentiful. Fruit, vegetables, meats, bread, and rice are easy to find. Markets are rare; *despensas*, the general stores, are where most people shop.

Restaurant prices are higher than the cost of buying provisions. Every village has at least one of the cheaper restaurants called *comedors*. Restaurants, although pricey, are excellent places for ordering dishes such as *lomitos*, meat steaks.

DRINKS. You must treat all water. Fortunately, mineral and soda waters are easy to find everywhere, as are soft drinks.

Mate, the traditional herbal tea of the *gaucho*, is the national Paraguayan drink. They drink it hot in the winter and cold in the summer.

Beer is tolerable, while most worthwhile wines are imported from either Argentina or Chile.

HEALTH. Since Paraguay is one of the poorer, less advanced countries of South America, diseases fester. You'll encounter health risks including tuberculosis, typhoid, dysentery, paratyphoid hepatitis, and cholera. Hookworm is also common, so you should avoid walking barefoot and pay strict attention to hygiene. From October to May, there is a risk of contracting malaria in departments bordering Brazil.

Pharmaceuticals are inexpensive and easy to obtain. Pharmacies also provide injection services, but ensure you buy a new needle.

PHOTOGRAPHY. Paraguay is an excellent place to buy film. Prices compare well to North America and Europe, so stock up here if you plan to continue to either Argentina or Brazil. Camera accessories, even the latest models, are also reasonably priced, particularly in the duty-free areas, such as Ciudad del Este.

MONEY. Two forces drive Paraguayan economics. The first is the massive hydroelectric projects shared with Argentina and Brazil. With little domestic demand for power, Paraguay sells much of its share of energy to its industrial partners.

The second economic principle driving the Paraguayan economy is the country's desire to become South America's largest duty-free zone. Paraguay offers attractive prices for international merchandise to its neighbors, who are restricted by heavy taxes and quotas on imports.

To smooth the way for these international transactions, Paraguay has adopted a free-market monetary system. In Asunción and border towns, you can exchange local currency or traveler's checks into hard American currency. The small 1 percent commission is an excellent value if you plan to continue to Brazil or Argentina with their flourishing parallel markets.

Paraguayans use the guaraní as their local currency. Changing most currencies and checks is easy in the capital and border towns; however, *casas de cambio* are sometimes reluctant to change American Express checks, a purely political decision. By shopping around, you can find someone willing to change Am-Ex checks.

Casas de cambio usually operate from 8:45 A.M. until 5:00 or 6:00 P.M. Shops and *despensas* open earlier, generally between 6:00 and 7:00 A.M., closing from noon to 3:00 P.M. for siesta, and then remaining open until 8:00 P.M. in the evening.

Paraguay observes the following holidays: January 1, New Year's Day; March 1, Heroes' Day; Maundy Thursday and Good Friday; May 1, Labor Day; May 14–15, Independence Day; Corpus Christi; June 12, Chaco Peace Day; August 15, Foundation of Asunción Day; August 25, Constitution Day; September 29, Battle of Boquerón; October 12, Dia de la Raza; November 1, All Saints' Day; December 8, Virgin of the Miracles of Caacupé; December 25, Christmas.

SECURITY. Paraguay has become democratic. After decades of dictatorial leadership, the people now choose their leaders freely. The military continues to exert a major influence. This power leads to a heavy-handedness among officials, but if you remain polite and act respectful, you should have few problems.

Paraguayans have respect for others, so encountering safety problems is rare. The country's most dangerous area is in Ciudad del Este, at Brazil's border.

Traveling in Paraguay, therefore, is extremely safe. Few threats endanger your personal security; drugs are a minor problem, and terrorist groups are nonexistent.

Security Rating: A.

CYCLING INFORMATION

BICYCLES. Most bikes in Paraguay are Chinese or Mexican roadsters, though occasionally you'll see Brazilian bicycles.

Routine bicycle parts are available in Asunción. The country's best shop is situated on Cerro Cora, between Tacuary and Anteguera. A wholesaler, the shop supplies parts to smaller shops and the public. They have an adequate selection of basic parts, but don't expect modern touring components. You can find 26- and 27-inch tires.

Outside the capital, locating parts is very difficult. Most shops are a mixture of motorcycle and bicycle stores, and although each city has a *bicicleteria*, providing repairs for both types of cycles, their expertise is limited.

In essence, in the populated Mesopotamia zone, there are a limited number of repair facilities and buses. In the Chaco, however, you must be fully independent. Don't rely on repair facilities, parts suppliers, or the transport network.

ROADS. The Paraguayan road network is rudimentary, comprising four main paved routes. The first, the primary international route from Brazil, connects Ciudad del Este with Asunción. This road is well maintained but busy. The second paved route connects the border town of Encarnación with the capital. This route is narrow, hilly, and quiet. The third paved route, pastoral and interesting, follows the Argentine border, connecting Ciudad del Este with Encarnación. The Trans-Chaco Highway is the final significant stretch of pavement. Presently, this stretch stops 75 kilometers before Mariscal Estigarribia, but the government continues its obsession with opening the area, paving with a frenzy in the hope that development and resources will follow.

All secondary roads are unpaved, with conditions that range from satisfactory to very rough. Some unpaved roads are impassable after a rainstorm because the clay surfaces turn into slippery mud-baths.

MAPS. The only worthwhile map to obtain is the Instituto Geográfico Militar tourist map. Although printed in a horrendous 1:3,000,000 scale, it describes (in Spanish) most of Paraguay's towns, lists tourist information, and most importantly, contains strip maps of every major road route in Paraguay. These strip maps are indispensable, describing facilities and listing the distances between villages. The IGM tourist map is available in most Paraguayan bookstores.

BIKE TRANSPORT. You can't rely on local buses for bike transport. Most cargo, live or otherwise, is carried in the bus. Don't even try to bring your bike along on a tightly packed local bus. Long-distance buses, especially the first-class buses, are much easier to travel on with a bike. Haggle over the bike fare, as drivers negotiate openly.

Hitching a ride by truck is impossible. You have to pay for any help you flag down.

Trains are a slow alternative. All the trains have turn-of-the-century steam locomotives, so long-distance travel by train is tedious and slow, slow, slow.

A last option for travel is by riverboat. Vessels regularly ply the Rio Paraguay, connecting the capital to the riverbank communities. Boats routinely sail to Concepción twice a week, and every two weeks a ship journeys as far as Corumbá in Brazil. You don't have to pay any extra fees for cargo, but arrive early, as good spaces are quickly taken.

PERU

Peru's image as a traveler's mecca is well deserved. Civilizations here reach back thousands of years. The mountain scenery rivals that anywhere in the world, and *campesinos* hang on to their mysterious traditions. The country's possibilities for intense travel could fuel every adventurer's dreams.

Sadly, though, Peru is a country in turmoil. Terrorist groups control a third of the country. Economically, its people barely get by. Morally, it's bankrupt. Healthwise, its lack of sanitation has resulted in a cholera epidemic. The country's problems seem limitless and unsolvable.

As a traveler you will hear wonderful stories about Peru. Some gush about the sights and the people they've met. But you may also hear strong warnings against traveling in Peru. Before deciding to visit Peru, your responsibility is to obtain as many facts as possible. Realize the risks and weigh them against the wonder and enchantment of the country. There are risks inherent in traveling anywhere—not just Peru. So base your decision to go to the Andean mecca by what is in your heart *and* head.

CYCLE ZONES

The Desert Coast

TERRAIN. The coast's terrain is flat to slightly hilly. In the north the road embraces the seaboard and connects the oases' cities. South, in the Nazca area, the road lays along more hilly terrain, at times climbing to 200 meters. The road deviates inland, near Arequipa, rising to 2,500 meters, but then immediately drops back to the coast.

SCENERY. The coast is not for the scenery aficionado unless you are fascinated by hundreds of kilometers of bare sand dunes. The land is stark, dominated by dusty hills. Punctuating the austerity are densely populated oases, a respite from the general bleakness.

CULTURAL INTEREST. Despite the area's unattractiveness and remoteness, the coast was a birthplace of eminent pre-Columbian civilizations. Races had lived and generations were forgotten long before the famous Inca civilization was born. Across the whole coast, remains of past nations endure. In the north, outside Chiclayo, you can explore the huge adobe pyramids the Spaniards named *El Purgatorio*. Southward, sitting placidly at Trujillo, is the vast necropolis of Chan-Chan. Edging central Peru, the Sechín complex near Casma engendered the mysterious rock-worshiping culture of Chavín. Still farther south, the world-famous Nazca lines, large geometric and animal figures cut into the desert floor, lie encrypted on the stony ground.

217

The entire coast, from top to bottom, is an absorbing area for discovering the origins of the later mountain civilizations.

WEATHER. The coast is cool and dry. The cold Humboldt current chills the desert air and sucks away its moisture. In the winter months, from June to August, precipitation arrives in the form of light dew. During this season a mist blankets the coast, infusing the landscape with a monochromatic dullness. Winds from the southwest prevail.

Approximately every seven years, the ocean currents shift to the south. The warm equatorial winds then gather large amounts of water from the ocean and dump heavy rains over the parched desert land. Floods and devastation follow. Known as *El Niño*, the effect last occurred in 1991.

The Altiplano

TERRAIN. Technically, the *altiplano* is the plateau above 3,000 meters in altitude between the mountains. The high chain of mountains stands on the land like a huge rectangular wall. Traveling in this area is difficult, but once you've scaled a mountain's wall and reached the north–south troughs, the climbing diminishes. Roads through the hills and valleys of the Andes are like roller coasters. The passes reach between 3,500 and 4,800 meters high. If you start climbing out of a valley at 3,200 meters, the climb to the summit will be short.

The difficulty of the area lies in the primitive road conditions and the diminished oxygen. You may have a 600-meter climb that is made more difficult by the terrible, rock-encrusted roads and literally breathtaking atmosphere.

SCENERY. In the north the Cordillera Blanca of the Huaráz region entices expert mountaineers and connoisseur hikers from around the world. Lake Titicaca, sharing the southern border with Bolivia, is the world's highest navigable lake and has lured Jacques Cousteau from his ocean habitat. Between the cordillera and the lake lies an area containing a multitude of snowy pinnacles. Peru's sierra is a glorious area, infinite in its views, humbling in its glory, and exalting in its grandeur. Few other places in the world can compare.

CULTURAL INTEREST. The rocks and ruins of the sierra emanate an eeriness, as if the dormant boulders were only waiting for a resurgence of life. Each civilization incorporated rocks into their beliefs. The early Chavín culture worshiped rock as a deity. The stone's life force rose from the ground and radiated up and out of the peaks. The last pre-Columbian civilization, the Incas, built fortresses perched on mountaintops that still maintain a lonely vigil for an enemy long since vanished. Terraces, walls, buildings, temples, and citadels dot the land in a systematic order typical of the Inca. Today exploring these ruins can easily become a passion.

A traveler in the sierra will be moved by the ruins and the people, who are immersed in a traditional way of life. The speech, dress, and values engender a sense of humility in the traveler. You admire their uncluttered lifestyle.

A group of excited boys helping over a rough spot on the road to Wilkawain

The *campesinos'* introversion is a way of protecting their tenuous culture. Each generation brings modifications that chip away at traditions. The Uros Indians, on the floating islands of Lake Titicaca, now subsist on tourist handouts. In the main square of Cusco, women in traditional clothes pose for photographs with their llamas. Along the Inca Trail, porters loaded down with tourists' camping gear and numbed by coca leaves scurry trancelike over slippery rocks. Each scene bites hard into the traveler's memory, leaving a melancholy taste.

If you want to make real contact, understand their shyness and suspicion. Try not to be too gregarious and allow an interaction to develop slowly. On public transport, offering to share your food or playing with their children helps warm the people's attitudes.

WEATHER. Carry warm clothes and expect cold weather. Temperatures during a winter night can drop to −15 degrees. Daytime temperatures are warmer year-round, but become cooler as the altitude increases or you go farther south. The rainy season extends from late November to March, and wind direction is a product of valley orientation.

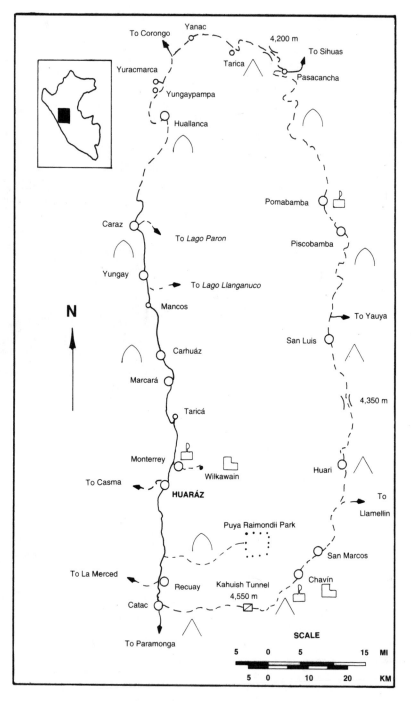

TOUR OF PERU

HUARÁZ

Distance: 613 km
Start/Finish: Huaráz/Huaráz
Season: April–December
Terrain: Hilly to mountainous
Scenery: ***
Interest: **
Difficulty: Difficult

Km	Location	Scenery	Interest	Comments
00	**Huaráz**	***	*	
17	Jct. to Puya Raimondii Park	**		
(26)	Excursion to Puya Raimondii	***		
08	**Recuay**	**		
10	**Catac**	**		
39	Kahuish Tunnel (4,550 m)	***		No provisions
36	**Chavín**	***	***	
09	**San Marcos**	**		
35	**Huari**	***		
71	**San Luis**	***		
70	**Piscobamba**	***		
24	**Pomabamba**	***	**	
86	Pasacancha	***		
(23)	Excursion to **Sihuas**	**		
30	Taricá	***		
18	Yanac	***		
38	Yuracmarca	***		
04	Yungaypampa	**		
10	**Huallanca**	**		
39	**Caraz**	***		
13	**Yungay**	**		
07	Mancos	**		
15	**Carhuáz**	**		
07	Marcará	**		
10	Taricá	**		
10	**Monterrey**	**	**	
(08)	Excursion to Wilkawain	**	**	
07	**Huaráz**	**		

Amazonas

TERRAIN. This area is known as *El Infierno Verde*. The Green Hell is the most challenging area of Peru to bicycle. The difficulty comes not from the terrain but from the terrible roads, the tropical weather, and the intense isolation. This is expedition cycling you should have a good reason for doing. It's unlikely you'd want to venture here if you weren't headed to Brazil.

SCENERY. Around the cities of the Amazon, devastation dominates. Logging lumber, drilling for oil, and slash-and-burn agriculture have led to the degeneration of the rainforest in areas touched by men seeking profit. Workers and settlers have swathed their way through the forest, and their routes have become funnels for destruction. To get a good feel for the Amazon rainforest and its cultures, you must take a river voyage.

CULTURAL INTEREST. Civilization has marred the native Amazon tribes. Forest cultures have had to either adapt to Western norms or retreat into the more inaccessible areas of the forest. Interestingly, archaeologists have speculated that the Amazon region was the cradle of the Andean civilizations, but don't expect to see or explore any traces of ancient cultures.

WEATHER. The weather is hot, humid, and very tropical. High temperatures and rainfall are constants year-round except for a drier period in July and August.

GENERAL INFORMATION

GETTING TO THE COUNTRY. Peru is a center for flights connecting North America with South America's southern half. Most flights in North America and Europe are scheduled through Miami. You must pay a U.S.$10 exit tax when leaving Peru by air. Any international tickets purchased by foreigners in Peru must be paid for in foreign currency and are subject to a 21 percent tax.

Via Ecuador, two overland routes connect Peru. The first is the Tumbes–Huaquillas crossing, a busy, dangerous route that is the easiest physically. The second route is through La Tina, a spectacular trip on the Ecuadorean side, but in Peru the desert road is rough and isolated.

If you want to go by road to Brazil, prepare yourself for exotic, rugged, and unpredictable conditions. The sole route begins near Cusco, drops dramatically to the Amazon basin, and ruthlessly continues to Puerto Maldonado. From here you must persevere over horrific roads to Inaparí in Brazil. Prepare documents beforehand, check conditions before starting, and don't attempt the expedition during the rainy season.

In the Peruvian north, two river routes cross into Brazil. Both begin by scaling the Andes and dropping into the Amazon basin. The first route, beginning in Lima and continuing by road to Pucallpa, reaches altitudes of 4,900 meters. From Pucallpa you board a riverboat going down the Ucayali River to Iquitos. The second route is through Cajamarca and then onward to Yurimaguas. This is the more difficult of the two routes because of the road conditions and the isolation. Once this road ends, it's onward to Iquitos by riverboat and then to Ramon Castilla. Riverboat transport throughout the area is frequent.

From Chile, one straightforward route crosses to Peru, the Tacna–

Santa Rosa crossing. This continuation of the Pan-American Highway from Ecuador, like Ecuador's main crossing, is an intense smuggling route.

To Bolivia, the Desaguadero crossing is the busiest, easiest, and least complicated route. This route accesses the Bolivian ruins of Tiawanaku. The second route, with spectacular views of Lake Titicaca, is through Yunguyo and Copacabana. The Bolivian section of this route is more difficult, requiring more climbing over rougher roads. There is also a ferry crossing in Bolivia. The third route into Bolivia is an obscure, difficult road around the northern tip of Lake Titicaca. Check road and crossing requirements before attempting this route. A long shot is to try crossing the lake by high-speed air-cushion vessel. Its schedule is unpredictable and baggage capacity is limited, so unless the boat is nearly empty, you can't load your bike.

DOCUMENTS. Most nationalities don't need a visa; however, everyone receives a tourist card, valid for ninety days. For U.S.$20 you can extend it for another sixty days at any Peruvian immigration office. Onward tickets are unnecessary if you're arriving overland by bike. If you arrive by air, officially you need an onward ticket, but this policy isn't consistently enforced. Border formalities are straightforward at the busier crossings. However, the more remote and obscure the crossing, the more important it is you have all your passport stamps and documents in order. If you plan to leave through the Amazonas region, ensure you have your passport stamped before reaching the crossing, as officials may not have the authorization to give you an exit stamp. Check exit and entrance requirements before arriving at any border.

Once in the country, you must carry identification with you. Embassies should authorize copies of your passport, and you should keep copies of all your travel documents, traveler's checks, and check receipts.

Borders are notorious for graft. Officials may fabricate any excuse for demanding a bribe before allowing passage. If you have time and determination, you may be able to get them to back down. Just remember, nothing is certain in this ensuing battle of wills.

Bicycles don't require any extra declarations or forms, but ask for a declaration form for your bike to eliminate an excuse for graft when you leave.

ACCOMMODATIONS. Hotels in Peru are called *residenciales*, *paradors*, *hostals*, or hotels. Finding cheap accommodations is easy in most towns and cities; by shopping around, for a little extra cash, you can get more value for your accommodations dollar. Peru offers even more pricey *hotel de turistas*, state hotels containing swimming pools and other luxuries.

In smaller villages, finding accommodations is more challenging. A *parador* may be an unmarked building where transient road workers are staying. Ask around the village to find what is available.

Youth hostels operate in Peru, but they cater to Peruvian school groups. Usually inconveniently located, they are as expensive as hotels and are noisy.

Although there are no official campsites, you will probably need to camp if you're bicycling in Peru. Even traveling the main Pan-American Highway, there are remote sections where, in a day's riding, you won't find a hotel. Most of the interesting areas of Peru are in remote areas, and for this reason alone, it is worthwhile to have camping gear.

Be very careful when you camp. Stay well out of sight of the main road, even if this means hauling your bike for 300 meters over scrubby hills. If locals are around, ask for permission to camp. Also ask if there is any current local criminal or terrorist activity. If so, ask if they know of a shed, barn, or side of a building where you can camp discreetly. No matter how isolated your campsite feels, lock your bike and put your gear away at night.

You can buy the best camping equipment in South America in Huaráz and Cusco. In the Huaráz region, climbers sell their gear after finishing an expedition. On Huaráz's main street, many outfitting stores sell all kinds of camping equipment at prices for used gear that are equivalent to new North American prices. In Cusco outfitters rent and sell camping gear for Inca Trail hikes.

Another place that sells used camping gear is the South American Explorer's Club in Lima. If you are a member, you receive discounts for camping gear, maps, guides, and traveling accessories, though nothing is available for bikes.

You can find white gas, *benzina blanca*, in Huaráz *ferreterías* and Cusco *farmacias*. Kerosene, *kerosina*, is available in pumps at gas stations. Bring a gas filter, as the gasoline is dirty. You can buy GAZ cartridges in both Cusco and Huaráz, but the GAZ system is not recommended because of its poor efficiency at high altitudes and in cold temperatures.

FOOD. For breakfast you usually get whatever they're serving. If you're in luck, they'll be making *sandwich de huevos*, egg sandwiches. In tourist centers you'll choose either a *desayuno continental*, a European continental breakfast, or a *desayuno Americano*, the same meal with eggs. If cooking for yourself, porridge, pronounced "Kwaker" whatever the brand, is easy to find.

Almuerzo or *menú* is the set meal of the day. Lunch is usually thin soup and a *segunda* of rice, meat, potatoes, and a minuscule amount of vegetables.

You usually order dinner, *cena*, from a menu at a restaurant. The smaller *comedors* do not serve supper.

On the coast you'll find a plentiful supply of fish; however, due to the outbreak of cholera, ensure restaurants cook all fish well. Avoid shellfish entirely, including the traditional dish of *ceviche*, an appetizer of marinated seafood.

In the mountains meat is the main source of protein. The poor-quality pieces of beef, llama, goat, or sheep are hacked into chunks and served untrimmed. Fortunately, chicken is good—it's always the best choice.

You should always check dairy products for pasteurization. You can buy yogurt, milk, and cheese from bakeries and sidewalk vendors.

Chinese restaurants can be found in every city, and vegetarian restaurants, in tourist areas.

Markets are a good source to buy food. You can buy either prepared meals from a kiosk or groceries from a vendor. Different areas sell their regional specialties, which means that fish is difficult to find in the mountains and plantains and yucca are difficult to buy on the coast.

Generally, food prices are low.

DRINKS. All water is unsafe. Don't trust any taps and don't drink from mountain streams without treating the water, as it might be contaminated from villages farther upstream.

Most of the local soft drinks (*gaseosas*) are syrupy. *Refrescos* and *jugos* are diluted fruit juices. Both are very risky to drink because of the added contaminated water. *Extractos* and *puros* are supposedly pure juices.

Coffee is made from *esencia*, an awful boiled sludge that you add to a glass of hot water. Herbal teas are common. The most interesting, *mate de coca*, made from coca leaves, is an uplifting drink to try.

Pisco, a brandy made from grapes, is the potent national liquor. Regional brands of beer are usually very good. Another interesting drink is *chicha*, the homemade corn beer found in the sierra villages. *Chicha* is sold either at traditional markets or from people's homes, which you can identify by the long pole with a ragged piece of colored plastic at the end.

HEALTH. Before leaving for Peru, find out the current health risks you face. You should definitely have typhoid, yellow fever, and hepatitis inoculations.

Mountain sickness, *soroche*, is common but affects individuals in different ways at different altitudes. The local remedies of *mate de coca* or directly chewing coca leaves helps alleviate symptoms.

The risk of contracting malaria occurs year-round at altitudes below 1,500 meters, excluding Lima and the southern coast. If traveling in the Amazon basin, take precautions for chloroquine-resistant strains.

Cholera has become the latest epidemic to ravage Peru. At root a disease of poor hygiene and sanitation, cholera subsides during the cooler winter months. Take necessary precautions and be extremely cautious about street food and fish.

PHOTOGRAPHY. Print film is surprisingly cheap in Peru. Slide film is exorbitant. Most major cities have a black market where you can buy imported items smuggled into the country. Film is 30 percent cheaper here than in stores, but always check the expiry date and inspect the box to make sure it is unopened.

Avoid having film developed in Peru. Work is usually done sloppily, and negatives and slides are returned scratched.

Accessories are very expensive. A lens cap can cost as much as U.S.$20. People expect a tip for posing, so carry small change.

MONEY. When I first arrived in Peru, the rate of exchange was 600 intis for an American dollar. Two months later, the exchange rate was 5,200. Six months after I had left, the exchange was 35,000 per American dollar. The inflation rate is difficult for a foreigner to grasp. To cope, only change as much money as you need, unless you plan to go through remote areas.

The invisible workforce and the black market drive Peru's economy.

Money itself is an ambiguous term. Blatant counterfeit notes, without the profiled silhouettes, are accepted, even at banks.

Money changers, in any town where there are tourists, are easy to spot. Look for people in the streets with huge bundles of bills and a calculator. You probably won't have to look for them, as they usually find you first. If you are careful, changing money can be entertaining. The cutthroat competition drives prices up by the hour. Most black marketeers work for a commission for travel agencies, who in turn sell the cash to people needing hard currency. Black-market exchange rates are three times the government-set official rate, but are less for traveler's checks.

Exchanging money at banks is not worth the time. Banks open for exchange from 10:00 A.M. to 1:00 P.M. You may change before 10:00, but the rate is the previous day's. Although banks offer the "parallel rate," it's less than the black-market rate. They accept traveler's checks at 20 percent of the cash rate. Despite the difference between cash and checks, take most of your funds in checks. Security risks are extremely high.

Opening hours vary by area. Most shops are open from 8:00 A.M. to 1:00 P.M. and from 4:00 to 8:00 P.M., although in the sierra, they open and close earlier. Smaller villages follow the "sun clock," opening when it is light and closing at dusk. Sundays in the sierra are usually market day, and most shops are open.

Sending parcels and letters from post offices is frustrating. Regulations are enforced at the clerk's whim. Depending on the contents, the clerk may demand you wrap your parcel in linen sacking, brown paper, or both. Luckily, any items you need are conveniently sold outside the post office. Mail prices depend on the last adjustment for inflation. If possible, avoid having mail sent to the *Lista de Correos*.

Peru celebrates the following holidays: January 1, New Year's Day; Maundy Thursday and Good Friday; May 1, Labor Day; June 29, St. Peter and St. Paul; July 28–29, Independence Day; August 30, Santa Rosa de Lima; October 8, Battle of Amgamos; November 1, All Saints' Day; December 8, Day of the Immaculate Conception; December 25, Christmas.

Each village celebrates its own special holidays and religious events. You usually just stumble on these unique, exciting occasions; few are advertised. However, one event that is renowned throughout South America is the Inti Raymi Festival in Cusco. This solstice festival, from June 24 to June 30, is the biggest religious event in the Andes.

SECURITY. Security is the biggest concern for travelers in Peru; not surprising, when you learn that 80 percent of all travelers are robbed or are a victim of a robbery attempt. Thieves now target tourists.

Peru has an unemployment rate of 70 percent. Inflation over the past two decades is 1 million percent. Government financial austerity programs have wiped out all social programs. So people are desperate. When they see wealthy tourists flashing expensive cameras and carrying the equivalent of a Peruvian's yearly salary, tourists become logical targets. Additionally, the risk for thieves is small. Even if they are caught, Peru's judicial infrastructure is shattered; and if criminals do go to court, their sentences are lenient.

Travelers must look out for themselves. You cannot expect citizens or police to help.

Most crime in Peru is the grab-and-run type, yet violence is increasing. As travelers learn the thieves' methods and take more precautions, the thieves become braver and more desperate. Now they'll wait for days for an opportunity to strike. In cities, keep alert; don't expose any valuables and avoid vulnerable situations.

While traveling by bike, try to stay in a group. Keep close enough so that you can see your traveling companions, but far enough apart that an ambush is difficult. Don't tell anyone your plans, as that information can be spread and an ambush arranged. Before leaving, get advice from locals, police, and tourist offices. At some point someone will attempt to rob you. In the three months I was in Peru, I was subject to four robbery attempts, but only once did I lose anything.

Another security factor is terrorist groups. In areas of Peru, the *Sendero Luminoso* and the *Tupac Amaru Revolutionary Movement* are active. At one time guerrillas did not involve tourists in their activities. Now trying to cripple the economy further, random attacks on tourists occur. The *Sendero* thinks that frightening tourists away from the country helps their cause. These guerrilla groups couldn't care less about their international reputation. Travelers must take precautions. The most effective way of minimizing your risk is to avoid areas where terrorists are particularly active. Your embassy and the tourist offices will advise you on an area's status. Presently, the central mountain regions should be avoided, including Ayacucho, Huanacaelici, Junin, Pasco, Huanuco, and the Huayhuash area of Ancash. If you are extremely unlucky and encounter a guerrilla group, cooperate fully, giving them anything they ask.

There is increasing evidence that drugs are a major source of capital for the terrorist groups. An estimated 20 percent of Peru's Gross National Product comes from coca's main derivative, cocaine. From the top down, kickbacks to politicians, judges, and police are common. These same authorities who accept or even benefit from these payoffs will still take a very hard stance on foreigners connected with drugs. Jail terms of fifteen years are given to Americans and Europeans. For politicians looking for scapegoats, foreigners are easy targets.

Choosing noninvolvement is the first precaution against potential drug problems. Police can arrest anyone just for associating with people carrying drugs. Therefore, avoid strangers appearing overly friendly. Sadly, in Peru trust only people you've approached, not those who approach you. Don't accept rides from strangers. Getting in a car with people you don't know invites trouble.

All these dangers may seem daunting, but this is the reality of Peru. Soon after arriving, you quickly feel the pain of the social and economic problems pressuring the people. Peruvians simply no longer know how to cope. Their social fabric has been destroyed, and their sense of conscience is lost.

Your embassy will overreact and tell you to clear out, but other travelers will tell you Peru was great. Be forewarned that there is a calculated risk in cycling in Peru—greater than in any other South American country. Be alert in Peru. Be paranoid.

Security Rating: F.

CYCLING INFORMATION

BICYCLES. Bicycles and bicycle shops are best viewed as a joke. Expect nothing for bicycles in Peru. I was in shops that only sold water bottles—no tires, tubes, or patches—just water bottles. With the country's restrictive import laws, a 26-inch tire is a unique find. In the mountains, market stalls devoted to selling bike parts sit beside hubcap dealers and banana vendors. These vendors, displaying chains, wheels, hubs, spokes, and bearings in neat organized rows, have parts compatible only with the cargo bikes used in towns as taxis.

There is a bicycle assembly shop in Peru that imports low-quality parts and builds bikes, ranging from BMX to mountain bikes. However, replacement parts are impossible to find, and the bikes are useless for touring.

The best chances for finding parts and tools are at independent organizations. Surprisingly, Peru has several bicycle racing clubs. You can ask at these clubs for information and help. For example, in Trujillo, Hugo at the Demarco Cafe enjoys helping visiting cyclists and has a guest book for all the foreign bicyclists who have pedaled through town.

It's possible to buy replacement parts from bicycle touring organizations in Huaráz and Cusco. In Cusco try the Explorandes.

The best bike shop in the country is near the intersection of Colmena and Avenida Mexico in Lima. Basic Japanese components are available.

This lack of parts and facilities underscores the degree of cycling self-sufficiency you need. If you leave the Pan-American Highway, you must have the most robust equipment possible. Road conditions in the sierra are tough, and parts, tools, and mechanical expertise are nonexistent.

ROADS. Peru's main road, the Pan-American Highway, embraces the coast from Ecuador to Chile. The highway's 3,000-kilometer length is a narrow, busy international route where you must cycle carefully. Visibility is the major key to safety.

Paralleling the Pan-Am, the sierra route stretches from Huanuco, in central Peru, to Desaguadero, on the Bolivian border. Most of this road is unpaved, unmaintained, and unpleasant for traditional bicycle touring. If cycling in the sierra, expect bad roads; rocks, potholes, and washboards can shake and jolt the most hardy bodies and bikes. Even worse, after rainy conditions, roads deteriorate further.

In some places, such as along the Cusco–Juliaca route, the locals have unofficially worn a bike track beside the main road. The track, longer but more comfortable than the road, meanders peacefully along the *altiplano*. It's also possible to bicycle along the railway bed.

Five main routes connect the coastal highway and the sierra. The only completely paved route links Lima and La Oroya. The northern route from Pativilca is paved to the Cordillera Blanca and afterward quickly erodes. From Nazca to Abancay the route is impassable because of the destruction of its bridges by the *Sendero*. Arequipa to Puno is a difficult journey but is as safe as possible for Peru. The last route from Tacna to Juli is also difficult because of road conditions and isolation.

All roads running in a north–south direction are relatively flat. You'll still find mountain passes and desert hills, but they're manageable because their switchbacks and grades are designed for large, poorly maintained cargo trucks, which wheeze and grind their way up the mountainsides. When you travel in an east–west direction, expect arduous climbing and exciting descents.

Finally, if your goal is to pass through Peru as quickly as possible, it is possible to travel entirely on pavement. Your only problem will be the occasional lack of provisions. However, by bypassing the rougher, more difficult roads, you miss some of the most beautiful, interesting parts of Latin America.

MAPS. Bicycling in the more remote areas of the country requires extensive planning. Having a good map is critical for getting information on altitudes, climbs, and distances between provisions. Along the roads, signs, directions, and distance markers are rare. You must carry that kind of information with you.

The South American Explorer's Club stocks a good selection of general planning and hiking maps. The English-speaking staff also help to plan itineraries, and they also have the latest information on dangerous areas. Become a member if you are using their services even though they welcome nonmembers to their clubhouses. They operate three clubhouses: in Lima at Avenida Portugal 146, Breña; in Quito at Toledo 1254, La Floresta; and in Denver, Colorado, at P.O. Box 18327, 80218.

The best cycling maps are produced by the Touring Automobile Club del Peru. You don't have to enroll as a member to get advice or buy maps. The club has offices in every state capital, and they keep a good stock.

The club distributes three types of maps. The first is the *Hoja de Ruta*. These pamphletlike maps detail specific Peruvian road itineraries, illustrating road conditions, distances, towns, services, provisions, and orientation features. Accompanying graphs detail populations, altitudes, gas stations, and medical, postal, police, and telephone services. The text describes the scenic features and towns along the route. The *Hojas* are by far the best maps available in Peru. However, they cover only major routes, and they're irregularly updated. These deficiencies are a small price to pay, considering the amount of detailed information.

The second series of maps the club produces is the *Cartas de Turistica*. These maps, covering a large circuitous area, are designed for specific tours. Presently, the maps cover the following areas: Arequipa, Iquitos, Lima, Cusco, Junin, Puno, and Cajamarca. The maps are an excellent alternative if the *Hojas* neglect a desired area.

The third map the club prints is a large-scale map. This overly simple map lacks details on road conditions, elevations, and facilities.

If you want an adequate planning map that is updated regularly, most bookstores sell the independent *Lima 2000* map.

The Instituto Geográfico Militar is not worth the effort. Their maps are colorful but twenty to forty years out of date.

BIKE TRANSPORT. Unless you are a hard-core cyclist determined to travel the country entirely on two wheels, you'll need to transport your gear between cycling locales. Lengthy, isolated distances and poor security are two reasons why you may need transport.

Buses are the first option. There are speedy long-distance buses that load their cargo either atop or below the bus. It's preferable for your bike to travel on top, in part because it allows you to watch it during the journey. Bicycle fares are 75 to 100 percent of the passenger price. Primarily used for cheap local transport, the slow second-class bus is better for bike transport, even though its journey is interrupted continually by passengers, cargo, or breakdowns.

Collectivos are small vans or station wagons used for short hops between cities. These have easy bike loading. Arrange passenger fares and transport fees beforehand.

In the sierra, trucks are very useful for distance travel. Sometimes dusty, noisy, and uncomfortable, they're an adventure. Truck drivers take any type of cargo and passenger. Prices vary, depending on local demand for a particular trip. Some routes have few buses, so you may pay the same price for a truck that you would for a bus to receive the privilege of getting bounced, jostled, and banged while atop a load of bagged potatoes. Despite the fundamental lack of comfort, trucks allow you the best possible views on public transport.

Trains are another alternative for overland travel. However, before choosing to travel by train with your bike, go to the station and watch the ensuing fray when a train arrives. After seeing the panic and disorder, imagine carrying your bags, trying to watch your bike get loaded, and then fighting to get a seat. Additionally, trains and train stations are notorious for robberies; the worst is the Arequipa–Juliaca route.

What if you don't want to travel overland through some areas because they're criminally infected or guerrilla-controlled? What if the areas that entice you are surrounded by dangerous zones? What if, for example, you want to get to Cusco from Lima? The solution is to fly. The two national airlines accept boxed bicycles as baggage for an extra 50 percent fare.

An excellent value-to-adventure ratio is to book a flight on the *Gruppo Ocho* airlines, the scheduled military cargo flights. Book well ahead and arrive at the airport early to iron out bike predicaments. Prices are half the regular fares, but as for comfort, you get what you pay for.

URUGUAY

In a forgotten corner of South America, Uruguay nestles between sophisticated Argentina and hedonistic Brazil. The most prosperous time for the country was between 1920 and 1950. This small, conservative country seems frozen and forgotten. The Art Deco architecture of Montevideo, the antique cars, and the peoples' values all contribute to a nostalgic ambience of South America in the 1950s, a time of affluence and hope for the continent's future.

CYCLE ZONES

The Coast

TERRAIN. The coast's terrain ranges from flat to hilly. The coast makes for easy cycling, but as roads turn inland or cross over headlands, hills emerge.

SCENERY. Uruguay's coast, encompassing hundreds of kilometers of small bays and isolated beaches that are separated by rocky headlands, is South America's French Riviera. From December to February, the tourist season, scores of Argentines flock to the coast's beaches and resorts.

CULTURAL INTEREST. Interest along the coast is limited. Uruguay is a land of the *gaucho*, the South American cowboys who exterminated all vestiges of earlier native cultures so that cattle ranching could dominate. To examine the romanticism of these renegade cowboys, visit the Gaucho Museum in Montevideo.

You can see another interesting subject on the country's streets and highways. Uruguayans had money in the twenties to fifties, and everyone bought cars. When the boom times ended, the vehicles remained as reminders of past prosperity. Today watching these beautiful old relics putter past is like traveling into a time warp.

WEATHER. The ideal period for visiting the coast is the summer, December to March. Although the area is busy, it's the best time to appreciate the scenery, relax in the sun, and enjoy the sea. Still, rainy periods occur any time of the year. Winters are damp and uncomfortable. Prevailing winds arrive from the east.

The Interior

TERRAIN. The interior's routes roll through hilly terrain. Two minor ranges of hills lie in the interior, Cuchilla de Haedo and Cuchilla Grande. The hills, neither of which rise above 500 meters, originate in Brazil, stretch southward into Uruguay, and sputter in Uruguay's heartland.

SCENERY. Ranchers use most of Uruguay's interior for cattle grazing. Bicycling past the herds of cattle that dot the green pastures is idyllic.

Hydroelectric dams create huge artificial lakes, which are used as resorts by Uruguayans, who like to participate in water sports, camping, and fishing—anything that gets them outdoors.

CULTURAL INTEREST. Cultural interest is minimal to nonexistent, as farmers and *gauchos* oversee the area.

WEATHER. Weather conditions are identical to the coast: easterly winds, cool winters, warm summers, and regular rainfall.

GENERAL INFORMATION

GETTING TO THE COUNTRY. Three major routes cross from Brazil into Uruguay, the most popular of which is at Chuy. This coastal crossing is a chaotic, duty-free town where Brazilians sell their manufactured goods to Uruguayans. The second, a central route that crosses at Rivera, is quiet and unpaved. This route necessitates a long trip through Uruguay's interior and an isolated section of Brazil's Rio Grande area.

If you arrive from Iguazú or Posadas, Argentina, the ideal crossing is at Bella Union, on the Rio Uruguay, 640 kilometers from Montevideo. In Uruguay you'll face unpaved sections between the border and farther in the interior at Salto.

Entering from Argentina, you have three options for roads crossing over the Rio Uruguay and two boat routes across the Rio de la Plata. If you arrive from northern Argentina, the three crossings are similar and depend on where you arrive from in Argentina and where you plan on going in Uruguay. Some bridges may charge a small toll for bicycles. Entering from central or farther south in Argentina, no direct road routes exist, and it's a long circumnavigation around a marshy delta to reach Fray Bentos, the first road crossing.

Quicker and easier are the two available ferries across the Rio de la Plata. One ferry route takes two and a half hours to cross from Buenos Aires to Colonia, 177 kilometers west of Montevideo. The second ferry route begins in Buenos Aires, chugs its way down the Rio de la Plata, and arrives the next morning in Montevideo. Both convenient routes cost the same (neither charges for bicycles).

DOCUMENTS. Few nationalities need visas; however, all non–South Americans must fill out tourist cards. Procedures for entering with bicycles vary: Some border posts will ignore a bike completely, while others fill out lengthy customs declaration forms. The entire process is moot, as officials ignore the customs issue when you leave the country. If you leave the country by air, you must fill out an exit card, but it's unnecessary when you exit overland.

ACCOMMODATIONS. Most hotels along the coast are expensive, although some reasonably priced ones are hidden away. Cheaper accommodations, known as *alojamientos, habitaciones,* and *residenciales,* are difficult to find because locals use the rooms as apartments for indefinite stays. In the summer you may run into problems with reservations. You can find youth hostels, *albergues de juveniles*, in most cities, but you need a Uruguayan or South American Hostel card. A YHA (Youth Hostels of America) card is not sufficient.

The cheapest and most convenient method for sleeping in Uruguay is camping. Paid or wild, camping is a popular, accepted activity. Most cities have paid camping facilities with varying amenities. Along the coast many private campgrounds operate, and in the interior, you can easily find cheaper sites. Municipal sites offering basic services are the least expensive.

Wild camping is usually as easy and as accepted as paid camping. On the coast, eucalyptus groves provide a comfortable, sweet-smelling spot to pitch a tent, and you may find yourself with neighbors. In the interior you'll find wild camping sites with difficulty because of the fenced land.

Typically, the low-quality camping equipment is a poor value.

Basic gasoline for stove fuel is also expensive. Kerosene (*querosene*) is sold at gas stations or supermarkets, while alcohol is sold only in supermarkets. GAZ cartridges, imported from Brazil, are expensive and sold in camping stores or *armerias*, weapon stores.

FOOD. The good news: Dairy and meat products are cheap. The bad news: Everything else is expensive. Fruit and vegetables top the list of expensive items, and prices vary, depending on the season. Imported and processed food prices equal those in North American and European countries.

Finding cheap lunches is easy; ask for the *menú económico*. Suppers are difficult to find, as Uruguayans tend to eat a light, early supper. Pizzas and *chavitos* (hamburgers) can be found everywhere, at almost any time.

DRINKS. Hurrah! Uruguayan water is safe. If you're unconvinced, the country's brand of mineral water is widely available and reasonably priced. Soft drinks, imported from Brazil, are very expensive. As in all the countries bordering the pampas, *mate* is the national herbal tea. Drinking *mate* is a Uruguayan obsession; slurping it constantly, Uruguayans are never without their ornate *mate* cups.

HEALTH. Traveling in Uruguay poses no specific health risks. Water is safe to drink, you can eat fruit and vegetables, and endemic diseases are rare. There is a slight risk of hepatitis and be careful of cholera.

Health services are expensive, and not all pharmacies sell drugs over the counter. For example, gamma globulin serum is available only with a doctor's prescription.

PHOTOGRAPHY. As with all imported items arriving in Uruguay, film and camera accessory prices are exorbitant.

MONEY. Banks and *casas de cambio* operate in every major city. In either facility it's easy to change cash or traveler's checks into pesos. There is only a small commission for changing either, and in some Montevideo facilities there is no charge. Shop around for the best rates at both banks and exchange houses.

Uruguay runs a free-market economy, so it's possible to buy American dollars with traveler's checks. If you plan to travel into Uruguay's neighboring countries, Argentina and Brazil, change as much money as you feel comfortable carrying.

Uruguayan banks keep bizarre hours, opening during the summer from 1:00 to 5:00 P.M. and in the winter from noon to 4:00 P.M. Rarely closing for the siesta, most stores keep regular hours, from 8:00 A.M. to 6:00 P.M. daily, except on Saturday's half day.

SECURITY. Uruguay is one of the safest countries in South America. People are respectful and unobtrusive. Still, in Montevideo don't take chances with your gear. Since the last election in 1989, the military has chosen not to intervene in politics. No terrorist groups operate, and drug-influenced violence is rare.

Security Rating: A.

CYCLING INFORMATION

BICYCLES. Uruguayan bicycles are basic. Finding bike shops is difficult, and when you do, they sell cruisers and BMXs. Occasionally, you can find mountain bike parts in motorcycle shops. In Montevideo, on 1171 Uruguay, a modest shop sells a tolerable selection of simple parts, including 26- and 27-inch tires and brake shoes. In the capital there's also a commendable shop for complex repairs, such as welding and truing, on Avenida Payamandu near Cuareim.

ROADS. The only road with heavy traffic is the coastal road, the Inter-Balenario. Along the road, the flow of traffic starts and stops, reacting to traffic lights at every busy intersection. Most roads have a paved shoulder, but Uruguayans use it as a slow lane, which adds an extra passing lane. This habit transforms a single-lane highway into a suicidal raceway. Traffic conditions are also intense during the summer rush, so use caution and a rear-view mirror. The good thing about the road is the consistent and accurate signs and kilometer markings.

Spur routes, notably the R-9, veer off to the coast. Roads away from the coast have little traffic and are well maintained. Most main routes running north from Montevideo are paved, but then lapse into gravel farther north.

MAPS. ANCAP, the state oil company, produces the country's best map, but finding a copy is difficult. Because of the country's size and its lack of major climbs, you don't need a small-scale map with detailed elevations.

The Uruguayan Tourist Office has comprehensive information for the country, including a free map that details distances, a strip map of the coastal highway, and exhaustive tourist literature written in Spanish.

BIKE TRANSPORT. Most buses traveling in Uruguay are huge Brazilian monsters, with massive amounts of cargo space. Your chances of using the space depend on the number of passengers and the amount of cargo the buses are carrying. Since few people use the inefficient post office, buses deliver mail and packages. Talking to the office's baggage personnel and the driver usually helps in getting your bike carried.

Hitchhiking is a popular form of travel in Uruguay, but your chances of getting a ride with a bike are remote. The few pickups and trucks are not likely to stop.

Passenger trains are nonexistent.

VENEZUELA

A decade ago travelers shunned Venezuela; its politics and extremely high cost of living made visiting the country dangerous and expensive. Times have changed. Venezuela's volatile political system is calmer, and because of the depressed oil market, prices have plummeted. Venezuela is now affordable for travelers, and the country is taking advantage of the fact by developing an extensive infrastructure. Thousands of sightseers visit the attractions in each region: Isla Margarita off the coast, the snow-covered Sierra Nevada of the interior, and the remote Angel Falls of the Gran Sabana. Venezuela has become more attractive, both for its beauty and for your wallet.

Leaving the Gran Sabana, the stunning highlands in Venezuela

CYCLE ZONES

The North

TERRAIN. Venezuela's northern zone includes the narrow Caribbean coast and the mountains. The coastal strip lies in a narrow band, bracketed by the sea and mountains. Around Maracaibo Lake, the most level section, is the country's oil source.

The mountains act like a wall. Abruptly, the land rises. Caracas, sitting close to the coast, is a surprising 900 meters above sea level. West of Caracas the terrain becomes more extreme. The highest peaks are over 5,000 meters high, and roads, following the valleys, alternately rise and drop. East of Caracas, altitudes decrease, with average altitudes under 2,000 meters. The terrain drops to sea level around Guanape and then rises to a short range around Maturín.

SCENERY. To fully appreciate the Caribbean beaches, leave the mainland. Most of the tropical paradises are on islands, so if you need rest or relaxation, they provide the best opportunities. Conveniently, ferries shuttle passengers between the islands and mainland.

Seizing most of the coasts, industries scar the landscape with ports, oil refineries, and petrochemical factories. The most attractive coastal area is through the Mochima National Park, east of Puerto La Cruz.

The mountains and its basins are scenic. Either heavily forested or intensely cultivated, the area is adorned in a thick carpet of greenery. Above the tree line, snow adds visual appeal.

CULTURAL INTEREST. A strong Caribbean influence pervades the coast, particularly in the ports. Along the Paraguana Peninsula, you can find indigenous people. The peninsula's road system allows you to complete a circular tour. Ultimately, unless oil fields and factories interest you, the coast is of little interest.

Venezuela was the birthplace of colonialism. San Martín, the liberator and icon of South American nationalism, was born in the Venezuelan mountains. The people, maintaining their proud past, uphold the colonial character of their cities and towns. Visit the cities of Valencia, Maracay, Trujillo, and Mérida.

WEATHER. The coastal area is scorching. The area around Lago Maracaibo boasts South America's highest average daily temperature. Away from the lake area, the high temperatures and humidity are tempered by an offshore breeze providing relief.

In the mountains temperatures are moderate, with July maximums of 34 degrees and January minimums of 9 degrees Celsius. Night temperatures are cool, but the greatest effect on the daily extremes is the altitude. Usually, rain falls in short bursts within the May-through-November rainy season.

Guyana

TERRAIN. The Guyana zone encompasses an extensive area from the Brazilian border to the foothills of the sierra. Geographically, the zone consists of three areas, the southern Gran Sabana, the central plains of the Llanos, and, nestled in the northeastern corner, the Amacuro delta.

The Gran Sabana, a large plateau, is punctuated by mesas and buttes of stunning beauty. Roads within this area are flat to rolling.

The Llanos, an area of forest and savanna, is flat to rolling, while the marshy Amacuro delta is level.

A curious pet parrot in Santa Elena de Uairén.

SCENERY. The Gran Sabana, Venezuela's most scenic area, is also its most unique. Colorful buttes rise out of the plateau, and waterfalls tumble over escarpments. Angel Falls, the world's highest waterfall, hides in this zone, but reaching it takes perseverance. Other waterfalls, each with unrivaled character, are within easy access of the main highway. Various national parks in the area offer the traveler unique adventures.

The Llanos region, although not as breathtaking as the Gran Sabana, holds a large variety of wildlife. Jaguars, monkeys, caymans, and thousands of birds inhabit the area, making it exciting to explore.

CULTURAL INTEREST. Similar to the sierra, the Amazon region of Guyana has its colonial reminders. If you visit the area, try reaching the castle near San Fernando de Atabapo, a gateway to the Rio Orinoco and the Amazon River. Today indigenous tribes exist within the more remote area of the Llanos plains, but more accessible are the Gran Sabana settlements. Located near the roadside, the groups live by subsistence farming and government funding. If you visit the villages, ask the chief's, *jefe's*, permission to stay or explore.

Other interesting aspects of the Llanos area are the gold diggers and diamond seekers. You can access their makeshift camps by four-wheel-drive vehicles. The miners are dispersed along the trails, and drivers deposit the fortune seekers among the camps. Women should be careful or even avoid venturing into these isolated, lawless areas.

You get a feel for the gold-digger's raunchy lifestyle by sticking around town on a weekend night. Drunken miners and brazen hookers party boisterously, backed by the sound of caterwauling country-western bands.

WEATHER. The weather is hot and windless within the Llanos, while Gran Sabana temperatures are cooler because of the higher altitude. The rainy season extends from May through November, with predominantly eastern winds.

TOUR OF VENEZUELA

THE GRAN SABANA

Distance: 746 km
Start/Finish: Ciudad Guyana/ Santa Elena de Uairén
Season: September–April
Terrain: Flat to hilly
Scenery: ***
Interest: *
Difficulty: Moderate, due to the scarcity of provisions

Km	Location	Scenery	Interest	Comments
00	**Ciudad Guyana**	*	**	
56	**Upata**	**		
140	**Guasipati**	**		
30	**El Callao**	**		
40	**Tumeremo**	**		
108	**El Dorado**	**	**	
88	**San Isidro**	**	**	
12	Piedra de la Virgen	***		No provisions
18	Salto El Danto	***		No provisions
16	Monumento al Soldado Pionero	***	*	No provisions
04	La Ciudadela	**		No provisions
60	Salto Kamá	***		No provisions
66	La Laja	***		No provisions
48	San Francisco de Yuruaní	***	***	
30	Quebrada Jáspe	***		No provisions
30	**Santa Elena de Uairén**	***		

GENERAL INFORMATION

GETTING TO THE COUNTRY. International airfares to Venezuela are some of the cheapest South American access flights available. North Americans discovering the resort areas have made charter flights easier to obtain.

Overland, from Colombia, two major routes cross into Venezuela. The coastal route through Maicao is a smuggling belt that comes under intense scrutiny on both sides of the border. Narcotics and black-market goods make this crossing dubious. The more difficult but more scenic crossing is at Cúcuta. This mountainous route is less stressful, having simpler procedures and easier entry than the northern route. A minor crossing exists at Arauca, in the Amazon basin. Expect a lot of questions

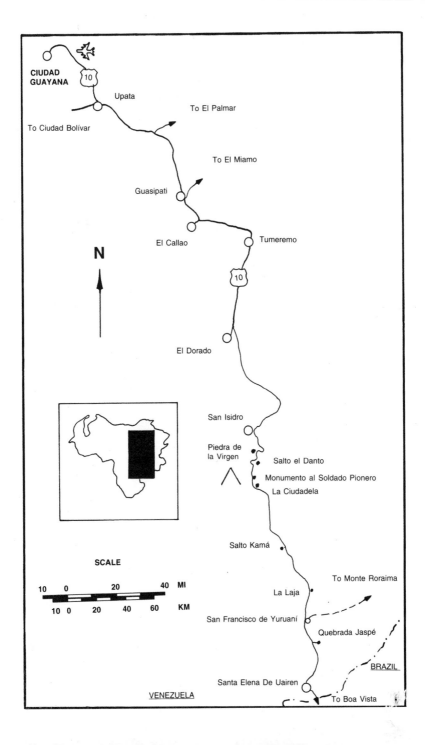

and formalities if you use this crossing. The route is difficult, and the Venezuelan road connects back to the Cúcuta route.

If you arrive from Brazil, you'll find enormous difficulty in traveling along the northern route. In Brazil, road conditions are rudimentary, provisions scarce, and the route potentially dangerous. On the Venezuelan side, the route passes through Venezuela's most magnificent scenery, the Gran Sabana. Although isolated, Venezuela's road conditions are excellent, the traffic scarce, and the riding glorious.

All crossings are subject to intensive baggage searches. Drug smuggling is rampant, and officials target the vulnerable.

DOCUMENTS. All entry is by passport. Tourist cards are only issued to those nationalities not needing visas and arriving by air. Everyone arriving overland requires a visa. Visa issuance varies depending on where you apply. Some consulates require medical certificates, letters from banks, onward tickets—the list seems endless. Other consulates require a minimum—only your passport and one photo. If you travel overland, try to obtain your visa before the last consulate on your route. Ask at the various consulates, and when you find a reasonable office, get your visa. Costs vary by nationality, but most visas have a fee, and processing takes at least a day.

If you arrive by air and don't need a visa, officials issue you a tourist card, a *tarjeta de ingreso*, valid for ninety days.

You don't require anything special when arriving overland with a bike. Usually, the bike itself is sufficient proof to waive any onward ticket requirements.

ACCOMMODATIONS. Finding cheap hotels in some areas is sometimes a problem. During the holiday season, the difficulty intensifies. The two problematical areas are the Maracaibo region, where oil workers guarantee a zero vacancy rate, and the few villages in the Gran Sabana that have no paid accommodations.

When you do find accommodations, it's possible to negotiate a price based on the amenities. For example, if you don't want the television or the extra bed, have the proprietor remove them to lower the room's cost.

From the capital to the gold regions of the Llanos, cheap rooms operate as brothels. At times it's worthwhile to pay a little more to avoid the inherent sounds of whispers, sighs, brawls, and puking.

Camping is a favorite pastime in Venezuela. People take to the beaches and mountaintops for the weekend, boldly erecting their tents with indifference. If you have the option, station yourself close to other campers to minimize the risk of theft. Few paid camping sites operate in the country. Camping in the remote areas of the Llanos and the Gran Sabana is easy.

Most camping equipment found in Venezuela is of the department store variety. You won't find specialty stores catering to the outdoors. However, you can find GAZ cartridges and five different grades of gasoline.

FOOD. Since Venezuela imports much of its food, costs are high. Food is plentiful in most towns except in the Gran Sabana, where supplies are limited to nonperishable items.

Restaurants limit breakfasts to pastries, bread, and coffee. Like most

Latin American countries, the day's main three-course meal, known as the *menú ejecutivo* or *cubierto*, is served at midday. Different from most other countries, you can find cheap evening meals in most cities. Restaurants post their menus and specials outside. Once inside, ask what you are going to be billed for, as waiters will offer you bread, butter, and appetizers and then charge you for them.

Finding meals is usually not a problem, as *fuentes de soda* and *cervecerias* also serve meals throughout the day. Browse for the best prices. One beer can cost three times the price at a different restaurant.

Seafood is popular on the coast, the Llanos produce excellent beef, and the Gran Sabana imports lots of cans. The traditional Venezuelan bread is *arepa*, *cachapas* are local pancakes, while the national dish is *sancocho*, a vegetable and meat stew.

DRINKS. Water in most cities is heavily chlorinated and safe to drink. In remote or dubious areas, treat the water. You can find bottled water easily, but in restaurants, water arriving in bottles could be from taps. Ask specifically for bottled water.

Venezuelan authorities seem to have subsidized almost every drink in the country. Milk is heavily subsidized and is inexpensive. The government apparently sets coffee and alcohol prices according to who is greasing whose palm.

Soft drinks are moderately expensive, while fruit drinks run the gamut from boxed artificial products to freshly made juices known as *batidos*.

HEALTH. Specific vaccinations are unnecessary to enter Venezuela. Recommended vaccinations include poliomyelitis, hepatitis, typhoid, and yellow fever. Cholera is active, so be careful with water and hygiene. A malaria risk exists year-round in the western section of the Apure state, all rural and urban areas south of Azauca, the state of Barinas, the state of Mérida in rural areas below 600 meters, Tachira, Trujilo around Lake Maracaibo, Zulia, Bolivar in the Orinoco river basin system and in the central and southern parts of the state below 600 meters, and in the territory of Amacuro.

Health care is adequate, with many English-speaking doctors and clinics.

MONEY. The best rates of exchanging foreign currencies into bolivars are at the *casas de cambio*. You can find the latest exchange rate in most major newspapers. The exchange houses are the most reliable places for changing either cash or traveler's checks. Take only American dollars into the country. You'll have difficulty changing anything else. Some banks won't change checks, and others won't even change American dollars. Most places exchanging money do so at a small 4 percent commission. You might try changing money at larger hotels, but rates are markedly lower. Changing money in the Guyana region is nearly impossible, and places that exchange moneys do so at a noncompetitive rate. No black market operates.

The bolivar has taken a pummeling. At one time the country was riding high; oil prices skyrocketed and Venezuela was an extremely expensive country. Since oil prices have dropped, the country has faced severe economic problems. Unemployment is high, most food is imported, and exchange rates have steadily improved. Venezuela has become significantly less expensive to visit.

Banks are open from 8:30 to 11:30 A.M. and from 2:00 to 4:00 P.M. Monday through Friday. Government offices are open from 9:00 to 10:00 A.M. and from 3:00 to 4:00 P.M. Most shops stay open from 9:00 A.M. to 1:00 P.M. and from 3:00 to 7:00 P.M. Monday to Saturday.

Venezuela celebrates the following holidays: January 1, New Year's Day; the Monday and Tuesday before Carnival; Thursday through Saturday of Holy Week; April 19, Declaration of National Independence; May 1, Labor Day; June 24, Battle of Carabobo; July 5, Independence Day; July 24, Birth of Simón Bolívar; October 12, Discovery of America; December 25, Christmas.

SECURITY. As the political scene heats up through attempted coups and economic austerity, people have become frantic. Criminal activity is rising, particularly in the large cities. A favorite tactic involves motorcycle thieves riding up on the sidewalk, grabbing your pack or a piece of jewelry, and then speeding away. Don't carry your bags loosely over your shoulder, don't expose your valuables, don't wear expensive jewelry, and avoid walking next to the curb.

Politically, demonstrations and riots are becoming more common. The two root causes to these incidents are groups opposing government policy and the desperate poor looting food stores. Tensions are running high, so stay alert.

Drugs are exploding into a greater problem. Venezuela is another funnel for Colombian and Brazilian drug smuggling. Police searches are thorough and indiscriminate. Authorities target travelers, who are easy marks, to score points internationally.

Security Rating: C.

CYCLING INFORMATION

BICYCLES. Although Venezuela has velodromes and an Olympic cycling team, you wouldn't know it looking at their bicycling equipment. Bike shops vary in their types of bikes and components. The best cycling resource is the Instituto Nacional de Deportes Associacion Venezolnaia de Ciclistas, Velodromo Teo Carpiles, Caracas 1021. Finding racing and mountain bike parts is possible, but you may have to look hard. Twenty-six- and twenty-seven-inch tires are available. Prepare yourself for complete bike independence outside the major cities.

The best bike shops in Caracas are at Avenida Theresa del Parma at Edificio Dante Santa Maria, at the end of Avenida Romulo Gallegos Esquina Calle Guacaipuro. One other shop is on Avenida Urdaneta on Block Veroes.

ROADS. Most of Venezuela's roads are paved. The exception to this is in the secondary roads of the Llanos and Gran Sabana. Freeways, *autopistas*, connect major cities although authorities prohibit bicycles, and they'll remove you if they catch you. Alternate roads to the expressways exist, but they're in a dilapidated condition and present poorly engineered routes and more difficult climbs. Cargo trucks, hoping to save a few bolivars, take these secondary highways, exposing you to exhaust-spewing trucks crawling up the mountains.

Through the Llanos area, you need to cross rivers on toll ferries. In the rainy season, these routes may be impassable; check beforehand.

MAPS. The best map is from the CVP gas stations. When available, the maps are reliable but have no elevation markings. The Cartógrafia Nacional offices have a good general map and a series of larger-scale maps with elevation markings. There are few good maps of Venezuela and even tourist offices aren't much help. Lacking a sufficient tourist infrastructure, few cities maintain a tourist office, so literature and maps are scarce. Be wary of the information regarding provisions and cities on maps of the Gran Sabana. A settlement may only be a few mud huts, so stay informed of the available provisions.

The best guide to Venezuela is the *Guide to Venezuela,* written by Bauman and Young. Widely available throughout Caracas, this large book is a comprehensive description of Venezuela's roads and tourist attractions. Whether you want to carry this heavy, 900-page book along with you is debatable, but it is an excellent resource.

BIKE TRANSPORT. Venezuelan bus travel varies. Buses plying the routes between major cities provide fast, efficient service. *Por puesto*, the fastest bus service, is also the most expensive. In the more remote areas, the dilapidated buses are usually slow, in part because the drivers stop for anybody along the road who wants a ride. Negotiate the fare for your bike on all buses. Generally, the prices are high, sometimes twice the passenger fare.

Because of the plentiful traffic on the road, hitching is possible.

The only rail line is the Batquisimento–Puerto Cabello line. This is a short route, so its usefulness is questionable.

Ferries run between the coast and the offshore islands. Carrying your bike is trouble-free. Riverboat service down the Orinoco River, starting at Puerto Ayacucho, is unpredictable and infrequent.

APPENDIX A: IAMAT ADDRESSES

Australia
575 Bourke Street
Melbourne 3000

Switzerland
57 Voirets
1212 Grand Lancy
Geneva

Canada
40 Regal Road
Guelph, Ontario
N1K 1B5

U.S.A.
417 Center Street
Lewiston, NY 14092

APPENDIX B: HEALTH RISK AREAS

• = risk
L = low risk

Area	DPT	Hepatitis A	Typhoid	Cholera	Malaria	Chloroquine-resistant malaria	Yellow fever	Poliomyelitis	Meningitis
Argentina	•	•	•	•	L				
Belize	•	•	•	•	•	•			
Bolivia	•	•	•	•	•	•	•	•	
Brazil	•	•	•	•	•	•	•	•	•
Chile	•	•	•	•					
Colombia	•	•	•	•	•	•	•	•	
Costa Rica	•	•	•	L	•				
Ecuador	•	•	•	•	•	•	•	•	
Guatemala	•	•	•	•	•	•			
Honduras	•	•	•	•	•	•	•		
Mexico	•	•	•	•	L	•			
Nicaragua	•	•	•	•	•	•			
Panama	•	•	•	•	•	•	•	•	
Paraguay	•	•	•	L					
Peru	•	•	•	•	•	•	•	•	
Uruguay	•	•	•						
Venezuela	•	•	•	•	•	•	•		

APPENDIX C: WHERE AND WHEN TO GO

Country/Zone	Scenery	Interest	Difficulty	Rainy months
Argentina				
Andes	**	**	Moderate	Dec.–Mar.
Pampas	*	**		Dec.–Mar.
Patagonia	*	*	Difficult	None
Belize	**	*	Easy	June–Jan.
Bolivia				
Altiplano	***	***	Moderate/Difficult	Dec.–Feb.
Eastern Valleys	***	**	Difficult	Dec.–Feb.
Lowlands	**	*	Moderate	Nov.–Feb.
Brazil				
Amazonas	**	*	Difficult	Oct.–June
Paranagua Basin	**	*	Difficult	Nov.–Mar.
Planalto	**	***	Moderate	Nov.–Mar.
Littoral	***	**	Moderate	Oct.–May
Chile				
Northern	*	*	Difficult	None
Central	**	*	Easy	None
Archipelago	***	*	Difficult	Dec.–Feb.
Colombia				
Caribbean Lowlands	**	**	Easy	Sept.–Nov.
Amazonas	***	*	Difficult	Apr.–Oct.
Central Mountains	***	***	Moderate	Oct.–Dec./Mar.–May
Costa Rica				
Lowlands	***	*	Moderate	May–Oct.
Meseta Central	***	**	Moderate	May–Oct.
Ecuador				
La Costa	*	*	Easy	Jan.–Apr.
Sierra	***	***	Moderate	Oct.–Apr.
Oriente	**	**	Difficult	Jan.–Dec.
Guatemala				
Petén	**	**	Difficult	May–Oct.
Sierra Madre	***	***	Moderate	May–Oct.
La Costa	*	*	Easy	May–Oct.
Honduras	**	*	Moderate	May–Sept.
Mexico				
Baja California	***	**	Difficult	Jan.–Mar.
Central	***	**	Moderate	June–Sept.
Southern	**	***	Difficult	June–Sept.
Yucatán	*	***	Easy	June–Sept.
Nicaragua	*	***	Easy	June–Oct.
Panama	**	*	Easy	May–Nov.
Paraguay				
Mesopotamia	**	**	Easy	Nov.–Apr.
Chaco	**	*	Difficult	Nov.–Mar.
Peru				
Desert Coast	*	**	Moderate	None
Altiplano	***	***	Moderate	Dec.–Mar.
Amazonas	**	*	Difficult	Oct.–Apr.
Uruguay				
Coast	***	*	Easy	Mar.–June
Interior	**	*	Easy	Mar.–June
Venezuela				
North	**	**	Moderate	June–Oct.
Guyana	***	*	Moderate	Apr.–Sept.

APPENDIX D: SAFETY AWARENESS CHART

Country	Personal	Property	Political	Drugs
Argentina	A	B	B	A
Belize	B	C	A	F
Bolivia	B	B	C	C
Brazil	B	C	C	C
Chile	A	A	B	A
Colombia	C	F	C	F
Costa Rica	A	A	A	A
Ecuador	B	C	B	B
Guatemala	B	B	C	A
Honduras	A	B	C	A
Mexico	B	B	A	B
Nicaragua	A	B	C	A
Panama	C	F	C	F
Paraguay	A	A	A	A
Peru	F	F	F	F
Uruguay	A	A	A	A
Venezuela	B	C	B	B

APPENDIX E: SPANISH PRONUNCIATIONS

Vowels

a   the **u** in *but*
e   the **e** in *felt*
i   the **i** in *marine*
o   the **o** in *god*
u   the **ou** in *should*
Note
When **i** occurs before another vowel, it is pronounced like the **y** in *yes*.
When **u** occurs before another vowel, it is pronounced like the **w** in *wind*.
After **q**, **u** is not pronounced; **u** is also silent in **gui** and **gue**.
ü is pronounced in **güi** and **güe**.

Consonants

Latin American consonants follow the same pronunciation as English consonants except in the following instances:

c   before **a, o, u** is like the **c** in *cast*
c   before **e, i** is like the **s** in *see*
ch   is like the **ch** in *chat*
d   is like the **d** in *dart*
g   is like the **g** in *government*
g   before **e, i**, is like a strong **h**
h   is silent
j   is like a strong **h**

ll	is like the **y** in *yawn* or the **j** of *jelly*
ñ	is like the **ni** in *onion*
q(u)	is like the **c** in *cat*
r	as the first letter is rolled
rr	is strongly rolled
y	is like the **y** in *yes*
z	is like the **s** in *sail*

Stress and Accentuation

For words that end in a vowel, **n**, or **s**, stress the second-to-last syllable.

For words that end in a consonant other than **n** or **s**, stress the last syllable.

Words that do not follow the above rules have an accent over the stressed syllable.

Differences in meaning between certain similar words are shown through the use of an accent (for example, **sí** [yes] and **si** [if]).

Question words carry an accent and are preceded by an inverted question mark: **¿dónde?** (where?).

APPENDIX F:
SPANISH BICYCLING VOCABULARY

axle: *eje*
ball bearing: *munición*
bicycle: *bicicleta*
bottom bracket: *copa*
brake: *freno*
brake handle: *manecilla*
brake shoes: *zapatas / gomas*
cable: *cable*
chain: *cadena*
chainguard: *plato*
chainring: *disco demultiplicador*
clamp: *abrazera*
crank: *multiplicador completo*
decals: *calcomanias*
derailleur, front: *descarilador*
derailleur, rear: *descarilador decambio*
fenders: *loredas*
fork: *tenedor*
frame: *chassis / marco*
freewheel: *piñon*
grease: *grasa*
handgrips: *esponjas*
handlebar post: *reversible*
handlebars: *dimon*

headset: *copa de dirección*
hub: *masa*
kickstand: *sostén*
light: *luz*
lock: *cerradura*
mirror: *espejo*
oil: *aceite*
pedal: *pedales*
pump: *bomba*
races: *cojinetes*
rack: *parilla*
reflectors: *reflectores*
rim: *aro / rin*
seat: *asiento*
seat post: *poste*
shifter: *mando de velocidad*
spokes: *rayos*
tire: *llanta*
toe clips: *clips*
tools: *herramientas*
tube: *tubo / camara*
water-bottle cage: *canastia*
water bottle: *amfora*
wheel: *rueda*

APPENDIX G: TRIP INVENTORY

Clothing
1 pair walking boots
2 pair socks
1 pair pants
2 pair cycling shorts
2 pair underwear
2 T-shirts
1 polypropylene shirt
1 cycling jacket (waterproof)
1 hat
1 pair walking shorts
1 bandanna
1 pair cycling gloves
1 pair sandals

*Additional Clothing for Cold
and Mountainous Areas*
1 pair wool socks
1 pair cycling tights
1 pair wool gloves

Camping Equipment
1 tent
1 ground sheet
1 sleeping pad
1 semi-mummy sleeping
    bag (−10°C)
1 stove
2 fuel bottles
lighter/matches
fuel filter
nesting pots (1-l., 2-l.)
tin mug
spices
pocket knife
candle lantern
flashlight
pot scrubber
cutlery

Bike
1 bike
1 rear rack
1 front rack
1 odometer
    3 oversized water bottles
    bungee cords

1 lock
rear panniers
front panniers
small internal-frame backpack
handlebar bag
1 side-view mirror
photocopy of passport in handlebars

Bike Parts
brake cable (long)
derailleur cable (long)
assorted bearings
assorted nuts and bolts
spare wire
folding tire
spare tube
pump
3 spokes to fit rear and front

Bike Tools
6-inch adjustable wrench
8-9-10mm Y-wrench
allen keys to fit bike
spoke key
2 tire levers
needle-nose pliers
chain-breaker
freewheel remover
crank remover
cone wrench
grease in film container
drive-train oil
patch kit

First Aid Kit
triangle bandage
tensor bandage
hemorrhoidal suppositories
hydrocortisone cream
Sulfatrim (amoebas)
antihistamines
anti-nausea pills
Fansidar
Imodium
alcohol pads
antiseptic ointment
thermometer

anti-fungus cream
analgesics
heat rub
gauze pads
bandages
adhesive tape
burn cream
sunscreen
toothache gel
lip balm
cough drops
IAMAT directory
iodine
insect repellent
insect coils

Personal Needs
brush
moisturizer
dental floss
nail file
soap
shampoo
nail brushes
deodorant
razor
blades
toothbrush
   toothpaste
   toilet paper

sunglasses
eyeshades
towel
facecloth

Documents
traveler's checks/directory
personal checks
passport
vaccination record
credit card
address book
money belts
birth certificate

Miscellaneous
batteries
souvenirs
postcards from home
day pack
small rope
pens
ziplock bags
sewing kit
duct tape

Maps/Books
journal
guide book
maps—general and specific

APPENDIX H:
LATIN AMERICAN CLIMATE CHARTS

	Jan	Feb	Mar	Apr	May	Jun	Jul	Aug	Sep	Oct	Nov	Dec
ARGENTINA												
Salta 24.51S, 65.29W; Alt. 1,258 m												
Temperature (°C)	22	21	19	17	14	11	11	14	16	19	21	21
Precipitation (cm)	19	14	10	03	01	00	00	00	01	02	05	13
Buenos Aires 34.35S, 58.29W; Alt. 26 m												
Temperature (°C)	23	26	25	17	13	09	09	11	12	15	19	22
Precipitation (cm)	08	07	11	09	08	06	06	06	08	09	08	10
Rio Gallegos 51.40S, 69.16W; Alt. 23 m												
Temperature (°C)	12	12	10	07	03	01	01	02	04	08	10	12
Precipitation (cm)	03	02	03	03	03	02	02	01	01	01	02	02
BELIZE												
Belize City 17.29N, 88.10W; Alt. 0 m												
Temperature (°C)	27	27	28	30	30	30	30	31	31	30	28	27
Precipitation (cm)	14	06	04	06	11	20	16	17	24	31	23	19
BOLIVIA												
La Paz 16.30S, 68.08W; Alt. 3,636 m												
Temperature (°C)	11	11	11	11	09	08	08	09	10	11	12	11
Precipitation (cm)	11	11	07	03	01	01	01	01	03	04	05	10
Cochabamba 17.23S, 66.09W; Alt. 1,173 m												
Temperature (°C)	20	19	19	19	16	15	15	16	19	21	21	20
Precipitation (cm)	11	10	06	02	01	00	00	00	01	02	04	10
Santa Cruz 17.47S, 63.11W; Alt. 448 m												
Temperature (°C)	26	26	26	24	22	20	20	23	25	26	27	27
Precipitation (cm)	17	13	10	10	07	07	05	03	06	09	12	15
BRAZIL												
Manaus 3.08S, 60.01W; Alt. 51 m												
Temperature (°C)	26	26	26	26	27	27	27	28	28	28	27	27
Precipitation (cm)	28	28	30	29	19	10	06	04	06	11	17	23
Corumbá 19.00S, 57.39W; Alt. 147 m												
Temperature (°C)	27	27	26	25	23	22	22	23	25	26	27	27
Precipitation (cm)	17	16	12	07	06	04	03	02	05	08	12	15
Belo Horizonte 19.56S, 43.56W; Alt. 968 m												
Temperature (°C)	22	22	22	21	19	18	18	19	20	21	22	22
Precipitation (cm)	27	19	17	07	07	01	01	01	04	11	21	35

	Jan	Feb	Mar	Apr	May	Jun	Jul	Aug	Sep	Oct	Nov	Dec
BRAZIL, cont.												
Santos 23.56S, 46.20W; Alt. 9 m												
Temperature (°C)	25	25	25	23	21	20	19	19	19	20	22	24
Precipitation (cm)	25	32	25	20	16	12	09	11	14	18	16	20
CHILE												
Antofagasta 23.26S, 70.28W; Alt. 899 m												
Temperature (°C)	20	20	20	18	16	15	13	14	14	15	17	18
Precipitation (cm)	00	00	00	00	00	00	.5	00	00	00	00	00
Santiago 33.27S, 70.42W; Alt. 550 m												
Temperature (°C)	20	19	17	14	11	09	08	09	11	14	16	19
Precipitation (cm)	00	01	01	02	07	07	06	06	02	01	01	00
Punta Arenas 52.59S, 70.58W; Alt. 3 m												
Temperature (°C)	10	10	08	07	04	02	02	02	04	07	08	09
Precipitation (cm)	04	02	03	04	03	04	03	03	02	03	02	04
COLOMBIA												
Cartagena 10.28N, 75.30W; Alt. 2 m												
Temperature (°C)	25	26	26	27	28	28	28	28	28	26	26	26
Precipitation (cm)	00	00	00	01	10	07	07	09	11	19	13	03
Arauca 7.04N, 70.44W; Alt. 125 m												
Temperature (°C)	26	27	27	26	27	26	26	26	26	26	26	26
Precipitation (cm)	00	01	02	18	23	24	24	18	16	16	06	02
Bogotá 4.38N, 75.04W; Alt. 2,650 m												
Temperature (°C)	13	14	15	15	14	14	13	14	14	14	14	13
Precipitation (cm)	06	07	10	15	11	06	05	06	06	16	12	07
COSTA RICA												
Liberia 10.39N, 85.28W; Alt. 48 m												
Temperature (°C)	27	27	28	29	28	27	28	28	27	27	27	26
Precipitation (cm)	00	00	00	01	24	27	27	16	42	38	12	02
San José 9.59N, 84.04W; Alt. 1,150 m												
Temperature (°C)	18	19	19	21	21	21	21	21	21	20	20	18
Precipitation (cm)	02	01	02	05	23	24	21	24	31	30	15	04
ECUADOR												
Guayaquil 2.12S, 79.53W; Alt. 6 m												
Temperature (°C)	26	26	26	26.5	26	25	24	25	24	24	25	26
Precipitation (cm)	19	26	24	16	3	01	01	00	00	00	00	00

	Jan	Feb	Mar	Apr	May	Jun	Jul	Aug	Sep	Oct	Nov	Dec
ECUADOR, cont.												
Quito 0.12S, 78.29W; Alt. 2,819 m												
Temperature (°C)	13	13	13	13	13	13	13	13	13	13	13	13
Precipitation (cm)	13	13	16	18	13	5	2	2	8	13	11	10
Mendez 2.43S, 78.19W; Alt. 620 m												
Temperature (°C)	24	24	24	23	23	22	22	23	23	25	25	24
Precipitation (cm)	15	15	24	30	31	27	23	18	20	26	16	14
GUATEMALA												
Flores 16.56N, 89.53W; Alt. 120 m												
Temperature (°C)	23	23	24	26	29	29	27	27	27	25	22	22
Precipitation (cm)	05	03	05	18	23	24	23	21	35	20	08	10
Guatemala City 14.38N, 90.31W; Alt. 1,590 m												
Temperature (°C)	22	25	27	27	28	27	25	26	26	24	23	22
Precipitation (cm)	01	00	01	03	15	27	20	20	23	17	02	01
Mazatenango 14.31N, 91.38W; Alt. 280 m												
Temperature (°C)	25	26	26	27	27	26	26	26	26	25	25	25
Precipitation (cm)	00	02	07	16	35	46	42	42	57	52	13	01
HONDURAS												
Tegucigalpa 14.05N, 84.17W; Alt. 975 m												
Temperature (°C)	25	26	28	30	29	27	27	28	28	26	25	25
Precipitation (cm)	01	00	00	03	18	18	07	08	15	09	04	01
MEXICO												
Mexico D.F. 19.26N, 99.08W; Alt. 2,437 m												
Temperature (°C)	12	14	16	18	18	18	17	17	16	15	14	12
Precipitation (cm)	01	01	01	01	05	10	13	10	12	03	01	02
Tuxtla Gutiérrez 16.45N, 93.06W; Alt. 567 m												
Temperature (°C)	21	23	25	26	27	26	25	25	25	24	22	21
Precipitation (cm)	00	00	00	00	08	24	18	16	20	08	00	00
Mérida 20.58N, 89.38W; Alt. 5 m												
Temperature (°C)	23	24	25	27	28	28	27	27	27	26	24	23
Precipitation (cm)	03	02	02	03	08	15	14	13	15	10	03	03
NICARAGUA												
Managua 12.06N, 86.18W; Alt. 40 m												
Temperature (°C)	27	27	28	28	28	27	26	26	26	26	26	25
Precipitation (cm)	00	00	00	00	08	30	14	13	18	24	06	00

	Jan	Feb	Mar	Apr	May	Jun	Jul	Aug	Sep	Oct	Nov	Dec
PANAMA												
Panama City 10.39N, 85.28W; Alt. 0 m												
Temperature (°C)	27	26	27	27	27	27	27	27	26	26	25	26
Precipitation (cm)	03	01	02	07	20	22	18	20	21	26	26	12
PARAGUAY												
Asunción 25.17S, 57.39W; Alt. 64 m												
Temperature (°C)	28	28	27	23	20	18	19	19	22	23	25	27
Precipitation (cm)	16	13	17	15	09	08	05	03	08	11	14	12
Mariscal Estigarriba 22.01S, 60.37W; Alt. 64 m												
Temperature (°C)	30	29	27	25	21	20	20	23	25	27	29	30
Precipitation (cm)	11	11	10	07	04	03	02	01	02	07	10	10
PERU												
Lima 12.02S, 77.02W; Alt. 147 m												
Temperature (°C)	23	24	24	22	19	17	16	16	16	17	19	20
Precipitation (cm)	00	00	00	00	01	01	01	01	00	00	00	00
Cusco 13.31S, 71.58W; Alt. 3,619 m												
Temperature (°C)	12	11	12	12	10	10	09	10	11	12	13	12
Precipitation (cm)	16	13	13	04	01	01	00	01	02	04	08	13
Pucallpa 8.25S, 74.37W; Alt. 159 m												
Temperature (°C)	28	27	27	26	26	26	26	27	28	28	27	28
Precipitation (cm)	14	17	19	19	15	10	04	07	11	19	23	13
URUGUAY												
Montevideo 34.55S, 56.10W; Alt. 3 m												
Temperature (°C)	22	21	20	16	13	11	10	11	12	15	17	21
Precipitation (cm)	07	06	10	10	08	08	07	08	08	06	07	08
Rivera 30.54S, 55.33W; Alt. 274 m												
Temperature (°C)	25	25	22	18	15	13	12	14	15	18	21	23
Precipitation (cm)	13	10	13	14	12	15	11	10	15	18	09	09
VENEZUELA												
Caracas 10.30N, 66.56W; Alt. 1,103 m												
Temperature (°C)	19	19	20	21	22	21	21	21	21	21	21	20
Precipitation (cm)	02	01	01	03	08	10	10	11	10	11	09	04
Santa Elena 4.36N, 61.07W; Alt. 959 m												
Temperature (°C)	21	22	22	22	22	21	21	21	22	22	22	22
Precipitation (cm)	07	07	08	13	23	24	22	17	12	11	11	12

INDEX

About the author:

Walter Sienko's first journey through Latin America lasted eight months. He was not home for long when he set off for Europe, almost encircling the Mediterranean in eighteen months of bicycle touring. Soon after this Sienko embarked on a two-year bicycle tour with his spouse Kathleen, which began in Inuvik, Northwest Territories, and ended in Tierra del Fuego, Argentina. A social worker, writer, and photographer, he lives in Toronto, Canada.